Video Nasty Mayhem

The Inside Story of VIPCO

James Simpson

DARK
RIVER

Published in 2019 by Dark River, an imprint of Bennion Kearny Limited.

Copyright © Dark River

James Simpson has asserted his right under the Copyright Designs and Patents Act 1988 to be identified as the author of this work

ISBN: 978-1-911121-70-1

Published by Dark River, an imprint of Bennion Kearny Limited
6 Woodside
Churnet View Road
Oakamoor
ST10 3AE

About the Author

Growing up in the aftermath of the Video Nasties 'scandal', during the late eighties and early nineties, James Simpson is from a small town in the North East of England where talking about grisly horror flicks was the norm in his school playground. For the last several years, he has written about cult cinema for different magazines and websites, as well as running his own now-defunct site *Infernal Cinema*. He has interviewed horror stars Emily Booth, Barbie Wilde, and the legendary Lloyd Kaufman, among others during this time. He appears in the VIPCO documentary *The Untold Story*. This is his first book and hopes it doesn't show that he is a dyslexia sufferer! His favourite VIPCO movie is *Spookies*.

Twitter: @VIPCObook

About The Book

At the end of 2017, on a cold and wintry night, I decided to watch *Spookies* (1986) on DVD. This was a film I'd always liked despite its muddled feel and often nonsensical plot. It's never dull and has always entertained me. After watching it, I looked into the film's background, and what I discovered was as interesting as the feature itself (more on that, later). It had also been produced by Michael Lee, the owner of the now-defunct home video distributor VIPCO.

It hit me – there and then – that the story of VIPCO would make an interesting book. As I had been writing about horror cinema for several years by this point, mainly reviews and the occasional feature or interview, I felt I should progress to working on something bigger. I wasn't intimidated by the thought of having to work towards a higher word count; it was *what* I should write about, exactly, that was intimidating.

I had grown up as a fan of VIPCO when a boy in my class at school, when I was eight years old, had snuck some VIPCO tapes into the playground from his older brother's horror video collection. The names of the movies and the sleeves enthralled us; we knew that, as we were kids, these were the sorts of things our parents wouldn't want us looking at. So we obviously went out of our way to seek them out.

That was in the early nineties. By the end of the decade, I was a teenager, and had now seen quite a few horror films (my parents cut me some slack, eventually) but still had only ever seen VIPCO titles on a shelf in a shop. The lurid and bloody front covers still grabbed my attention, though. Late at night on the Sci-Fi Channel (now Sy Fy), an advert for VIPCO aired repeatedly, usually at least once per ad break. I absorbed every moment; now I had seen brief clips of their films within this commercial, I was ever more determined to see what was on those tapes.

Thankfully, I didn't have to wait nearly another decade for this to happen. I stumbled upon a copy of *Zombie Flesh Eaters* in a charity shop (thrift store to any transatlantic readers) in 2001. The title, the cover, and the fact it had VIPCO on the packaging meant I quickly bought it, for a steal, at 99p. By this point, I had access to the internet and, of course, used it to read up on all manner of horror films. I was fascinated by the Video Nasties moral panic of the 1980s (more on that later) and learned how several of the 'nasties' had been released on tape thanks to VIPCO. As a result, I felt like I had Nazi gold as I left the charity shop with *ZFE*, despite knowing the infamous splinter-to-the-eye scene was butchered (it turned out I had a still heavily-cut 1992 release of the VHS).

About a year later, I turned 18, and one of my gifts was the cheapest DVD player available, at a 'bargain' cost of £65 (this was 2002), to the horror of my poor old gran who decided she'd get me this as a gift. With a new toy to play with, and birthday cash burning a hole in my pocket, I went to the local Blockbuster store and looked at their 'cheap' ex-rental line of DVDs for sale. Amongst these was

House by the Cemetery. Again, I knew instinctively that I had to have it. It was a former Video Nasty, it was VIPCO, and it was a Lucio Fulci flick (by now I was a fan of the director). It also cost a modest, by 2002 standards, £9.99.

With that, I was unleashed. I had an accumulating fascination with VIPCO, and sought out the VHS and DVD releases of their titles, any chance I could. HMV was usually a safe bet, despite new discs being sold at a staggering £24.99. Being a workshy student, and having no money as a result, I would usually look at the sleeves of these titles before putting them back on the shelf and trying to find them for less money via Music Zone, MVC, eBay, or Amazon.

I hope what I have detailed in the prior paragraphs shows I have a *genuine passion* and 'history' for the company. As I began to write, however, I realised I had a lot of VIPCO knowledge gaps. I knew it had gone out of business in either 2006 or 2007, which I admit had passed me by, but didn't know exactly when or why.

I procrastinated and let other things, such as learning to drive at the tender age of 33, get in the way of actually starting to write the book. In February 2018, I finally had a basic plan, and 'started' with a working list of movies that had previously been released by VIPCO. I found the number of films to be far greater than I had anticipated.

Then, a couple of weeks later, I learned of independent filmmaker Jason Impey. He was in the midst of making a documentary about VIPCO and was on various social media sites trying to raise awareness about it. I took this as 'a sign' that a book about VIPCO was needed, and I should actually do some bloody proper writing too. The timing of our projects, happening at roughly the same time without either person being aware, was serendipitous. I got talking to Jason, who is based in Milton Keynes, by email and Facebook about our shared love for the video firm. We both strongly believe that VIPCO and its owner Mike Lee are, despite the flaws, vital parts of horror and exploitation cinema history in the United Kingdom.

Now, several months later, the book is complete. In the time it has taken to accomplish this, I have re-watched many films that VIPCO had previously sold. Some of them I hadn't viewed in nearly 15 years. Time has been kind to a number of efforts, but hasn't for others.

Researching the background of the firm and piecing it together from old interviews, websites, and first-hand knowledge from the people involved has allowed me to find answers to my own questions about VIPCO. Questions that I think other fans have long wanted answered. The answers are, it should be noted now, tragic and emotional.

But all of that is to come within the following pages, and I hope this book is a satisfying experience for anyone who has decided to give it a go.

Now, let's enter the VIPCO Vaults of Horror once more...

Thanks

Time to do the clichéd thing here, and thank people who have helped me during the course of researching and writing this book. Everyone is equal in my eyes, and the order in which I thank people is no reflection of anything.

Thank you to director Jason Impey. Interviewing him for my former website, Infernal Cinema, in March 2018 was the boot up the bum I needed to take the idea of a book about VIPCO seriously. His knowledge as a fan, and as a friend of Mike, brought knowledge to my attention not previously known about VIPCO. I still consider it a huge compliment that, in October 2018, he would film me for an interview as a 'VIPCO expert' for inclusion in *his* VIPCO project *The Untold Story*.

James Simpson (left), and Jason Impey

Torstein Karlsen for his information on VIPCO activities in Scandinavia during the early nineties. He is also a lifelong fan and collector of all things VIPCO.

Marc Morris, not just for his insight on the British home video distribution industry, but also for being very frank and honest about VIPCO when he could have easily sugar-coated his opinions.

Barrie Gold helped me gain an insight into Mike's vital working and personal relationship with S Gold & Sons that helped both firms over the decades.

The delightful Graham Humphreys was willing to speak to me at length about his time with Mike and the finer points of the sleeves he designed for him. Graham also kindly consented for me to use some of the artwork he designed.

Arrow Video's Ewant Cant took time out of a busy schedule to have a very lengthy phone conversation in order to talk VIPCO, horror movies, and the current climate for distribution firms in the UK.

Former VIPCO employee Jay Slater who laid bare the inner workings of the company and spoke from the heart. He also allowed for the book's inclusion of the *Suicide* press release, and jumped at the chance to write the Afterword.

Martin Myers was brilliant in talking about his school days and friendship with a young Mike Lee, and his father's helping hand in the early days of VIPCO. As Martin was keen to point out to me, Michael Myers in the *Halloween* movies was named after his dad as a tribute for helping John Carpenter!

Also, a huge and very heartfelt thank you to Mike himself. Sir, your firm has enriched my life and that of others in ways you will never fully understand. It has been a pleasure and I hope you enjoyed reading this book.

Finally – James Lumsden-Cook, at the book publisher Bennion Kearny, for giving this book a chance when the usual suspects turned their noses up at it!

Viva VIPCO!

James

Table of Contents

The Films

Foreword

VIPCO will always hold a special place in my heart.

By trade, I'm an independent filmmaker who has a passion for movies, both making them and collecting/watching them. I have a particular interest in horror and obscure films, especially when I was younger – I was always trying to seek out extreme and bizarre flicks.

Having been born in 1984, I grew up in a strict United Kingdom in which the BBFC was scissor-happy, cutting and banning films left, right, and centre following the Video Nasties scandal. There was one film distribution label that always had a presence in my early years of collecting due to this. I remember always seeing titles in high street shops with obscure crazy titles and they were usually sold by the same label, that label being VIPCO.

This indie boutique label was offering hidden gems, classic weird horror, and Video Nasties.

One of the only true 'proper' ways to own and watch these kinds of films in the UK, while I was growing up, was buying releases by VIPCO. I later found out that they had made an impact in the pre-certification days of VHS, 'the good old times' that were made infamous by the Video Nasties scandal. To be honest, this 'Nasty' reputation gave some of the movies a status and reputation that can be argued as not being fully deserved. However, the DPP list that was drawn up acted as a collector's guide of must-own horror movies, many of which were being sold by VIPCO.

After raids, arrests, and prison sentences, the home video industry was shaken up, leaving many firms too nervous and afraid to touch such 'hot' titles; some features, it was feared, would not get through the strict new guidelines of the BBFC. Many distributors got off the bandwagon of churning out horror flicks on VHS as a result. Yet one man rose from the ashes, a character like no other… that man was Michael Lee, founder of the notorious VIPCO!

Yes, most of the titles they sold from the early nineties onwards suffered cuts, but this couldn't be helped following the Nasties panic. Despite this, at least the movies were getting British releases, something many of them would not have received until decades later, otherwise. A lot of VIPCO's releases from this period inspired me to make my own films which I started doing as a child with my father's camcorder. I progressed to studying filmmaking at college, after which I ended up becoming an independent filmmaker and embarked on a journey of making a zombie film entitled *Zombie Village* that I shot in 2004 and completed in 2005.

It was around this time that Michael started to release some new indie films as well as the old classics on VIPCO DVD. This addition of independent cinema to the 'vaults' encouraged me to reach out and contact Michael about getting behind some of my productions. I emailed him regarding *Zombie Village* and, to my amazement, I got a quick response about meeting up to discuss it further! A series of lunch meetings followed in which I proposed a zombie film focusing on the disease being spread sexually – putting a then-new, modern-day, twist on the sub-genre using S.T.I.s as an allegory.

Michael loved this and wanted to fund it with the new name *Revenge of the Dead*. He even phoned me up one day, telling me to get a close up of a zombie cock when shooting! This surprised me considering the censorship issues he had come up against. However, times had begun to change, and the BBFC was letting more through. When I figured this out, I suggested to Michael that he should seek out *Absurd* and release it via VIPCO. He agreed and got as far as looking into getting the rights for the title.

As I embarked on this new film project, tragedy struck, leaving Michael distraught. This ultimately resulted in the ending of VIPCO. As for *Zombie Village*, I was left with making a short version of the film, shot on Super 8, that ended up having a screening at my local cinema in September 2007; it was also released on an anthology called *Tales Of Terror Part Three*.

Years went by, and I went off and made a number of films, many in the horror genre. Although I lost contact with Michael, I was sat on a shoot one day in deep thought about what could have been regarding *Revenge of the Dead*. I've always felt it was such a missed opportunity. At the time, I had also seen many posts on social media about VIPCO, and it struck me there was not much information publicly available. I decided I would track Michael down and get his story told on camera.

After a long search, I finally made contact with the legend again. I located him in London, recovering from a spell of ill health. He agreed to be filmed and tell his story on camera. In the spring of 2017, the interview took place in which he was brutally honest and really did tell all. This was the start of what was to be a passion-driven documentary; a thrilling journey I embarked on to create my new film – *VIPCO: The Untold Story*.

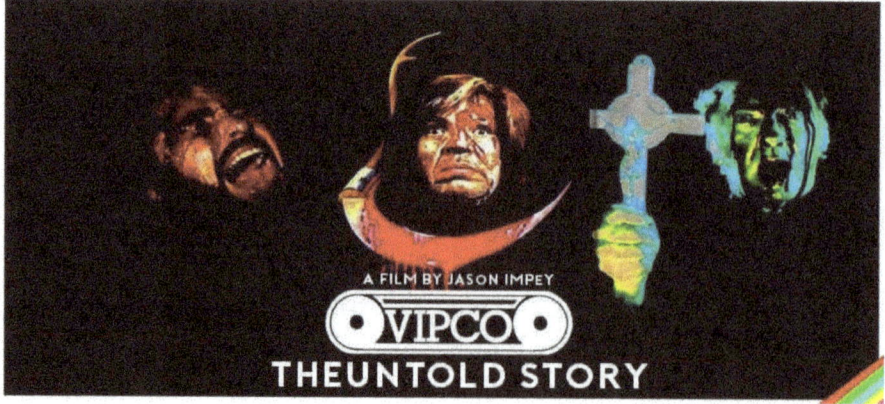

After releasing an early teaser trailer for *The Untold Story*, in early 2018, a writer named James Simpson reached out to me to do an interview for his website Infernal Cinema. He wanted to help promote my documentary but also speak to me about VIPCO as he was writing a book on the company! I was very happy to be asked to contribute to such an exciting project when he later asked me to write this very foreword.

Long live VIPCO!

Jason Impey

The History of VIPCO (Part I)

I was a bit of a naughty boy!

Michael Lee, VIPCO founder

Over the years, Michael Lee has been described as many things, some negative and some positive: an entrepreneur, a wheeler-dealer, a charlatan, an idiot, a loving father, a straightforward guy who just wanted to make a living, and a man who went against the grain in the Video Nasties Era. It is fair to say that Michael Lee is a polarizing figure.

Born in London in the 1950s, Michael – or Mike to his friends – was a salesman for many years at the Oxford Street branch of now defunct British hi-fi chain Laskys (it was taken over by Comet in 1989). By the late seventies, however, VHS and Betamax had entered the British marketplace, and Mike became all too aware of the impact these new technologies were likely to make. He studied up as more and more Laskys customers became interested, and wanted to know about them; in doing so, he foresaw how home video was likely to become commonplace. (Of course, this knowledge no doubt helped Mike shift a few units for his employer, too.)

At the time, home video in the United Kingdom was limited to a projector and a white sheet across a wall for a screen, and Mike rightly guessed that people would pay to watch a film on their televisions at their own convenience. It would be, he discovered, rather cheap to do as well.

Keen to make money and exploit the still fledgling market, Mike decided he could get a bigger slice of the pie than VCR sales at Laskys could provide. He used his savings, alongside borrowed money from his disapproving father, to try and crack into the world of home video. In an era before the internet and smartphones, he did something that many a person in the late seventies did – he got out a copy of the Yellow Pages. This telephone book of business numbers was a vital bit of kit for many a wheeler-dealer or shrewd businessman, and Mike Lee was both of these things.

Going through his Yellow Pages meticulously, Mike contacted every film distributor he could find. He hoped that distributors were not too aware of the power of video, and would be keen to sell him the rights to their movies instead of putting their films to tape themselves. It turned out that none of the distributors he contacted were too keen on cold calls from a cockney talking about "tapes". Luckily, for Mike, he had an ace up his sleeve.

He was going to call his old school friend Martin Myers.

Martin Myers is the fourth generation of his family to be involved in cinema; his great grandfather and grandfather ran cinemas across the south of England, and his father – Michael Myers – had a helping hand in the career of John Carpenter and ran *Miracle Films*. Martin is now a well-respected name in cinema distribution having worked for the likes of 20th Century Fox, CIC, Miracle Films, Vestron, and First Independent as well as being involved in films such as *Princess Bride* (1987), *Dirty Dancing* (1987), *Dumb and Dumber* (1994), and more.

But before this, Martin lived in the same street as his school friend – Mike Lee. "We were often in trouble with the Deputy Head for doing naughty things such as filling up water balloons and throwing them out of the fifth-floor windows and soaking pupils," Martin would say of his time at school with Mike.

The two friends lost touch once Myers moved to Chile to work for United International Pictures, but he learned that Mike had been in contact with his father at Miracle Films. "I remember him telling me he went through the Yellow Pages to find film distribution companies and he came across my dad's firm."

At the time, Mike had no idea that Miracle Films was run by his old mate's father. It was only when he dropped by Michael's office in Wardour Street, London, that he came across the man in person. The two recognised each other and, thanks to the old school link, Myers decided to help out Mike with some titles.

As mentioned, Mike Lee had hoped that distributors had little knowledge of home video; something that was confirmed by Martin. He recalls, "My father, as well as other distributors, was very unsure about this new business. He was happy to sell the rights outright for a flat fee which, in hindsight, was a terrible mistake but great for Mike!" A handful of titles went to the wannabe video distributor.

In fact, these titles turned out to be 'gems'. Mike Lee had obtained the video rights to cut-price smut and skin flicks *Bed Hostesses* (1972), *Caged Women* (1976), *Hot Sex in Bangkok* (1976), plus *Sweet and Sexy* (1970). Out of all these titles, it is only Jess Franco's *Caged Women* (aka *Barbed Wire Dolls*) that has not sunk into obscurity.

With some titles in hand, Mike decided his home video company needed a name. Many years later, in an interview with The Dark Side Magazine, conducted by Jay Slater, Mike explained that Video Instant Picture Company was chosen as his new firm's name when he approached his accountant about the matter. He also had a chat with his solicitor as, having got into a little bit of trouble (to say the least) for selling bootleg videotapes previously, Mike was keen to ensure that everything was above board.

While the company was known as the Video Instant Picture Company at first (and its initials of VIPC), it would eventually become better known by a name that would become synonymous with the time of Video Nasties in the UK: VIPCO. Although Mike refuses to go into detail about this, he is alleged to have had to come to a legal agreement with, of all people, Ringo Starr! The former Beatles member had supposedly registered the name 'VIPCO' in the past for a long defunct firm he once financed. In my research for this book I spoke to a couple of people that 'know' more about this intriguing piece of VIPCO history but they all refused to divulge any more details, citing Mike not wanting more to be known. Moving on….

The original four videos sold by the newly-founded VIPCO were knocked out cheap and sold at a relatively low – for the time – price of £19.95. Mike then shilled these videos and Betamax face-to-face, or via phone calls, with retailers or newly-established video rental stores. No longer working for Laskys, the entrepreneur spent his days selling the tapes and, at night, would make copies from the master tapes to sell the next day!

VIPCO was very much a one-man workforce with Mike Lee seemingly dedicating his every waking hour to making the company work. Eventually, it would add a couple of other employees to its ranks (Mike claims they once had 14 people). One of those hired early on was Jay Slater (who, for the most part, worked from home); he described Mike as a one-man army who did "pretty much everything" for his business.

Mike Lee was on a roll. The company was selling videos, and any money that was made during this time was invested back into VIPCO. Soon, however, something was to come along that would drastically change the distributor's fortunes. In fact, it would change the course of not only VIPCO's history, but horror cinema in Britain as well.

*Michael Myers (furthest left) with wife Pamela, plus director
John Carpenter and then-wife Adrienne Barbeau*

Cannibals

Better to be in the warm body of a friend than in a cold hole in the ground...

VIPCO tag line, *Cannibal Holocaust.*

Mike loved a cannibal movie.

From the eighties to the noughties, he obtained several grisly skin-munching pieces of celluloid, and although he managed to release some of the biggest and best-known titles of the cannibal boom that ran from 1972 to 1988, he also snapped up some of the movies that marked the end of the genre; shoddy films from other genres, repackaged as if they were cannibalistic cinema. The following are VIPCO's cannibal movies, examined.

Disclaimer. All spelling and grammatical errors that appear in the synopses taken from VIPCO VHS and DVD sleeves remain in place for added authenticity. Proof reading must have not existed at VIPCO...

CANNIBAL HOLOCAUST (1980)

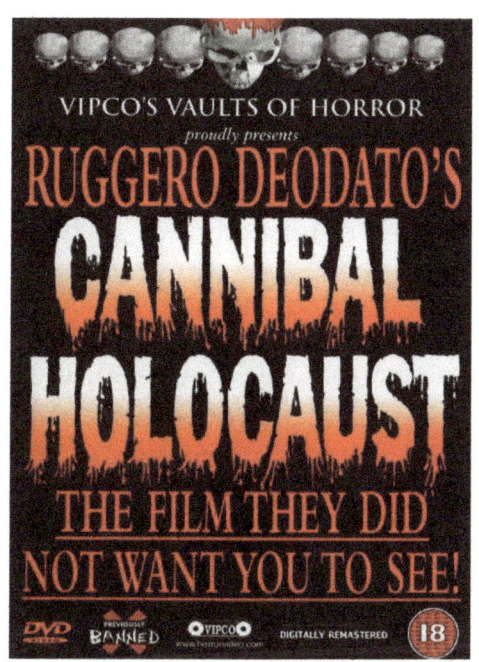

Director: Ruggero Deodato

Writers: Gianfranco Clerici, Giorgio Stegani

Stars: Robert Kerman (Prof. Monroe), Luca Barbareschi as Luca Giorgio Barbareschi (Mark), Francesca Ciardi (Faye), Perry Pirkanen (Jack)

VIPCO Release: 2001

Also Known As: *Hell of the Cannibals, Holocausto Canibal, Ruggero Deodato's Cannibal Holocaust*

VIPCO Plot Synopsis: *In 1979 four documentary film makers disappeared in the Jungles of South America while shooting a film about cannibalism... Six months later the New York University along with the Pan American Broadcasting Corporation sent a search team in looking for the film makers. They could never have been prepared for what they found...*

One of the most notorious films ever made, VIPCO did not get its hands on *Holocaust* until 2001. The movie was banned in the early eighties in the United Kingdom amid the Video Nasties panic that saw numerous movies outlawed for excessive violence, explicit sex, real animal murder, and other delights usually associated with horror and grindhouse cinema. *Holocaust* was one of the Nasties to get the most flak, due to the killing of animals on screen, and its realistic depiction of human death.

VIPCO, of course, saw itself at the centre of the Nasties scandal due to other genre classics such as *The Driller Killer* (1979), *Zombie Flesh Eaters* (1979) and other, legendary cannibal picture *Cannibal Ferox* (1980). Mike would have – no doubt – wished to add this to his catalogue of releases during the eighties, based on reputation alone.

When *Cannibal Holocaust* was finally released (presumably the British public had become hardier since the ban was first implemented 20 years earlier), it was heavily cut by over five minutes to remove the footage of animal killings. Some people were grateful as this edition of *Holocaust* allowed them their first chance to see the exploitation epic; others, who had previously seen it, had a chance to revisit it for the first time in years. Admittedly, others decried the new version, saying the edits weakened the feature and took away from the power of Deodato's work.

The VHS and DVD that went on sale in 2001 featured some eye-catching artwork. The film's logo, in dripping blood, is given centre stage with the director's name printed above. With Mike always keen to exploit the notoriety of his releases, the text 'The film they did not want you to see!' practically screams along the bottom of the front cover. Who 'they' are is open for debate. Are 'they' the BBFC… despite lifting their own ban? Or perhaps 'they' are the establishment – the British politicians of the area that attached themselves to the moral panic to enhance their public image?

As referenced at the start of the chapter, 'Better to be in the warm body of a friend than in a cold hole in the ground...' is written on the back cover. Whoever came up with this piece of black humour must have been rather pleased with themselves!

Frivolous hype aside, *Holocaust* is clearly a film with a message. The meaning behind it could be a book in its own right; in fact, books *have* been published on it and the movie's legacy. For the sake of brevity, we shall cover the message briefly.

The movie explores the way that so-called civilised man treats the natives in the jungle – and the acts they do – and how he casts a scathing eye on the developing world at the time. Deodato felt that the media played a part in overstepping boundaries and indulging in the violence that was happening around the globe during this period. Out of all the cannibal boom movies to be produced, this is probably the most cerebral and thought-provoking.

Deodato also empowers his viewers to an extent. The manner in which we are shown the Westerners' trek up the Amazon, and the build-up to them finally arriving, signposts how they are approaching their doom. Which, of course, they are, but it is depicted in such a way that it feels like everyone but the characters are aware of this.

Kerman, as the voice of reason, seems like he is losing a battle he was never destined to win as the TV studio execs practically have a group orgasm at the footage of the documentary makers being absolute villains to the less intelligent natives. It is only when they are shown the footage of the same crew having the tables turned on them, and in a way making the execs relate to the suffering of the (now) victims of violence, that they see things on an equal level. It is rightly decided that what happened is dreadful and not fit for transmission. Those two-faced swines!

The found footage does lend a certain authenticity to those moments of violence, which no doubt added to its power back in the day. As a genre that was relatively underdeveloped and barely known of at the time, this found cannibal footage flick would have been highly original and trailblazing. An early example of found footage horror can also be seen at work with Charles B. Pierce's *The Legend of Boggy Creek* (1972), although it lacked the punch of Deodato's masterpiece.

The violence is not as extreme as it was once considered – when held up against films of today – but in the early eighties, it was innovative and realistic. The most iconic moment of gore must surely be the scene of a woman impaled on a huge wooden spike that rises up out of her mouth as if she is a human kebab skewer. Deodato illustrates how powerful this shot is, as he has the camera linger on the shocking scene for an extended period of time. The effect was actually accomplished by the actress simply sitting on a bicycle seat and tilting her head back. She then placed part of the pole into her mouth and played dead.

The feature ends on the loaded question of "I wonder who the real cannibals are?"

VIPCO's packaging states that people have tried to better *Cannibal Holocaust* but have failed. For once, a claim of superiority on a VIPCO sleeve is actually 100% true! There have been many attempts to snatch the crown away from *Holocaust* and some of these were even released by Mike Lee, yet none can wrestle away the title of 'The King of Cannibal Flicks' from Deodato's ground-breaking work. A must see.

CANNIBAL HOLOCAUST II (1988)

Director: Antonio Climati

Writers: Marco Merlo, Francesco Prosperi as Franco Prosperi, Federico Moccia, Lorenzo Castellano, Antonio Climati

Stars: Marco Merlo (Fred), Fabrizio Merlo (Mark), May Deseligny (Jemma), Roberto Ricci (Prof. Korenz)

VIPCO Release: 2002

Also Known As: *The Green Inferno, Paradiso Infernale, Natura Contro, Against Nature*

VIPCO Plot Synopsis: *Jemma, a reporter hires a couple of men to find a professor who is lost in the jungle and she suspects may still be alive. The two men steal a plane and the three of them head off to a place called Fort Angel. They find a guide called Garcia in a bar and off they go deeper still, into the Amazon. Naturally there's a few mishaps on their way!! One of them has a fish swim up his arse that has to be plucked out, and amongst other things there's a bat attack during the night! After hunting some monkeys with blow darts they are captured by some savages. One of them has ants put all over his body and another is put up a tree and is blow darted himself, just like the monkeys were!*

Welcome to Fort Angel where you can enjoy the stunning scenery, get a tan, enjoy the exotic nightlife, watch toad racing, experience the local delight of a flesh-eating fish forcing its way into your rectum, or have a python chomp off your penis!

That opener is written in jest, in case it is not apparent. Why? Because the first half of this movie feels like it is a travel documentary gone wrong, promoting the exotic destination of Fort Angel (actually Leticia, Colombia). The opening of *Cannibal Holocaust II* starts off in this bland manner until the more disturbing elements creep in, and the cheesy holiday video vibe is no more. Even then, events prove boring and plodding, with a lack of any real excitement.

Quite how it was hoped people would believe this was a sequel to *Cannibal Holocaust* is lost on many. Indeed, the originally titled *The Green Inferno* merely feels like a vacation-gone-wrong flick and not the gritty and absorbing grindhouse picture that would be *expected* of a 'sequel' to Ruggero Deodato's hard-hitting exploitation epic.

It is directed adequately enough, with some passable performances; however, this is not enough to make *Holocaust II* a must see. Sadly, the feature is not even something completists of VIPCO or diehard fans of the cannibal genre should seek out. Stick with the memories of the original. Exploitation cinema has itself been exploited with this movie, by using the *Holocaust* name. That's marketing for you...

The only real highlight is a scene where two male characters try to catch pythons and anacondas in a river. One such giant snake escapes and starts to swim away into the Amazon River as the two cut-price Chuckle Brothers proceed to dive in and swim after it. Clearly unaware of how dangerous anacondas are, they only stop when it wraps itself around a crocodile and kills it. Very wise.

No cannibalism happens, nor is it really a holocaust; due to this, *Cannibal Holocaust II* has been pinpointed by many as the end of the cannibal boom that had trundled along for almost a decade. In all honesty, the boom had already slowed down to a crawl before this mess.

This was the last film by Antonio Climati. The Italian had strong links to the mondo sub-genre, having directed several features in this area of exploitation film.

The movie's original English title – *The Green Inferno* – is perhaps now more known due to Eli Roth using it on his own Amazonian cannibal flick from 2013; a film which *is* entertaining.

The *Cannibal Holocaust II* label had already been used in 1985 for Mario Gariazzo's *White Slave*. *White Slave* is also known as *Amazonia – The Catherine Miles Story* on some DVD and Blu-ray releases. It is passable.

The synopsis on the VIPCO VHS and DVD release in 2002 reads like it had been written by some bloke down the pub, who was drunkenly trying to tell his mates about a film they watched late one night on Channel 5, while drinking Carlsberg Special Brew. As Mike often thought of his fan base as a group of mates coming back from the boozer to watch a VIPCO tape, this ties in perfectly with his ideal customer.

CANNIBAL FEROX (1981)

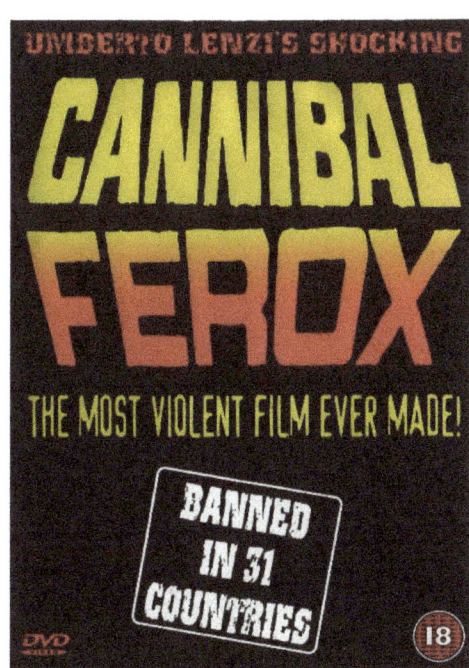

Director: Umberto Lenzi

Writer: Umberto Lenzi

Stars: Danilo Mattei as Bryan Redford (Rudy), Lorraine De Selle (Gloria), Giovanni Lombardo Radice as John Morghen (Mike), Robert Kerman (Lt. Rizzo)

VIPCO Release: 2000

Also Known As: *Make Them Die Slowly, Woman From Deep River*

VIPCO Plot Synopsis: *Gloria Davies is writing a thesis and she believes, unlike most people, that cannibalism is merely a myth which has been invented by whites. In order to test her theories she sets out for the jungle of the Amazon River, with her brother Rudy and her friend Pat. They go as far as Panaguaya in a Range Rover, and then proceed on foot. What they then experience is too terrifying to imagine but you can be sure is enough to chill the spine!*

The hype machine is at full steam with this one and with such a controversial film who can blame Mr. Lee? When VIPCO gave *Ferox* its first official release since its ban in the UK, the sleeve for the VHS and DVD stamped the following proudly across the bottom: 'BANNED IN 31 COUNTRIES'. 'The most violent film ever made!' then hammered home the point.

While both claims are hyperbole, they do have a ring of truth to them. Certainly, *Ferox* was one of *the* most violent films made upon its initial release, and due to the nature of the violence in question was banned in many countries the world over as a result.

A poster boy of the Video Nasties storm that filled the newspapers and broadcasts of the United Kingdom in the mid-eighties, *Ferox* was first put out on VHS uncut, and was followed by a cut edition with most of the animal cruelty erased. But Umberto's work was still to be banned despite this, and would remain so until the BFFC became more lax and less highly strung in 1999.

Although the ban was eventually lifted, VIPCO still had to follow BBFC orders of getting rid of the animal killing and maiming, as well as six seconds of further cuts to an animal bouncing around on the side of a Jeep. The British Board of Film Classification would enforce similar cuts almost two decades later when Shameless Films issued *Ferox* on Blu-ray in July 2018.

As for the feature itself, it is obviously a classic of exploitation cinema and is still held in high regard decades later. While debate still rages as to whether it is equal or pretty much as good as Deodato's *Cannibal Holocaust,* when viewing both notorious cannibal flicks back-to-back, it is glaringly obvious that Ruggero Deodato's flesh-munching opus is superior. This is not to say Lenzi's rival for genre fans' affections is a shoddy film. It stands on its own two feet in terms of the visceral delights expected, and provides food for thought.

The 'civilised' characters are mostly entitled and arrogant people that feel they can go into the native people's village and do what they like (because the tribe is inferior to them). It is a message that can easily be aimed at the first world of the time with western civilization and consumerism overpowering, and taking from, those that they deem to be inferior and – in their view – subhuman.

Giovanni Lombardo Radice, as Mike, is the biggest culprit and, in all fairness, is a nasty piece of work. He is a character that, no doubt, is supposed to embody the sentiments mentioned above. Radice's performance is fierce and done with a gleam in the eye. This makes a change when compared to his other appearances in VIPCO titles, where he was usually cast in roles as a low-brow simpleton or the innocent victim of violence. Here, the fate of Mike is warranted after his rampage of attacking the natives. His eventual demise gains no sympathy.

Another person in this movie is Lorraine De Selle. This came in the middle of De Selle's short onscreen career, 1977-84, that saw her co-star in another Video Nasty, *The House on the Edge of the Park* (1980). It is a strong outing and no doubt, at times, Lorraine was not actually acting; just reacting to what looks like a genuinely gruelling shoot.

For its director. Umberto Lenzi, *Ferox* came quickly after another well-known cannibal exploitation flick of his – *Eaten Alive!* Lenzi even reused the music from that feature. *Ferox* is the better remembered of the two although that is undoubtedly due to the controversy it would attract.

CANNIBAL FEROX II (1985)

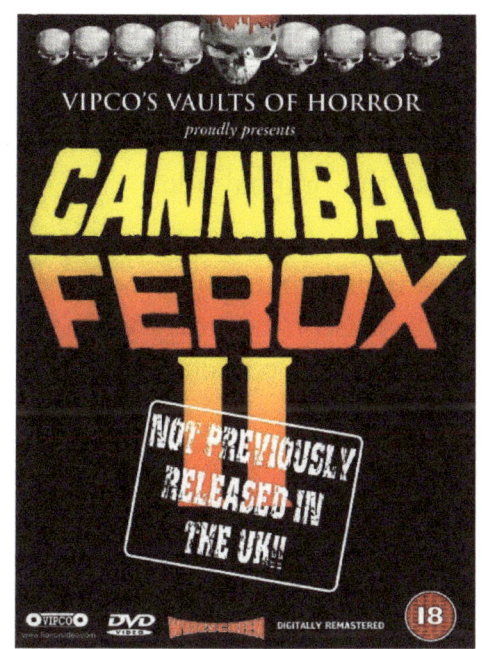

Director: Michele Massimo Tarantini as Michael E. Lemick

Writer: Michele Massimo Tarantini

Starring: Michael Sopkiw (Kevin), Milton Rodriguez as Milton Morris (Cpt. Heinz), Marta Anderson (Betty), Suzane Carvalho as Susane Carvall (Eva)

VIPCO Release: 2002

Also Known As: *Massacre in Dinosaur Valley, Stranded in Dinosaur Valley, Nudo e Selvaggio* (original)

VIPCO Plot Synopsis: *A charter plane crashes into the middle of the Amazon jungle in an area known as "Dinosaur Valley" so called because of a substantial fossil find in the area. Assorted archaeologists, models, alcoholic wives, Vietnam vets etc, have to battle their way through flesheating Voodoo tribes, piranhas, quicksand, crocodiles and more in this flesheating, entrail rending, bullet hitting, bloody impaling, previously unavailable tale!*

By renaming the original movie as *Cannibal Ferox II*, VIPCO were able to recreate the attention-grabbing sleeve of the original *Ferox*. While not previously banned in the UK, a 'Not Previously Released in the UK' stamp (remarkably similar-looking to the original 'Ferox's Banned in 31 Countries' stamp) is on the cover, plus a warning about the 'representation of violent and repulsive subject matter'.

Like *Cannibal Holocaust II*, *Ferox II* starts off feeling like a holiday travelogue with shots of beautiful scenery being shown, as cheesy music plays in the background, and the Prof's pretty young daughter is eyed up on the bus. This actually happens a lot during *Cannibal Ferox II*: women being eyed up.

An incredibly large amount of the screen time is dedicated to male characters having a good old perv at half naked or completely naked young women. If not that, then the same young women are getting frisky with male characters or being molested in some form. The camerawork during these many, many sequences make the viewer feel as if they are in on the action too, or at least complicit. Tarantini lunges the lens right in on most of the nudity when it occurs, from shots of the women showering, to being sexually assaulted, or having a lie down after surviving another attempt on their lives.

It is not just the men that seem to be desperate to get in the hapless girls' knickers; other female characters do so too, when a spot of forced lesbianism crops up in the final act. Michele Massimo Tarantini sticks with what he knows hereafter, having directed countless smut-filled flicks in his career previously.

The titular cannibalism barely takes place and seems to be more of a way of getting some gore in the mix when it does happen. Apart from a heart-munching scene, and some minor bloodshed, *Cannibal Ferox II* concentrates on campy nudity and bad acting.

Of course, this will be due to the fact this is not an actual sequel to the epic *Cannibal Ferox;* this movie started life as *Massacre in Dinosaur Valley*. It is a standalone flick that is so far removed from Lenzi's classic that it is absurd that VIPCO re-stickered it as a sequel. The name was suggested as a joke by Jay Slater, only for it to be taken seriously by Mike as he did not like the original title.

Along with the pseudo-sequel to *Cannibal Holocaust*, VIPCO's release of *Ferox II* is undoubtedly a low point in the cannibal film boom. It is fitting that both would be the last entries into the genre's golden period. Is it perhaps also fitting that VIPCO would try to exploit the two biggest names in cannibal cinema by repackaging two of its weakest names as pseudo-sequels?

The movie itself could have been a lot better, for cult cinema hero Daradano Sacchetti was a writer for *Dinosaur Valley*. He is uncredited, perhaps to save the embarrassment of being attached to this. Marta Anderson, in what would be her final film role, gives the best performance despite the fact her acting chews the scenery and is frivolous.

VIPCO released *Cannibal Ferox II* with nearly two minutes of cuts, and it would not be until 15 years later that the movie would be picked up for another UK release by 88 Films as *Dinosaur Valley*. This time around there would be just 13 seconds of cuts. Said cuts were the usual BBFC no-no of animal cruelty. To save confusion, and ignore the VIPCO *Ferox* sequel spin, 88 Films gave the feature its original name for their DVD and Blu-ray editions.

EATEN ALIVE! (1980)

Director: Umberto Lenzi

Writer: Umberto Lenzi

Stars: Robert Kerman (Mark Butler), Ivan Rassimov (Jonas Melvin), Janet Agren (Shelia Morris), Me Me Lai (Mowara)

VIPCO Release: 1992

Also Known As: *Doomed to Die, Eaten Alive by the Cannibals!, The Emerald Jungle*

VIPCO Plot Synopsis: *The renowned Italian director Umberto Lenzi tells a tale of cannibals at play in the Jungles of New Guinea, starring Robert Kerman, Janet Argen and Mel Ferrer. When a young woman's sister disappears, the only clue to her whereabouts is a glimpsed appearance in a bizarre film showing scenes of cannibalism, left behind by a hitman murdered on the streets of New York. The trail soon leads to*

New Guinea, where the subject of the film, the self styled spiritual leader 'Mr. Jonas', is teaching his cult followers ancient cannibal rites...

Considering this is a cannibal flick, not much flesh munching takes place. *Eaten Alive!* feels more like a wacko cult movie than anything, with the Jim Jones-esque Jonas setting up camp in New Guinea, and taking advantage of his followers, as well as the locals.

The Jonestown Massacre gained worldwide attention in the winter of 1978 when cult leader Jim Jones gave his followers drinks spiked with cyanide in their settlement in the South American country of Guyana. 909 people died in total although 300 of them were by gunfire when the followers refused to drink up. *Eaten Alive!* was made and released less than 18 months later. Director Umberto Lenzi not only capitalised on the cannibal film boom of that period, but real life events too, with this offering.

Ivan Rassimov, as the leader Jonas, has a Jim Jones look to him, and is a charismatic figure throughout. That's important since cult leaders tend to be charismatic. The methods of Jonas are not quite that of his real-life counterpart however; this, of course, is the work of Lenzi who inserts a lot of titillation and bloodshed.

There are copious amounts of nudity with the native women wearing very little. Burmese-British actress Me Me Lai is given the most screen time out of them, and lives up to her reputation for taking her clothes off. Admittedly, she is stunning throughout, and manages a good performance. But she meets a bloody end, as can be seen on many VHS/DVD covers of *Eaten Alive!.*

Eaten Alive! not only had its bloodletting and effects censored for the VIPCO release but its footage of animal death also met the same fate. This certainly was more in keeping with other cannibal boom pictures of the era. In the United Kingdom, the BBFC have never been too fond of real animal killings on camera. The exclusions, or edits, to these moments do not really detract from the movie, though.

What's certain, however, is that the scriptwriters are guilty of providing some truly duff dialogue. When there are lines like 'That's the $64 question', 'How odd, how very odd' and '...he's out of his cotton-picking head', unintentional laughs are to be had.

Eaten Alive! could perhaps be seen as a test run for Lenzi in the cannibal genre as his next feature would be one of the most iconic and controversial entries into that subgenre (as well as being another VIPCO title): *Cannibal Ferox.*

Mike got his hands on this cannibal flick in the early nineties with a Cult Classic release which had great artwork by Graham Humphreys; it was followed by a summer 2000 reissue with the familiar Me Me Lai photo sleeve. It was given one more cash grab DVD release as part of the Screamtime Collection in 2003.

THE MOUNTAIN OF THE CANNIBAL GOD (1978)

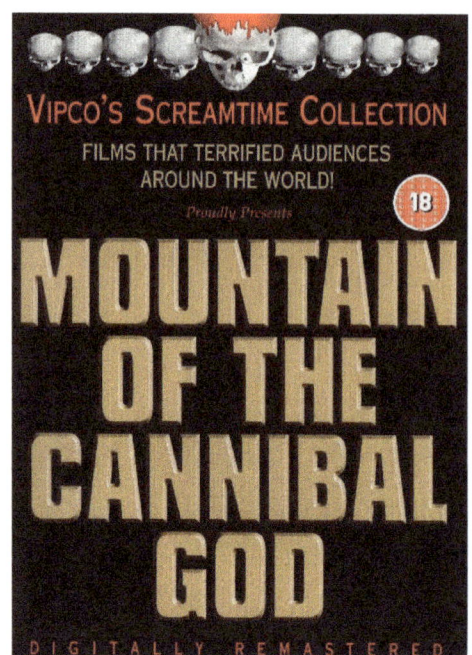

Director: Sergio Martino

Writers: Cesare Frugoni, Sergio Martino

Stars: Stacy Keach (Prof. Foster), Ursula Andress (Susan), Claudio Cassinelli (Manolo), Antonio Marsina (Arthur)

VIPCO Release: 2001

Also Known As: See main text

VIPCO Plot Synopsis: *Susan Stevenson and her brother Arthur go to Manilla for the purpose of organising a search party for Susan's husband, a famous anthropologist, who has disappeared during a mysterious expedition, on one of the larger islands of the archipelago. No one knows for sure the purpose of his expedition, not even Dr. Foster, Stevenson's close friend and collaborator. By examining the last parts of the film shot during Stevenson's expedition, they are able to ascertain that he penetrated the jungle right up to Mount Rarami, the Mountain of the Spirits, considered taboo by the natives. Set in the jungles the story unfolds of the Mountain and its curses.*

Made and released in its native Italy under the *Mountain...* name, this feature would be marketed initially as *Slave of the Cannibal God* in the United States and, when first released in the United Kingdom, it was as *Prisoner of the Cannibal God*. VIPCO opted for the *Mountain...* handle in 2001, when the BBFC finally lifted the ban on Martino's work. Whatever the name, they all ensured that the words *Cannibal God* were mentioned to take advantage of the lure that 'the C-word' had.

While it languished for nearly two decades as a banned video nasty, the eventual VIPCO DVD and VHS of *Mountain...* did contain cuts. The BBFC were not so keen on Martino's use of real animals being killed on camera; two minutes of this type of footage were snipped. Oddly, some animal cruelty does remain, real or otherwise. However, the boar fucking scene is gone and if people were disappointed by its absence then that raises some serious questions about why they wanted to view it.

The artwork used on this title features one of the natives chomping on a snake which, of course, is gone from the Screamtime edition. Considering that Ursula Andress is nude during the film, it is a shock that an image of her in the buff was not used instead; Mike was always fond of a bit of titillation. Shameless Entertainment made sure this was the case for their 2018 Blu-ray edition with Ursula in the mud-rubbing scene on the sleeve cover. It should be noted that the boar fucking *is* in the Shameless version.

Martino was no stranger to VIPCO over the years with his 1979 flick *Screamers*, aka *Island of the Fishmen,* receiving a VHS issue from the firm under the title of *Island of*

Mutations in 1980, and his 1973 classic *Torso* hitting VIPCO video in 1993, amongst others.

With *Cannibal God*, his direction and style were nowhere near his early seventies purple period. Regardless, there are moments where Martino does up the ante and bring tension to proceedings. There is a sequence when Susan and the others climb up a waterfall with all the actors seemingly doing their own stunts, and the scenes within the caves of the mountain have a tense atmosphere and sense of urgency.

Outside of those remarks, the rest of the feature is clichéd and predictable. Martino relies on the violence associated with cannibal flicks to liven things up as well as Andress getting her clothes off. Indeed, the director seems to take great delight when she is rubbed all over with what appears to be mud, yet is meant to be honey.

Who can blame him though? Andress was still a name at the box office at this point in her career, due to her looks and body. Her performance is not completely abysmal, but it is safe to say her acting ability was not the main reason why she was cast. Stacy Keach and Claudio Cassinelli, thankfully, are more than capable in the acting department. Cassinelli would sadly die in 1985 in a helicopter crash while filming another Martino film: *Hands of Steel* (1986).

The write-up on the back of the Screamtime edition of the movie ends with the typical VIPCO hard sell: '*Mountain of the Cannibal God*, one of the most sought after Video Nasties is at long last available to take home. Don't resist – take your copy home today!'

3

The History of VIPCO (Part II)

I got caught by The Rank Organisation, and others, who took a lawsuit out against me for illegally selling their films on tape. I knew a couple of air hostesses, too, that had the films from the planes, and they'd phone me up. I'd give them a bit of money for them tapes.

Mike Lee

Mike's gamble to start his own video company was a modest success. But he knew that he needed something that would sell more copies, and quickly.

Although he did not enjoy horror movies – despite publicly saying otherwise – Mike rightly figured out that horror films on VHS were the way to go. He would have no doubt seen how well his rivals were doing with this genre on tape, and it made the businessman's next decision a lot easier as a result. VIPCO was to sell its first horror film.

Mike turned again to Michael Myers of Miracle Films, and the father of his former school friend Martin, in the hope he would part with a horror movie that he had on his firm's books. Indeed, Mike was thrilled when Myers informed him that he did have a horror flick he would sell to him. This one film would make VIPCO and, in turn, Mike a lot of money and steer the young company in the direction for which it would become famous. It would also cause VIPCO to release titles that would be at the centre of the yet-to-happen Video Nasties scandal; a period which would see Mike victimized by an overzealous press and police. But that was in the not-too-distant future.

The title which Mike had bought the rights to? *Zombie Flesh Eaters.*

Lucio Fulci's 1979 zombie masterpiece had been a worldwide hit. The relentless Fulci had shot a movie which was gruelling and bloodthirsty with plenty of gore and flesh-munching; the special effects had made the movie a must-see among cult cinema fans all over the globe.

Mike fell in love with *ZFE* as soon as he saw it, at the Prince Charles Cinema he claims – especially the infamous eye-splinter scene – and decided that the film *had* to be sold on tape by VIPCO. He was also impressed with Fulci's style and direction, supposedly appreciating the godfather of gore for more than just the bloodshed on screen. "Wonderful stuff," Mike would say of *ZFE* in his 1993 Darkside interview. This admiration for Lucio's efforts would see more of the Italian director's works being released by VIPCO in the following decades as Mike

17

believed these were "worthwhile films in anyone's collection." While some were just as strong as *ZFE*, others were terrible; yet Mike was a fan with the means of getting his new-found favourite director's other features a British release. And it all began with *Zombie Flesh Eaters*.

"It was my father that 'brought' the feature to the United Kingdom after acquiring distribution rights of *Zombie Flesh Eaters* from its Italian producers," Martin Myers pointed out. "He even commissioned the famous 'hand out of the soil' poster [by Tom Beauvais] that is forever linked with it." When it came to VIPCO releasing it on video, and the impact it had on his friend's business, Myers had this to say, "It made Mike very rich and gave him a good lifestyle. VIPCO should be remembered for the success and impact in Britain that that movie had. But the plaudits should also be shared with my father as he was the one who had the rights to begin with, before passing them onto VIPCO!"

ZFE was indeed a success and made the owner of VIPCO wealthy. Mike would sell up to 10,000 copies in some months and would end up running out of the materials needed to make more tapes. He had two versions made of his new toy; one which was the cut cinema version he had initially bought; and the second which was a completely uncut version (which did not have to be censored due to the lack of policing of the still-growing home video market). Mike decided that this 'strong uncut' version of *ZFE* would be sold for more money, making even more cash on an already lucrative release! That edit was usually sold under the counter; its reputation was that notorious already. Mike has said the success *ZFE* and other Nasties made him a millionaire by the age of 27; as he explained, "Our sales went through the roof! First year we made £78,000, second year we did £239,000, and after the third year it was almost £1.5 million... I would go to the casino, play poker, then go clubbing. I had a great time!"

In a way, VIPCO had seen the light with this hit title. Mike decided that he had to have more horror films for his firm and obtained the rights for other movies that would become forever linked with VIPCO. *The Driller Killer* (1979) – Abel Ferrara's cult exploitation flick – did great business, and *Psychic Killer* (1975, again from Myers) followed soon after. More and more horror was added to the growing catalogue of VIPCO videos, a number of which were just as bloody or controversial as *Zombie Flesh Eaters* or *The Driller Killer*. Other genres would get a look in, too, with the likes of *King Frat* (1979) and *The Rise and Fall of Idi Amin* (1981) being offered, although VIPCO was quickly becoming the firm that genre fans knew was responsible for some of the goriest and mad-looking VHS sleeves on rental store shelves.

It was the perception that VIPCO sold the most extreme titles to buy or rent in the United Kingdom that would see it gain publicity that helped sales to rocket. It was this perception that also, ultimately, saw the distributor become the poster boy for Video Nasties in the witch hunt of the day.

The press and government of the era, slow as always to catch on to what the British people wanted, or were interested in, finally started to take notice of the now strong video rental market, and the influx of controversial and often realistic horror movies that helped these stores thrive. The competition to get the casual viewer to buy or rent a title was fierce with other distributors designing ever more over-the-top and bloody covers for their output, in an effort to stand out from the shelves.

These factors coupled with a gloriously eye-catching picture on the sleeve of *The Driller Killer* (along with its related advertising) would propel VIPCO into the eye of the raging Video Nasties moral storm.

I couldn't make the tapes quick enough!

Michael Lee on the success of Zombie Flesh Eaters

There is no denying that VIPCO relied heavily on the zombie genre during its lifetime. Mike, after all, first gave horror a shot after seeing *Zombie Flesh Eaters*. He must have felt anything similar would be just as good and, boy, was he wrong as this led to VIPCO selling some right clunkers on tape and disc.

This fondness for the subgenre also saw him change the name of *Flesh Eater* to *Zombie Nosh* and *Burial Ground* to *The Zombie Dead* just to ensure 'zombie' was in the title of the eventual release. As you are about to find out, the quality of these features was often on the… ahem… low side, yet they always managed to have some type of strange entertainment value.

ZOMBIE FLESH EATERS (1979)

Director: Lucio Fulci

Writers: Elisa Briganti, Dardano Sacchetti, Chuck Smith

Stars: Tisa Farrow (Anne), Ian McCulloch (Peter), Al Cliver (Brian), Richard Johnson (Dr. Menard)

VIPCO Release: 1980

Also Known As: See below

VIPCO Plot Synopsis: *In Hudson Bay a sailing boat that has a neglected appearance is drifting slowly out to sea. A coast guard boat draws up alongside and a policeman goes into the cabin. His colleagues do not see him come out again and one is about to go into the cabin when a terrifying sight appears out of the hatchway — a man, covered in blood, walks towards him menacingly. Only after being hit repeatedly by bullets from the policeman's gun does he fall overboard and disappear amid the waves. This news causes a* *sensation and panic in the whole of America, also because the sailing boat belonged to a famous scientist who disappeared rather mysteriously in the Caribbean. The scientist's daughter Ann together with Peter West, a famous American journalist, set out to look for him. The two of them set sail on a schooner belonging to Brian, a young American ethnologist, and Susan, a young underwater photographer. Far out at sea, Susan dives to take some photographs, but is attacked by a huge shark: however, she is saved by a Zombie who unexpectedly appears out of the depths of the ocean. In the meantime, on a Matul Island, in the Antilles, Professor Menard is carrying out strange experiments. What follows in the Caribbean and later in New York is terrifying – ZOMBIE FLESH EATERS are here!!*

The synopsis on the original VHS box is so long and boring, it is a genuine wonder how potential punters in the early eighties did not simply put the video down, or fall asleep. Or both.

Those that managed to wake up and buy the thing made the right decision. *Zombie Flesh Eaters* aka *Zombi 2* is one of the definitive movies of the Video Nasties era and considered one of the best (if not *the* best) work by Lucio Fulci.

Starting life as a script written by Dardano Sacchetti, in the summer of 1978, one of Fulci's most famous gore epics was not intended to be directed by him at first. Other Italian directing legends, Enzo Castellari and Umberto Lenzi, had originally been rumoured to be in the director's seat. Fulci came on board, later, following a couple of name changes that would see Sacchetti's story being retitled *Nightmare Island* then *Zombi 2* – based on the success of George A. Romero's *Dawn of the Dead* in Italy under the title *Zombi*.

The movie itself begins with violence, and it continues throughout. With a shopping list of gore effects to tick off during proceedings, the viewer is treated to point-blank gunshot blasts to heads, throat ripping, blood spraying, eye gouging, and gut munching. The intensity with which they happen, and their cinematic qualities, proves gratuitous in nature and unflinching. Lucio gives this work an aesthetic that had been unseen in zombie cinema at this time. While *Dawn of the Dead* before it had bloodshed and a gritty nature, they were presented in a slightly subdued manner. Romero proffered a deeper meaning that cast a critical eye on consumerism.

Fulci, however, does not go as deep with the subject matter and context. Instead, he batters viewers over the head with sheer violence. In a way, proffering so much gore and so many grisly deaths, creates a zombie flick that threatens to be as mindless as the consumerism that Romero saw evident during the time of his masterpiece. The zombies have different appearances, too. Romero's are mainly blank-eyed actors with pale make up, while Fulci's are rotting, disgusting, and look as if they are genuinely the walking dead.

It would be this excessive (and rather realistic, at times) gore that irked the BBFC at the time. The movie had already been cut when it was first released in the United Kingdom back in 1980 but when it made its way to VHS – where anyone could rent or buy it – the blood and flesh eating that did remain became cause for concern, despite being deemed suitable years earlier. VIPCO would tout this on every *Zombie Flesh Eaters* release from the early nineties onwards. As well as this,

VIPCO would slap big eye-catching banners on the boxes, proclaiming a release to be the 'EXTREME VERSION' or 'STRONG UNCUT' regardless of any actual cut.

When censorship laws in the United Kingdom began to mellow by the late nineties, and the moral panic over 'video sadism' had faded/become ignored, *ZFE* was reissued with fewer edits – although a full actual uncut edition did not see the light of day until 2005. Uncharacteristically of VIPCO, they slipped up when it came to this title being given a DVD release; Mike was 'too busy' (his words) to renew the rights on *ZFE*.

Zombi 2 benefits from the strength of its main actors. In other words, the feature holds its own away from the gory glory. Tisa Farrow, who was about to enter a series of well-known exploitation cinema roles that would mark the end of her career, earns herself praise in her performance as Anne. It is a shame Farrow would retire so shortly after this, although her post-cinema profession as a nurse is a career she no doubt found to be much more rewarding.

Fans are also treated to horror flick stalwarts Al Cliver and Ian McCulloch. Cliver had appeared in many a Fulci work and his presence in this film is welcomed. McCulloch, who was an established British television actor, with some film experience by this point in his career, is serious if a little hammy here, but gives a credible and memorable performance as Peter. He followed this role up with other, hammy-yet-serious turns in *Zombi Holocaust* aka *Doctor Butcher, M.D.* (1980) and *Contamination* (1980). Out of those three flicks, it is his talents in *ZFE* which are most superior. McCulloch would work in the realms of horror and exploitation cinema until he returned to the relatively normal world of British television, several years later.

Of course, *ZFE* is enhanced by the ever-capable skills of the Italian musician and composer Fabio Frizzi. The legendary Italian composer delivers the goods with his score for this feature, and has stated that he (strangely) found inspiration from The Beatles. He is also another long-time Fulci collaborator.

Zombi 2 would be followed by *Zombi 3* aka *Zombie Flesh Eaters II* that was part-directed by Lucio Fulci. This, in turn, would then see various films related to each other (or not) being labelled as *Zombi* sequels.

ZFE is one of the titles that, alongside *Cannibal Ferox* (1981), *Cannibal Holocaust* (1980) and *Driller Killer* (1979), would be most closely linked with the moral panic of the early- to mid-eighties in Britain which led to the Video Recordings Act 1984 and the BBFC excessively censoring films. The now iconic sleeve of the green mangy hand grasping from a grave is an image that is forever linked with everything that era of exploitation film means to British fans; for some, it is a strange, morbid reminder of their childhood (which is the case for me) or coming of age. The power *ZFE* had is not to be underestimated, certainly not in the case of VIPCO. Not the best movie to be featured within the company's catalogue, but it is undoubtedly the title that provided the greatest momentum for the firm, helping them move towards forming their identity. It made Mike very rich indeed.

As can be seen at the beginning of this section, the VIPCO synopsis is tediously long and moribund. When re-released in the early nineties, it got worse as Mike decided more was needed to sell the tape. This starts off with a doubtful claim about it having never been available before, and the addition of widescreen. It reads (errors included): 'For the first time ever on video you can enjoy the full atmosphere and excitement of Lucio Fulci's Classic zombie movie, *ZOMBIE FLESH EATERS* – shot in super wide Cinemascope and presented here in its original screen ratio. There's never been a fully 'Widescreen' version of a horror movie let alone one previously banned! Here for the first time is *ZOMBIE FLESH EATERS* in all its widescreen gory glory!'

No mention though that this was the personal favourite (out of all the titles VIPCO would release) of owner Mike. This fact could help explain the company's fondness for *ZFE* and the money grab retitling of other zombie flicks that VIPCO would later do. Fulci's zombie epic was the biggest-earning title VIPCO would have by quite some margin. The firm would reorder thousands of copies, every month, at one point.

Barrie Gold of S Gold & Sons, VIPCO's distributor, nearly passed on handling the title for Mike. "When Mike asked if I would help with his first horror film – *Zombie Flesh Eaters* – I said I would do it, but only if he took back all the stock of those four other movies he got off Michael Myers that we were still stuck with!" Those four titles were the initial tapes VIPCO sold at launch and, thankfully, Mike agreed with Barrie's demand and *ZFE* would be sold in the UK!

Producer and horror historian Marc Morris cites the sale of *ZFE* as the best thing VIPCO did for genre fans in this country. His sentiments are shared by this writer. If Mike and his now defunct company are to be remembered for one thing, it is for bringing Fulci's epic to British shores. Everything else is a distant second.

The movie has since been released on DVD and Blu-ray several times in the UK and the world over. Its impact on horror cinema as a whole cannot be underestimated; the feature retains its power 40 years later.

ZOMBIE FLESH EATERS 2 (1988)

Directors: Lucio Fulci, Claudio Fragasso,

Writers: Claudio Fragasso, Rossella Drudi (uncredited), Lucio Fulci (uncredited)

Stars: Beatrice Ring (Patricia), Deran Sarafian (Kenny), Massimo Vanni as Alex McBride (Bo), Ottaviano Dell'Acqua as Richard Ramond (Roger)

VIPCO Release: 2002

Also Known As: *Revolt of the Living Dead, Zombi 3, Zombie 3, Zombie: Hell on Earth*

VIPCO Plot Synopsis: *Somewhere in South East Asia a cloud of toxic waste escapes from a nuclear power plant and quickly contaminates everything around. Immediately the military take charge and are faced by a growing army of contaminated men who die awful deaths and return as*

ferocious *Flesh Eating Zombies!* The arm goes ballistic and all hell breaks loose... What follows is terrifying...

"It has been done by a group of idiots, who are Claudio Fragasso – natural born cretin: Bruno Mattei – who before becoming a director was a house painter." Lucio Fulci on *Zombie Flesh Eaters 2*, interview quoted in *Beyond Terror* by Stephen Thrower.

As can be gathered by the above statement, Fulci was not happy with his movie *Zombi 3* aka *Zombie Flesh Eaters 2*. In fact, he refused to finish it, and the aforementioned 'group of idiots' was drafted in to finish it for him. The result is a zombie flick far more in keeping with Mattei's 1980 movie *Zombie Creeping Flesh* (Fragasso also did script duties on this) than being a continuation of Fulci's classic *Zombie/Zombi 2/Zombie Flesh Eaters* saga.

Lucio reportedly tried to finish his feature but felt the script was just too dreadful, despite trying to get it changed. He eventually pulled out and cited illness as his reason (in an effort to play down his departure). For many years, it was believed Mattei completed the movie although it has since come to light that Fragasso also had a hand in directing. The pair were asked to complete *Zombi 3* by worried producer Franco Gaudenzi (who Fulci *also* felt was an idiot). Gaudenzi must have liked what he saw as this trio would go on to make other movies together in the same roles.

The result is a bit of a mess; it's a muddle of other horror flicks and most viewers will recognise how much better the ripped off titles are. George Romero's works such as *The Crazies* (1973), *Dawn of the Dead* (1978) and *Day of the Dead* (1985) heavily colour the story. Other aspects of the plot seem to have been taken from *The Fog* (1980), *Return of the Living Dead* (1985) and *Demons* (1985).

But it is George Romero who casts the largest shadow over *ZFEII*. The military trying to contain the outbreak, and the way in which those suspected of infection are rounded up or killed – plus other numerous plot points – all reek of the famed director's previous output. Furthermore, the movie has a feeling of *Zombie Creeping Flesh* which, of course, borrows heavily from Romero too, and was (as mentioned) also directed by Mattei.

This is perhaps why *ZFEII* lacks the trademarks of Fulci's direction, as it is essentially not his work, and he has even publicly disowned it. The eerie atmosphere that often helped give some of his most nonsensical works at least some artistic value, is gone. Instead, we have typical Mattei, and a simple approach to directing. There are some points of interest such as the 'biting skull scene' or the pregnant woman having a zombie arm burst out of her stomach. But that's about it. The zombies here are quick-paced and vicious which would become a standout attribute of the hit *28 Days Later* (2002) where Danny Boyle's undead act in a similar fashion.

It is also no wonder Fulci tried to alter the script because the plot is often stupid or outright illogical. At the start of the runtime, the military urgently try to contain the virus and kill anyone with it. They illogically decide to dispose of the infected by cremating them which results in their ashes being blown out into the surrounding area, increasing the risk of exposure instead of reducing it. This is actually *pointed out by other characters* but the god-damn military (two of which are played by Mattei and Fragasso) refuse to listen. One infected character chops off his hand to stop the disease spreading despite it clearly having done so… his face is rotting!

Blue Heart (voiced by Del Russel in the English dub) is a charismatic character that meets a zany-but-absurd fate. This character is perhaps the only positive thing within this saga.

When VIPCO welcomed this title to its line-up in 2002, with a VHS and DVD release, the packaging was a blatant recycling of the *Zombie Flesh Eaters'* Tom Beauvais-designed artwork with slight modifications. The tagline drives home the message too: The Hand Returns! Those expecting it to be as good as the first entry will have been in for a shock. The title eventually found its way to the bargain bin Screamtime Collection, which is rather fitting for a feature of this standard. *ZFEII* would rise from the dead again thanks to an 88 Films Blu-ray release in 2015, as *Zombi 3*.

ZOMBIE FLESH EATERS 3 (1988)

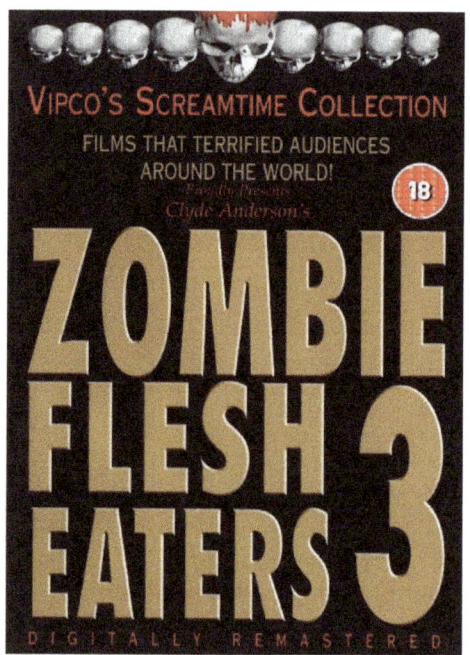

Director: Claudio Fragasso (as Clyde Anderson)

Writer: Rossella Drudi

Stars: Jeff Stryker as Chuck Peyton (Chuck), Massimo Vanni as Alex McBride (David), Candice Daly (Jenny), Jim Gaines (Dan)

VIPCO Release: 2002

Also Known As: *After Death, Return of the Living Dead Part 3, Zombie 4, Zombie 4: After Death*

VIPCO Plot Synopsis: *A team of researchers are studying immortality on a remote island feel the wrath of the Zombies when a Voodoo plague makes the Dead Ones rise again! Hearts are torn pout, faces are ripped off and heads explode as the gut munching, flesh eating dead have their wicked way! Wonderfully fast paced, gorier than hell with a meaty helping of dismemberments and mutilation makes this the best Zombie Flesh Eaters EVER!!*

Another alleged sequel to Fulci's *Zombi* where VIPCO tried, again, to tie into the success and name-value of *Zombie Flesh Eaters*. Released as *ZFE III* in the UK, in other parts of the world it is sold under its original title *After Death* or another Fulci cash-in name *Zombi 4*.

It was shot in the same location as *Zombi 3* – the Philippines – and features the undead. Those are the only connections between the two.

There was no involvement from the Godfather of Gore and this meant that *ZFE III* was just as bad as the film it followed. With Fragasso being solely responsible for directing duties this is no shock; his writer wife Rossella Drudi (who was uncredited on *Zombi 3*) provides her husband with a shoddy script to add to the misery. A scene that sums up how bad things really are is when two characters are in a semi-darkened room and light a candle to see better. They are terrified when it illuminates a group of zombies that were stood DIRECTLY IN FRONT OF THEM the whole time. The fact the viewer is meant to believe the characters had not spotted them prior to this is, quite frankly, an insult.

The movie does have one good thing going for it, and that is the music. It opens with a Dokken-esque rock song performed by Italian metal band Shout. The song is an adequate slice of eighties heavy metal and initially gives one the impression that – for an Italian zombie flick – *ZFE III* might be different. Al Festa's soundtrack is in keeping with similar undead flicks of the era but has a funky disco-like slant to it. It certainly perks up several moments of the feature.

The plot, despite being predictable as well as unoriginal, does have an element that is interesting. Once the group of friends start dying and coming back as zombies, they try to convince their living friends to join them as the undead. The zombies here do not just want to eat the living, they want to recruit them as well!

Gay porn star Jeff Stryker co-stars using the name Chuck Peyton and, out of all the bland performances, is fairly efficient. His character meets a ludicrous fate, and I won't spoil the surprise here.

For a zombie flick, the walking dead are not only extremely quick but are also throwing themselves around like ninjas. When they attack the living in the jungle, it feels like an episode of *Mighty Morphin Power Rangers*. The actors portraying the undead seem like stuntmen extras.

ZFE III ends in a rather frivolous manner, which again will not be spoiled, and it is questionable whether Fragasso and Drudi decided to use it. Something better could have been thought of, surely?

VIPCO first released *Zombie Flesh Eaters III* on VHS and DVD in 2002. Of course, the classic artwork used for the original *ZFE* is recycled here with the addition of a gravestone being clutched by 'the hand'. That gravestone is either tiny or the zombie hand is massive for this to happen. The image was ditched for the re-release as part of the Screamtime Collection. 88 Films put the movie out on Blu-ray in October 2018.

Fragasso and Drudi would go on to direct and write the abysmal *Troll 2* (1990) a film which has developed a cult following for all the wrong reasons. *Troll 2* would make *ZFE III* feel like *Citizen Kane* (1941) in comparison.

ZOMBIE CREEPING FLESH (1980)

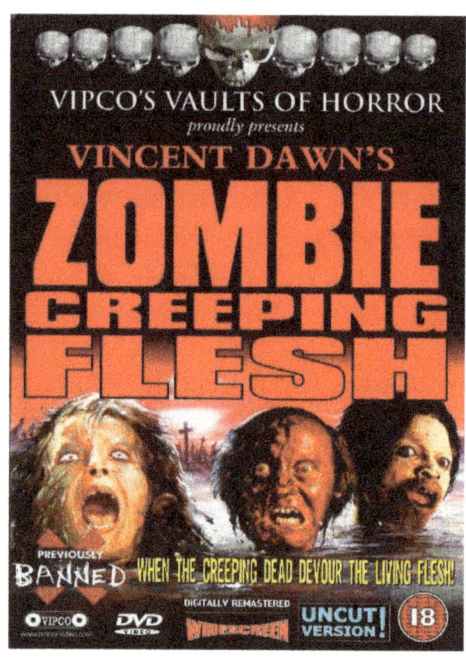

Director: Bruno Mattei (as Vincent Dawn), Claudio Fragasso

Writers: Claudio Fragasso, Jose Maria Cunilles as J.M. Cunilles

Stars: Margie Newton as Margit Evelyn Newton (Lia), Frank Garofalo as Frank Garfield (Zantoro), Gabriel Renom as Gaby Renom (Pierre), Jose Gras as Robert O'Neil (Lt. London)

VIPCO Release: 2001

Also Known As: *Hell of the Living Dead, Night of the Zombies, Virus*

VIPCO Plot Synopsis: *A centre producing synthetic nourishment for the Third World is rocked by a huge explosion. A cloud of toxic gas fills the air and asphyxiates the workers. They return as flesh-eating zombies – destroying villages and quenching their thirst for blood on the inhabitants... DEVOURING THEM ALIVE! A special squad is sent – their mission is to destroy the energy formula... and end the blood-crazed zombies reign of terror...*

When originally released by VIPCO in 2001, the packaging for this Mattei opus bared the following statement after the plot synopsis: '*Zombie Creeping Flesh* actually makes a serious point – that if you don't feed the Third World, THEY'LL COME AND FEED ON YOU!'

It is hoped Mike was joking when he came up with the above observation; it would be worrying if he believed a movie about zombies (by old Bruno) would prompt viewers to consider the poverty of the less privileged in the world… and that they would come eat you if you did not.

It is a shock, though, that Mike did not jump on the movie's efforts to rip off the far better-known and loved *Dawn of the Dead* (1978). *ZCF* is a watered-down version of that Romero classic, which is what the producers of the film wanted; Mattei even used some of the Goblin soundtrack from that feature (as well as other works by the legendary band). As *Dawn* was still fresh in people's minds in 1980, there were many attempts to emulate or riff on its instant classic success. Bruno Mattei will have easily gone where the money was. This was a key characteristic of the Italian's career.

In fact, another characteristic (of sorts) which would appear several times throughout the exploitation director's career, is in full swing with *ZCF*. Claudio Fragasso is on script duty. Fragasso would do similar work on many Mattei works during the eighties without much critical praise. Here the dialogue and *Dawn*-lite plot is in keeping with what is expected of the man that gave the world *Troll 2* (1990). Fragasso has since claimed that he part-directed the movie as well. The pairing of Mattei and Fragasso would generate several films that would grace the VIPCO catalogue over the years.

Whatever the shoddy backstory of *Creeping Flesh*, as well as what came after it, this yarn found itself in hot water in the United Kingdom in the early eighties. Banned as a 'Video Nasty', the strict BBFC did not take kindly to some of the violence and bloodshed that, candidly, was often the only interesting thing within the feature. That ban would be lifted at the start of the new millennium, and VIPCO jumped on the title, as the firm was prone to do, with anything linked to the 1980's moral panic.

Hitting VHS and DVD, the eye-catching and colourful sleeve made the release look far more interesting than it actually was. A few years later, it would not even have the interesting sleeve, as it was re-released as part of the Screamtime Collection and given the hideous and unexciting artwork which 'blessed' the series. 88 Films re-released the movie in 2017.

THE ZOMBIE DEAD (1981)

Director: Andrea Bianchi

Writer: Piero Regnoli

Starring: Gianluigi Chirizzi as Gian Luigi Chrizzi (Mark), Antonella Antinori as Antonietta Antinori (Leslie), Pietro Barzocchini as Peter Bark (Michael), Karin Well (Janet)

VIPCO Release: 2002

Also Known As: *Burial Ground, Burial Ground: The Nights of Terror, The Nights of Terror*

VIPCO Plot Synopsis: *The Zombie Dead are unleashed when a professor's thirst for knowledge seals his own demise when he unwittingly unseals a cursed underground crypt in an ancient burial ground. The desecrated graveyard erupts with a ground swell of ravenous, rotting, flesh hungry zombies that shamble into the night in search of living human prey. On the adjoining grounds, a group of clueless, decadent socialites are enjoying a wild weekend retreat of debauchery. Among the eccentric guest are a nympho mother and the freakish, incestuous son. Unfortunately for the guests, their isolated country villa lies directly in the path of the flesh eating horde that have party plans all of their own!!*

Having just read the plot synopsis, it is safe to say VIPCO seemed positively giddy that they got this one. In turn, perhaps courtesy of Mike, the line about 'a group of clueless, decadent socialites' seems like a dig at the upper classes. Normal service is resumed when reference is made to the 'freakish, incestuous son' – that being the legendary Pietro Barzocchini aka Peter Bark.

For those not in the know, Bark was in his mid-twenties when he filmed his role in *The Zombie Dead* yet – due to his unique appearance – he was cast as a child. He had the height and facial features of a pre-teen and it made for a strangely unnerving appearance. His role of Michael is perhaps best-remembered for all the wrong reasons, due to Bark's image and his character's role.

For those who have seen *The Zombie Dead*, then you know why VIPCO included the term incestuous in the synopsis. Those who have not, then all that will be said is *SPOILER ALERT* Bark 'gifts' the viewer the most memorable moment of not only the feature, but one of the most memorable moments of the entire Italian zombie boom, when he sexually molests his own mother. *SPOILER OVER*

The rest of the feature is entertaining in its own right, mainly for the gruesome look of the zombies plus the bloodshed and gore which they bring. The plot is the usual fare of existing/surviving with the sole intention of padding out the film until the next zombie attack. The effects used for the onscreen splatter are of a better standard than other similar titles that VIPCO would also unleash.

However, both at the time and now – almost four decades after the originally titled *Burial Ground* was made – there are some that cite this as a poor effort in the Italian zombie boom. Personally, I believe this is a fun movie and it could have been a lot worse. Thank goodness for Peter Bark.

Director Bianchi would spend much of his career in the world of exploitation with *Strip Nude for Your Killer* (1975) and *Maniac Killer* (1987) being some of his better-remembered works.

The Zombie Dead was originally released in the United Kingdom as *Nights of Terror* and was heavily butchered, with 12 minutes removed! VIPCO would give the feature its first re-release in 2002 with all the missing footage reinstated. 'Artistic licence' was used as the VIPCO release would be the only time the movie would be known as *The Zombie Dead*. Jay Slater remembers how this happened: "Mike asked me what we should call it. 'Nights of Terror, Mike?' was my answer. He said no, so I then asked 'What about Burial Ground, which is the US title?' No, again, and Mike then went for Zombie Dead, which made no sense whatsoever – zombies are already dead, so 'Zombie Dead *Dead*'? – but this is exploitation cinema and it stuck." 88 Films would release *The Zombie Dead* under its *Burial Ground* title in spring 2016 on DVD and Blu-ray. Thank goodness.

Hail Peter Bark!

ZOMBIE NOSH (1988)

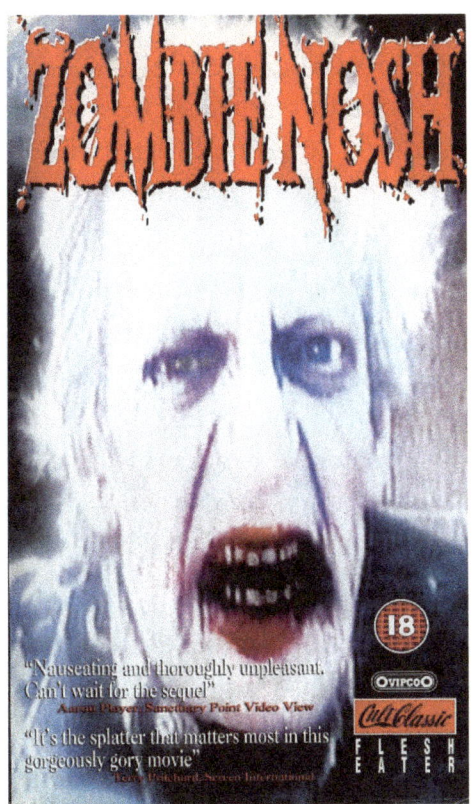

Director: S. William Hinzman as Bill Hinzman

Writer: Bill Hinzman

Stars: Bill Hinzman (Flesheater), John Mowod (Bob), Leslie Ann Wick (Sally), Kevin Kindlin (Ralph)

VIPCO Release: 1993

Also Known As: FleshEater, Revenge of the Living Dead, Revenge of the Living Zombies

VIPCO Plot Synopsis: *A group of attractive college kids with lust at the top of their agenda set out on a hayride. They come to rest at a picnic site, unbeknown to them once the setting for barbaric satanic rituals and rumoured cannibalism. By accident, the sinister forces of a bygone era are unleashed and a blood-lusting Zomole (sic) emerges from its tomb. And he's peckish...*

Critical reception for the movie has been mainly negative with the main bones of contention being the acting, the script, the tiny budget, and its lack of originality. So, a lot, as it happens. These are all certainly true as well; *Zombie Nosh* is bad in all of these areas. It is safe to say this is a flick that should have been left to 1980's zombie fodder obscurity. The reason this fate has not befallen *Zombie Nosh* is no doubt thanks to its star/director/producer/editor/writer: Bill Hinzman!

For those unfamiliar with Hinzman, he was the man that portrayed the 'original' zombie in George A. Romero's 1968 classic *Night of the Living Dead*. He played the undead man staggering around the graveyard, at the beginning of the feature, who attacks Barbara and Johnny. For one of the most iconic screen zombies ever seen to make his own zombie movie is an intriguing thing, and undoubtedly provided the hoped-for hook to lure fans in with.

Hinzman had previously done work as DP on another Romero flick: *The Crazies* (1973). He had also directed the feature *The Majorettes* (1987), and other more local work by this point in his career. It would be 20 years after appearing on screen – in his career-defining role – that he decided to create this movie *NotLD* character for the home video rental market. Hinzman claimed his part in *Zombie Nosh* was not exactly the same as his role in Romero's movie despite the fact anyone watching this will think, "Hey, that's the zombie from Night of the Living Dead!" and that Hinzman did this to cash-in on that very thought.

Since *Zombie Nosh* was Hinzman's creation, the limitations of the feature can be attributed to him. He wore numerous hats for *FleshEater*, on and off screen. As the director, his style is bland, as the editor he is sloppy; and considering he wrote the script, he fails to do anything other than rip off *NotLD* while leaving plot holes

31

throughout. The ending is galling in its recycling of the ending of Romero's superior original. Hinzman even has family members in key parts… probably to save money.

At least the few gore scenes that happen are effective considering the film's budgetary limitations; hearts get ripped out of people and eaten, and hatchets are delivered to heads, in addition to a couple of other bloody moments. Hinzman's zombie seems to possess super human/undead strength during such occurrences and also gets to grope a busty nude woman following a shower scene that serves no purpose other than being blatant T&A.

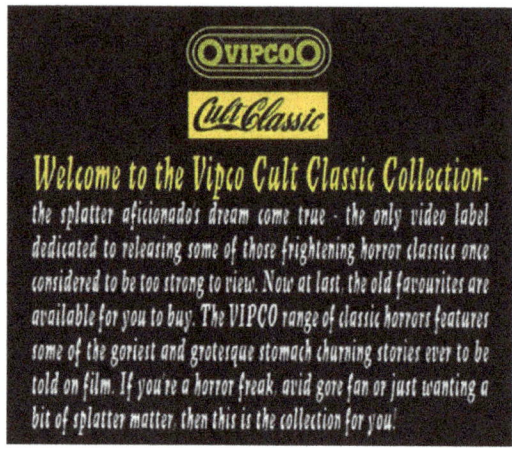

When VIPCO first released *FleshEater* as *Zombie Nosh* in 1993, as part of its Cult Classics label, several of the gore sequences had been cut. They would be restored for the DVD re-release a decade later. Staggeringly, Mike once stated in an interview that this movie is 'a classic'!

VIPCO changed *FleshEater* to *Zombie Nosh* as a reference to the undead desiring the consumption of human flesh as 'nosh': something to snack on. It should also be mentioned that 'nosh' is now also considered a term for giving or receiving oral sex e.g. "She noshed me off." Thankfully, no zombies are seen offering oral delights. Oo-er. *Zombie Nosh* was released on DVD, again, in 2005, under its original name by Stax Entertainment. No more noshing off for *FleshEater*.

5
The History of VIPCO (Part III)

They made me rich!

A laughing Michael Lee about the Video Nasties.

The term "Video Nasties" first appeared in a Sunday Times article by the now late Peter Chippendale. The feature – along with others like it in the tabloid newspapers – whipped up a frenzy amongst gullible and suggestible readers.

Parents and do-gooders alike were mortified that their children/the nation's youth were being 'exposed' to such harmful video violence as *The Driller Killer, I Spit on Your Grave* and *Cannibal Holocaust*. The self-righteous Mary Whitehouse, founder of The National Viewers' and Listeners' Association, jumped on the bandwagon. "I have never seen a video nasty… I actually don't need to see visually what I know is in [them]" she admitted on national TV at one point. It did not matter to her that she would never see one, because she (and other moral crusaders) felt 'assaulted' by knowing of such works very existence. Campaigners such as Whitehouse seemed very keen on hunting down those that peddled such filth in the first place.

When a nationwide scandal happens – in which those with an over-inflated sense of self-worth try to position themselves as potential heroes – it is only a matter of time before politicians join the fray. As always, some used the Video Nasties shitstorm to further their political careers and pat themselves on the back, such as interview-happy MP Graham Bright who made sure the voting public knew he was doing his best to stop this celluloid corruption. The grisly tapes were now being discussed at the very highest level of power in Britain; the line being that these movies would warp the fragile and still-forming minds of any children who happened to see them.

Video rental shops were also identified as baddies in this alleged crisis. These often family-run businesses were now commonplace in Great Britain, and as they were the very places that the apparently damaged children could get hold of harmful material, with relative ease, then they were also partially responsible for the ensuing scandal. "I'll never forget Dillons, the newsagents over the road from my mum and dad's, stocking *Cannibal Holocaust* next to the Slush Puppy machine!" recalls Scarred for Life's Stephen Brotherstone. "Were these films easy to get hold of as kids? Yes, yes, they were. My mates also knew people who could get hold of *Shogun Assassin* and *The Driller Killer*, no problem, or we had older siblings do it for us!"

At first, this bad press actually helped the stores; the more the press and MPs screamed outrage over the Nasties, the more people wanted to see them and sought them out in their local rental shops. The most infamous and long-lasting headline was splashed across the front page of the Daily Mail in July 1983; it read 'BAN THE VIDEO SADISM NOW'. If anyone was unaware of Video Nasties before this, they certainly weren't now.

The BBFC at the time had no power or authority over the censorship or classification of movies on home video formats. With no authority to refer to, people like Mike Lee jumped in with both feet in what they sold on tape to such outlets, and video stores turned no customer away because of their age. As Mike explained in his Dark Side magazine interview, "There was no clear structure and no referring authority. There was no one to turn to, but cinema had a clear legalisation. So, they couldn't blame me for putting out movies on a new medium when they were too slow to get off the mark and do something about it". With the growing and mounting pressure of a country seemingly on the brink of an absolute meltdown (because of the belief that anyone could see and – laughably – re-enact what was on these dastardly videos) the BBFC, Director of Public Prosecutions, and the British government finally took drastic action.

The Director of Public Prosecutions drew up a list of movies that were deemed 'obscene' and which could, therefore, be banned or prosecuted under the Obscene Publications Act 1959. MP Graham Bright spearheaded a campaign to have parliament establish a new bill to place heavy restrictions on the Nasties, and home video, as well.

Eventually, in 1984, the bill would be passed, and that meant the BBFC could now have a say over what happened to home video in the United Kingdom. The blandly named Video Recordings Act 1984 meant that any films to be released on VHS or Betamax were now to be submitted to the BBFC for classification. The BBFC would then assign the content to the most appropriate age group. It also meant the BBFC had the chance to remove footage before any release, which was a way of ensuring that anything they deemed too controversial would not see the light of day.

VIPCO had many of its titles seized. Some videos had severe cuts made before they were eventually allowed back on sale. But the firm faced a backlash from this scandal that was far greater than that experienced by rivals. During the entire time this had been happening, Mike's release of *The Driller Killer* was used by the press as the ultimate example of the extreme nature of these films. The simple, yet highly effective, image of a man appearing to be drilled in his forehead on its sleeve was intended to be eye-catching to draw punters in; now it was attracting adverse attention.

There were frivolous fears that anyone seeing this Nasty would go out and recreate what they saw on their TV screens. More broadly, the argument was that child viewers could be left disturbed by them, and that the images would potentially spawn violent killers. One news report showed kids claiming they had seen movies that the reporter had actually fabricated. Figures were manufactured to illustrate the widespread consumption of these grisly flicks.

Years later, Mike would publicly ridicule the press around *The Driller Killer*, "I can't think of one incident when someone saw *Driller Killer* and went out into the streets with a drill... It just didn't happen." He also rightly pointed out that there were no zombies attacking people nor cannibals on the prowl. It did not matter, though, as people with power had a vested interest in the Video Recordings Act 1984 being passed, and firms like VIPCO being harassed.

One person was even sent to prison for selling illegal tapes. Controversial film and porn distributor David Hamilton Grant received an 18-month sentence for having copies of *Nightmares in a Damaged Brain* (1981). A prime case of making an example out of someone, the prosecution was a massive waste of public money, held up as a major victory by the moral crusaders. Barrie Gold, of S Gold & Sons, witnessed his factory being raided, too. Not just for having possession of hundreds of copies of the uncut *Nightmares in a Damaged Brain* but VIPCO title *The Driller Killer*. "I believe it happened in 1982 or 1983," he recalled with disdain in his voice when I questioned him about it. "I chose to plead not guilty [to obscenity charges] and elected to go to trial by jury at Snaresbrook Crown Court. After a week-long trial, I was acquitted!"

Mike also faced court cases and the threat of jail. His home was raided a couple of times for the likes of *Shogun Assassin* and *Zombie Flesh Eaters*. He ended up being on first name terms with the DCI carrying out the raids – Peter Krueger – who 'promised' Mike he would make the last raid go as smoothly as possible and that no other VIPCO staff would be dragged into any legal proceedings. The emotional and financial burden was getting too much for Mike, though, which was perhaps the intention of the shit-stirrers to begin with. Mike felt it was obvious they were trying to force him out of business in the hope that the Nasties would 'go away'. Within mere days of these raids happening, VIPCO's sales would drop drastically, and making ends meet – to keep the still-growing company afloat – became more and more challenging. With the big sellers now banned, VIPCO seemed likely to close within months.

Video rental shops had been in the UK for several years by this point. The government and BBFC could have acted sooner to stop the mass hysteria of the mid-eighties. Yet they did not. Ultimately, they used firms such as VIPCO to divert attention away from themselves while they formulated a plan to become the heroes of a country in crisis.

The newspapers, mostly the same tabloids that were putting themselves at the heart of the anti-Nasties movement, did not have a problem earlier when they accepted payment from video firms to feature adverts. They never turned them down, and Mike claims that despite all the outrage shown over *The Driller Killer* poster, not one outlet refused his money and they all ran his advertising as a result. It was only when they decided they could sell more copies by exploiting the growing hysteria that they suddenly took the moral high ground. Money talks, and bullshit walks.

The harm had been done, and the course of British video distribution had been changed. The casualties either went out of business or dropped their offending titles to try to deflect the bad press. Mike was not about to do either. He decided that while the British marketplace had become toxic for his firm, he would go somewhere that would not reject VIPCO...

A lot of 'Nasties' were released by VIPCO in the early eighties and – as detailed previously – they got the company into a lot of hot water. To this day, they remain the most high-profile of VIPCO's releases, and many are now available in uncut form; some have even garnered critical reappraisal. The following is a look at some of the 'corruptible' pieces of cinema, although some of the nasties, such as *Cannibal Holocaust* and *The Beyond,* are in different sections of this book. Prepare to be corrupted.

ANDY WARHOL'S FRANKENSTEIN (1974)

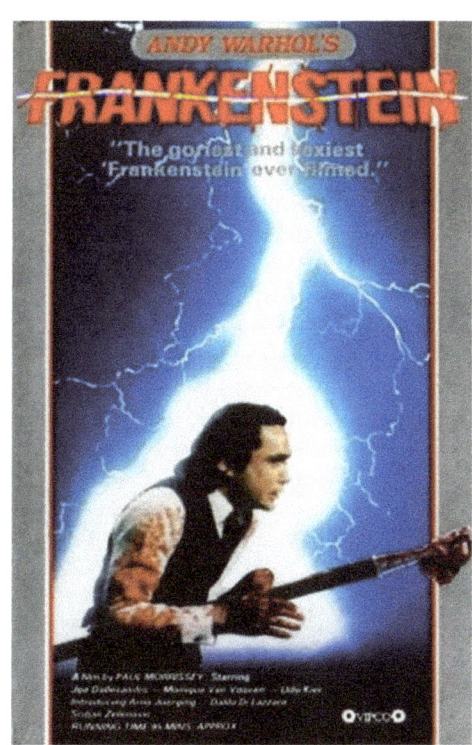

Director: Paul Morrissey

Writer: Paul Morrissey, Tonino Guerra (uncredited), Pat Hackett (uncredited)

Stars: Udo Kier (Baron Frankenstein), Monique van Vooren (Baroness Frankenstein), Arno Jurging (Otto), Srdjan Zelenovic (Sacha/Monster)

VIPCO Release: 1982

Also Known As: *Andy Warhol's Young Frankenstein, Flesh for Frankenstein, Frankenstein*

VIPCO Plot Synopsis: *Writer-director Paul Morrissey, director of Andy Warhol's FLESH, TRASH and HEAT, brings to the screen the most outrageous version of FRANKENSTEIN ever. "Swooping bats, severed limbs, gobs of livid human entrails, a hideously efficient decapitating gadget, some well turned breasts and buttocks, plus assorted spare parts are among the treats that slither off the screen. Andy Warhol's FRANKENSTEIN is the most outrageously gruesome epic ever unleashed. Horror fans can get a kick from this one." PLAYBOY MAGAZINE.*

Andy Warhol in a book about British home video distributor VIPCO? Yes, as outlandish as that may be.

Better known as *Flesh for Frankenstein* this movie was directed and written by Paul Morrissey. Supposedly, the movie came about after Roman Polanski told Morrissey he would be the ideal director for a 3D film based on *Frankenstein*. Morrissey subsequently set about making what is meant to be a parody or spoof of the *Frankenstein* subgenre of horror.

Morrissey was a friend of the legendary pop artist Andy Warhol and had helmed features produced by Warhol prior to this. With a name like *Andy Warhol's Frankenstein*, the viewer would think that the artist also produced this movie or had some heavy input. This was not the case; his involvement was zero. He visited the set once to see pal Morrissey, and then to the editing suite. Yet this 'limited involvement' was blown up into something designed to attract as much attention as possible. Lord knows what will have happened if the Chuckle Brothers somehow stumbled onto the set one day...

Morrissey tries to deliver a *Frankenstein* feature unlike anything seen at the time in the genre; the movie has tongue-in-cheek humour that the social crowd of Warhol would have found frightfully funny. Sadly, this is lost in the 'taking itself too seriously' aspect of the film's vibe. While it achieves its intentions of being different – in an era that saw Hammer run the name *Frankenstein* into the ground – this version has little link to the source material of Mary Shelley's classic novel because it is so far removed from it.

This *Frankenstein* is almost as po-faced, in parts, as the Hammer movies it is trying to distinguish itself from. The writing, the direction, the score, the locations and costumes all feel like a Hammer horror production minus Christopher Lee and Peter Cushing. The feature makes its own mark by upping the blood and nudity to an over-the-top and gratuitous degree.

The best example of both blood and nudity coming together at the same moment is when the Baron is having sex with the nude and prone body of the female 'creature' (Dalila Di Lazzaro) while he thrusts his hand into a bloody wound on her torso. Later, this same wound (now crudely stitched) up is caressed and licked. When *Frankenstein* gained a UK cinema release in the early seventies, much of this (and other gory scenes) was cut, with eight minutes removed. The movie was then prosecuted by the DPP and became a Video Nasty due to the no-no of fake blood appearing on naked breasts when a VIPCO VHS release was attempted in the mid-eighties. Finally, in 1996, the ban was lifted and it hit First Independent VHS with the cuts now at only 56 seconds.

Michael Lee had publicly vowed to get this re-released by VIPCO during a spring 1992 interview for Video World. He considered *Flesh for Frankenstein* to be an 'all-time great'. His promise never came true.

Frankenstein was shot in 3D and premiered in some countries in this format. This will explain why there are numerous occasions where human innards flick out or splatter onto the camera.

This entry into the VIPCO Vault is perhaps one for pre-cert completists only. Tatty old big box VHS copies of this title sell for quite a bit of money on sites like eBay. The contents of such purchases are typically not worth the advertised price tag.

THE BOGEY MAN (1980)

Director: Ulli Lommel

Writers: David Herschel, Suzanna Love, Ulli Lommel

Stars: Suzanna Love (Lacey), John Carradine (Dr. Warren), Nicholas Love (Willy), Llewelyn Thomas (Father Reilly)

VIPCO Release: 1981

Also Known As: *Mirror of Fear, Spectre, The Boogeyman, The Boogey Man*

VIPCO Plot Synopsis: *It begins with a horrifying killing and then starts to get bloody!! The Bogey Man is the chilling story of concentrated evil and its gruesome effect on a small American farming community. The evil is so great that even exorcism cannot stop the blood bath. Pray before you next look in a mirror!!*

A favourite of VIPCO, and perhaps one of its best-remembered releases, this former Video Nasty is a remarkable film for the often unhinged direction that Director Ulli Lommel brought to bear. Still showing some of the flare he had utilised early in his career, the German crafted a film that is as violent as it is frivolous. Decried upon its original release, and still lacking in critical praise decades later, The Bogey Man is undoubtedly entertaining and has moments of merit. Out of the many movies lumped together as a Video Nasties, this is one of the better titles to be caught up in the madness.

It has to be admitted that the plot is a cobbling together of other horror yarns and has moments of absurdity. For example, the spirit of the violent boyfriend of Lacey's mother being trapped in a mirror only to then be freed once said mirror has been smashed is a strained way to lead to a haunting/possession story. That pieces of the broken mirror can cause people to be killed, or possessed, more so. It leads to silliness and moments that border on the camp. See Love's possessed acting for proof.

It is spirited (no pun intended) though, and the runtime does not drag as Lommel treats viewers to people being impaled by floating pitchforks and screwdrivers; indeed, there is the now iconic image of an astounded looking Father Reilly oozing blood from his hairline all over his face. The haunting/possession scenes are eye-catching not just for the bloodshed and shrieking but also for the cinematography. This is a colourful movie.

The legendary John Carradine appears as a doctor helping the disturbed Lacey. Carradine was a veteran actor who had been performing for a staggering 50 years by this point of his career. While not his best performance, his presence in *The Bogey Man* is welcomed.

Nepotism is in effect; the director's wife Suzanna Love (who supposedly married the German so he could get a green card) plays the lead role. She is not a terrible actress although that possession scene is so naff it is funny. As she co-wrote the script, it should be assumed she tailored the script to her abilities. Also benefiting from nepotism is Suzanna's brother, Nicholas Love, as the mute Billy; several of her other family members play smaller parts. It should be noted that Suzanna did finance the movie.

The opening scene of children spying on adults having sex only for this to end in murder is a plot device that would be used as the opening for Lommel's other VIPCO release *Prozzie*, with some variations. The consequences of the sex/murder will then play an important and deadly role in the children's lives when the narrative jumps to them being adults. Again, as seen in *Prozzie*.

Lommel not only recycled parts of *The Bogey Man* story for his other works but he also simply reused chunks of the actual feature for the woeful sequel *Boogeyman II* in 1983. He did not direct part two as that 'honour' goes to Bruce Pearn (as Bruce Starr).

In *Boogeyman II*, Lommel is uncredited as directing yet appears on screen for a spot of acting. Love plays the same character as before who (this time) is in Hollywood working on a potential movie chronicling the 'real' events of the original *Bogey Man*. Instead of simply having Lacey retell what happened in one short scene, the film uses multiple flashbacks which reprise footage from the first outing. It is a shameless way of padding out the runtime. A flashback-happy third film came out in 1994 with *Return of the Boogeyman* directed by Deland Nuse. Both sequels are abysmal. IMDb has *Boogeyman: Reincarnation* listed as being completed in 2016 and directed by Lommel although it is yet to be released.

VIPCO would give *The Bogey Man* (ignoring the American spelling of its title) a VHS release in 1981 during those Wild West days of the pre-cert area. The film was banned in 1984 with it finally being deemed 'fit for public consumption' in 1992 with 44 seconds of cuts. Somewhat naughtily, the infamous 'STRONG UNCUT VERSION' logo appears on that VHS sleeve. It would then get the sub-par VIPCO DVD treatment in summer 2000 with 'BANNED SINCE 1982' on the top-left of the front cover despite being available from VIPCO for several years.

88 Films gave this movie a great Blu-ray release in 2015.

THE BURNING (1981)

Director: Tony Maylam

Writers: Harvey Weinstein, Brad Grey, Peter Lawrence, Bob Weinstein, Tony Maylam

Stars: Brian Matthews (Todd), Leah Ayres (Michelle), Jason Alexander (Dave), Lou David (Cropsy)

VIPCO Release: 1992

Also Known As: *Cropsy, The Cropsy Maniac, The Flames of Revenge*

VIPCO Plot Synopsis: *The scenario of this notorious 'splatter' movie may be familiar: A group of teenage counsellors at a lakeside summer camp face the vengeance of a twisted psychotic – but the nail-biting tension and graphic gore sequences of this bloody shocker will certainly not be.*

Labelled by some as a *Friday the 13th* rip-off, those involved with this movie claim plans were already in place for *The Burning* before Sean S. Cunningham changed the cinematic landscape with his seminal work. Anyone who has seen both will no doubt be aware of this; although there are slight differences, the basic plot outlines are the same.

The stories concern themselves with large hulking figures getting revenge after some horrible wrong that happened to them years before; revenge that leads them to massacre a summer camp full of frolicking teens. (And yes it was not really Jason in *Friday the 13th* killing everyone even though we were led to believe that.) With *The Burning*, it is actually the disfigured, wronged man called Cropsy: This film was the first feature to be produced by Harvey Weinstein, plus brother Bob, who was a man (then) at the start of a career that would see him become one of the biggest and most feared names in Hollywood. He is also credited as the 'creator' for the story of *The Burning*.

It is strange to think that such an innocuous start would be within the confines of the horror genre, and while many big stars or directors cut their teeth in the world of horror, it is unusual that someone who would become such a 'big shot' would emerge here. As we know – post-sexual misconduct revelations – Weinstein now holds little power and is the king of his own ruined kingdom and legacy. But that legacy started here with *The Burning*. It is quite the start, too. Maylam has said that after working with Harvey in a different capacity previously, the young would-be movie producer approached him about making a film which he and his brother would back. Harvey even had an idea in mind for the subject matter: Cropsy.

Tony Maylam had previously directed the successful Olympics documentary *White Rock* (1977) which had prog rocker Rick Wakeman involved with the score. That is why the Yes band member ended up providing the score for *The Burning*. Maylam took advantage of his friendship with the musician, stemming from *White Rock*, which is why this Video Nasty got such a unique and rewarding soundtrack.

Maylam has said he agreed to do a horror film as it was a good 'gateway movie' to learn how to direct a structured fictional feature, compared to non-fiction documentaries. He believed horror is the easiest genre to make due to no stars or a large budget being needed. Simply dot the dots, and the story will take care of itself, was his theory. That is often the case for horror flicks; however, Maylam is selling himself short. In *The Burning*, he takes advantage of the myth the plot is based around and adds to it significantly as well. *The Burning* is also fun and exciting as a result and, since 1981, it is rightly remembered as one of the better slasher fad flicks. Despite this, Tony has expressed he would do things differently now if he could make the feature again as he feels it has not aged very well. A modern-day version of *The Burning*, with the original director attached, could be something for hardcore Nasties fans to relish if it were to happen.

The special effects legend Tom Salvini also worked on this movie. The best example of the gory delights he offers up is the iconic raft massacre when Cropsy rises up from a river and lays waste to the unlucky campers on a raft. The climax of this scene is when one poor sod puts his hands up in self-defence and his fingers are chopped off with garden shears. The BBFC edited this out with the cuts remaining until 2002.

Much has been made about the talent involved behind the camera, or in the making of the feature, but this cult gem has a lot going for it on screen as well.

The young cast is actually good actors – something of a rarity for the genre at the time – and most appear to be having a genuinely good time. Brian Backer, Fisher Stevens, Holly Hunter, and Jason Alexander all began their careers with this feature.

Somewhat embarrassingly for distributor Thorn EMI an uncut version of *The Burning* was accidentally put on sale after the BBFC told them to sell it in a cut form (mainly due to the raft scene). There must have been a lot of swearing and sweating in the Thorn EMI offices when that blunder was discovered.

VIPCO distributed *The Burning* a couple of times once they obtained the rights. The first was in late 1992 on old faithful VHS; the firm then waited a decade until they reissued it on videotape again, as well as on the typically shoddy VIPCO DVD. At least, this time, it was uncut.

The Burning is one of the better and more fondly remembered titles that would grace VIPCO's Vaults. There was talk of a sequel for a time but, due to the film's initial poor box office performance, this was abandoned. Maylam has stated publicly that he thinks *The Burning* is a standard feature and does not see it as being worthy of a remake. Almost four decades since its release, it looks like a remake is unlikely as one would have surely happened by now which is a shame as other Nasties titles have had the remake treatment, *I Spit on Your Grave* (1978) was remade in 2010 for example, yet Cropsey is left sulking in his cabin.

THE DRILLER KILLER (1979)

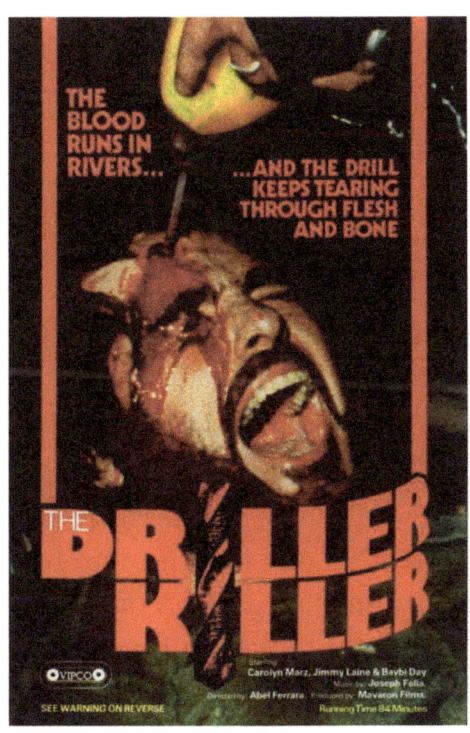

Director: Abel Ferrara

Writer: Nicholas St. John

Stars: Abel Ferrara (Reno), Harry Schultz (Dalton), Carolyn Marz (Carol), Baybi Day (Pamela)

VIPCO Release: 1982

VIPCO Plot Synopsis: *As the screaming drill closes on its victim you don't really believe what you are seeing... until the blood starts pouring and another tearing scream joins the drill. A steel stomach is required to watch the final scenes of mayhem.*

For those who noticed, the VIPCO synopsis is lacking any real plot points so to help here is a quick write up for the benefit of those who are unfamiliar with *The Driller Killer's* plot: a struggling artist named Reno (Ferrara) mentally unravels due to the strains of just about every aspect of his life. He eventually snaps and takes it out on the homeless of New York City with the deadly aid of a power drill.

Another heavy hitter for VIPCO, *The Driller Killer* is one of the most controversial movies ever made. Well, at least in the UK it is. In the decades since Abel Ferrara unleashed this Video Nasty on the world, it has seen countless re-releases (it is in the public domain) and has had countless articles and features written about it. And in the eighties, it was the movie that nearly ruined VIPCO.

Much has been made about Michael Lee's 'marketing brainwaves' in this book. From his 'beat them over the head' blurbs to renaming a film as something more attention-grabbing, Mike knew that catching a potential buyer's eye was important. When his firm's titles were on the video rental stores shelves with dozens of other over-the-top horror tapes, he rightly realised he needed something special to make VIPCO stand out. He definitely did this with *The Driller Killer*.

The iconic image of some hapless bloke being drilled in the head with blood trickling down his face was used by VIPCO as the cover work for their pre-cert VHS release of Ferrara's work. Not only that, but Mike thought it would be a good idea to have the same said image appear on the advertising to try and create more interest in *The Driller Killer*.

It worked. A little too well.

When the press adverts ran, and the video was released, that head drilling image was like a red flag to a bull with the moral crusaders of the time. The amount of negative press and hassle Michael Lee received was fierce. He himself has admitted he did not expect the level of criticism. National tabloids, politicians, and the easily outraged/manipulated, all zeroed in on *The Driller Killer*. Now anything wrong in the country was pinned on this title and its distributor.

Forget the fact that the people who were so outspoken against *Killer* had not actually seen it, a scapegoat was needed. Michael Lee was prosecuted for possessing 'illegal booty' (Mike's words, not mine) and his house was even raided; an act that nearly ruined him mentally and financially. *The Driller Killer* was banned, and the BFFC would use it as a prime example of why they should create the Video Recordings Act. If these busybodies had actually bothered to see the film behind the poster, they would have felt a little silly at how worked up they became.

"If people thought they (the adverts) were excessive, I'm surprised the magazines ever accepted them in the first place," Michael was to say about the matter in a 1992 Video World interview. But these magazines wanted a slice of the video nasty profit pie, and this was their indirect way of further exploiting the scandal they helped stir up.

The Driller Killer is not the wall-to-wall drill kill and blood fest that it appears to be. Its 'reputation' is perhaps the most extreme thing about the feature. As a movie, it is acceptable and adequately directed, yet dated, and is more interesting for being early in the career of Ferrara when he was still cutting his teeth as a director. The supposed violence on screen is not as savage as one would expect, whether viewing the flick in the seventies or in 2019. The arthouse influence also bogs down proceedings, more so for those wanting to see drills-to-the-head spills.

A decade later he would begin to direct feature films on a more mainstream level. In the early nineties, for example, he directed movies that would also become cult classics with *King of New York* (1990) and *Bad Lieutenant* (1992).

The ban that was forced on *The Driller Killer* would be lifted in 1999 (with some cuts in place), and the once-controversial flick finally received an uncut release in 2002. In the space of two decades, this movie had gone from public enemy number one to fit for uncut public consumption.

Due to its status as a public domain film, Ferrara's movie has seen numerous VHS and DVD releases over the decades all over the world. Out of all of these, Arrow Video's winter 2016 dual format edition is the most interesting and worthwhile as it incorporates a previously unseen version that contained an additional five minutes of footage.

THE HOUSE ON THE EDGE OF THE PARK (1980)

Director: Ruggero Deodato

Writers: Gianfranco Clerici, Vincenzo Mannino

Stars: David Hess (Alex), Giovanni Lombardo Radice (Ricky), Annie Belle (Lisa), Lorraine De Selle (Gloria)

VIPCO Release: 2002

VIPCO Plot Synopsis: *Nice type, Alex. If you didn't know him you could even be fooled when he amuses himself playing the "nice guy". For some time he's been wearing one more necklace. He ripped it off a girl; Susan, whom he then raped and killed. Alex is just a dangerous vicious animal. He wants to go out and have fun with Ricki (sic). Ricki's a strange guy. They're about to leave their garage when two kids arrive. Their car has something wrong with it. Alex refuses to fix it. His tone changes when he hears the two are going to a party. If they invite him and Ricki the fun is guaranteed. But they are two hoodlums who rape and are prepared to kill.*

Kicking off with David Hess raping then killing a young woman (heavily edited in the case of VIPCO releases), this is a movie that has a reputation that has not softened over the decades since its first release.

When VIPCO released *House...* on VHS and DVD in summer 2002, the movie had almost 12 minutes of cuts. That is certainly a fairly large part of the runtime considering it was only 90 minutes originally. It should not be a surprise though as the BBFC had a habit of wanting any sexual violence removed from films they gave certificates to. And *House...* is definitely a movie about sexual violence. This is why the VIPCO release saw most of it edited out, most notably the harassment of Cindy (Brigitte Petronio) and the rape of Lisa which is admittedly disturbing. Back in the early eighties when this title was put forward for a cinema release, it was refused and eventually banned. Interestingly, in 2011, nearly all of this footage was reinserted when Shameless put out *House...* on DVD.

The opening scene actually loses some of its power due to the heavy cuts made as Hess simply gets in the car and grabs the terrified girl by the throat. Considering a major plot twist at the end of the story has a lot of its power derived from the initial murder, the movie does not have the desired impact at first. For a large part of *House...* Alex and Ricky come across as likeable guys who are the butt of an upper-class joke. If that cut scene had been left intact, this would not have been the case.

The two mechanics end up going to a house party of some would-be preppy customers and are made to feel inferior (especially Ricky) by them. The vibe created is that Alex and his violent temper are close to boiling over due to this belittling and the victims-to-be have only brought it on themselves. Alex and Ricky seem to want to have a good time, but when the privileged friends play on the gullible Ricky's simple intentions, and mercilessly mock him, it leads to their downfall. Meanwhile, a different type of teasing is played on Alex when the flirty Lisa gets him sexually wound up, only to deliberately leave him worked up to the point of steam literally coming out of his ears.

The feckless Ricky is then cleaned out at a rigged game of poker; an event which presses the launch button on Alex (so to speak) unleashing his vile and mean streak. At first, the suffering the toffs experience feels almost invited and they come across as unsympathetic. The way they lead along Ricky, and mock him to his face knowing full well he is not the brightest of men, certainly makes the viewer feel sympathy for him. When Alex has had enough and snaps, the smirks being wiped off their faces is welcomed.

It is only when Deodato has Hess turn up his nasty guy act, and things head down the exploitation route, that *House* becomes the movie that it is remembered for… controversial. Hess shines in this character, from that point on, which is no shock considering he played a similar role in *The Last House on the Left* in 1972. He has a genuine screen presence that leaves some viewers feeling uneasy. He seems to take great delight in sadistically abusing his captives and, although mainly cut here, the torture of Cindy hammers home how bad a man this character is. Even Deodato would be unsettled by the events he directed in his own feature, with the director stating in an interview some years later that he was not fond of this movie because it was 'packed with violence' as well as considering it weak next to some of his other directorial efforts.

Ignoring the scandal and uproar that surrounds *House,* it is actually a fairly accomplished effort. The limited cast mostly give good performances with Hess, Radice, and De Selle all being impressive. The story, which is admittedly flawed, has an arc that runs throughout the whole film and the ending packs a punch that also makes more sense out of the edited opening sequence that was used by VIPCO.

The full synopsis on the VIPCO video/DVD sleeve for *House* (too large to be reprinted here) is something to behold. The last paragraph gives away the ending of the film. It can only be assumed that Michael Lee must have been oblivious to the fact that this would spoil the flick for anyone reading it. Consider what was used for this book as the 'abridged version'.

ISLAND OF DEATH (1976)

Director: Nico Mastorakis

Writer: Nico Mastorakis

Stars: Jane Lyle as Jane Ryall (Celia), Robert Behling as Bob Behling (Christopher), Jannice McConnell (Leslie), Jessica Dublin (Patricia)

VIPCO Release: 2002

Also Known As: *A Craving for Lust, Cruel Destination, Devils in Mykonos, Island of Perversion, Killing Daylight*

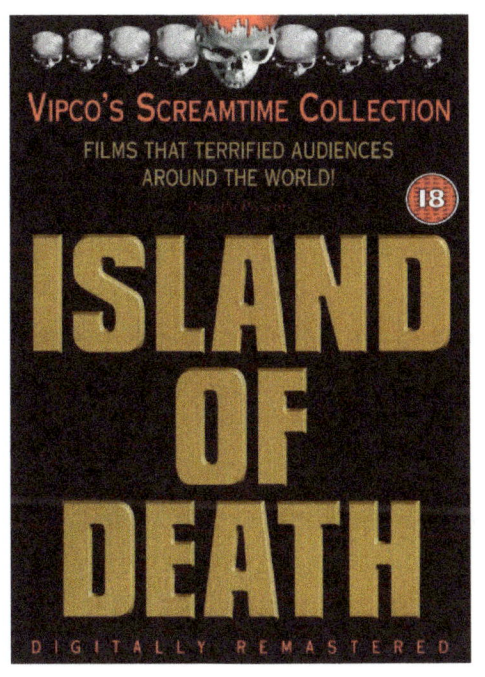

VIPCO Synopsis: See main text.

The write up on the sleeve of this release has not been featured in this book for a couple of reasons. One is that it is just way too long to be reproduced here. Another reason is that it contains nearly every crucial and minor plot development. It actually gives away the shocking final twist that ends *Island of Death*, and if anyone had read it before viewing the movie, the movie would have been entirely spoiled for them. Of course, Many people watching the film will have no doubt been aware of what takes place anyway. Banned in the 1980s, when put forward for a video certificate, the feature already had a reputation amongst diehard horror and exploitation fans.

VIPCO first released *Island of Death* on VHS following the end of its 15 year ban in 2002. The movie had actually been given a cut cinematic release in 1976 as *A Craving for Lust* but, following a 1987 attempt to see it issued on VHS (following the Nasties scandal), the BBFC outright banned it. While VIPCO did manage to see the ban lifted, it was under the condition that there were over four minutes of cuts.

It is not difficult to see why the quick-to-react BBFC came down hard on this movie. There is a shopping list of exploitation cinema-happy murders, and scenes of cruelty, that exist to deliberately offend those watching. Mastorakis has said as much himself, having been inspired to make a film that would shock after he had seen *The Texas Chain Saw Massacre* (1974). But Tobe Hooper's classic work had a level of talent and value to it, *Island of Death* is just crass for the sake of it.

Mastorakis has his actors depict some bizarre and outrageous actions. Once seen, who can forget Christopher raping then killing a goat? Or the sight of Christopher urinating on a naked elderly lady only for her to revel in his golden stream? If these moments were considered good enough to include in the movie, then the rejects must have been really bad.

Most of the onscreen killings have an almost equal level of absurdity to them. Celia and Christopher are inventive, it has to be said. They nail a hapless bloke to the floor and pour paint down his throat, chase down homosexuals, and decapitate one victim by dropping the scoop of a tractor across the neck of their prone body. It is difficult to comprehend the supposed influence of *The Texas Chain Saw Massacre* after enduring these scenes.

The reputation of *Massacre* and the cash it generated will have been the real inspiration behind *Island* and the many ludicrous moments of the movie led to a reputation of its own. Being labelled a Video Nasty has added to this, and it is fair to say that Mastorakis's film would not be as well remembered were it not for this.

Despite its flaws, the feature's two stars are passable actors. Jane Lyle (Celia) handles the duality of her role very well. One moment she acts like the pretty girl next door, the next moment she is urging Christopher to rape or kill. Robert Behling deserves special praise for being willing to act a character who was forced to have sexual intercourse with a goat. Sadly, Behling committed suicide in 2011; he was allegedly troubled by his sexuality.

Former radio host/news reporter/TV host turned director Mastroakis would go on to have a career in film despite the reputation of *Island of Death*. Most of his features would be made in the US and typically ripped off more popular films or genres of the time with the likes of action flick *The Zero Boys* (1986) and *Police Academy* (1984) knock off *Ninja Academy* (1988)

Mike originally issued the movie on VHS in 2002 before dumping it onto the Screamtime Collection for a DVD release. Arrow Video would re-release it in DVD format in 2011and, in 2015, Dual Format.

THE NEW YORK RIPPER (1982)

Director: Lucio Fulci

Writers: Dardano Sacchetti, Vincenzo Mannino, Gianfranco Clerici, Antone Pagan, Gene Luotto, Lucio Fulci

Stars: Jack Hedley (Lt. Williams), Andrea Occhipinti (Peter), Howard Ross (Mickey), Paolo Malco (Dr. Davis)

VIPCO Release: 2001

Also Known As: *Beauty Killer (working title), Manhattan Ripper, Psycho Ripper, The Ripper*

VIPCO Plot Synopsis: *One day the body of a woman is found on the bank of the Hudson. The post-mortem shows that the woman was killed by a maniac, and the police fear that this is the first of a series of brutal murders. Their fears are not without foundation for within one week a girl is killed on a ferry, then a strip-tease actress in a night club. The killer has left no traces whatsoever! His next intended victim manages to save herself and identifies her attacker by the fact that he has two fingers missing... the manhunt commences and soon grinds to a halt as the suspect is found having committed suicide... but the attacks continue...*

The write up on the VIPCO VHS release, as you may have read, gives away a lot of the plot. But when this was eventually released in the UK in 2002, it is safe to say anyone picking up *The New York Ripper* in their local HMV would have already been well aware of the story and what happens.

A movie that was denied a cinema – as well as a home video – release back in the early 1980s when Eagle Films tried to obtain a classification, *Ripper* caused bother the world over due to its violence and subject matter. The fact that this is a movie that was heavily cut in the usually lax Germany, speaks volumes.

Fulci took a break from zombies and supernatural nastiness with this effort. It is an exploitation movie that is set in the home of exploitation cinema: New York City. During this era, NYC and 42nd Street were not the tourist-friendly places they would become. Crime was rife, and grindhouse was prevalent.

Using the same intense approach to violence that he would use in other genres, Fulci directs a story that has been labelled as glorifying violence towards women, as well as being nihilistic and bleak.

Even fans of the director have admitted this is quite unlike his other works and is difficult to defend. This writer thinks it is one of his finest works for his no-bullshit approach to a city that had a reputation for being seedy and exploitative of anyone susceptible enough to fall within the company of its many low life inhabitants. Admittedly, I struggle to justify some of the content within, regardless of the director's meaning or the actual context which it is based upon.

If anything, Fulci handles everyone within the cityscape of this work with the same disdain and contempt. All male characters – even the 'heroes' – are unlikeable; Lucio even treats some of the victims of the titular Ripper as if they are hapless and perhaps deserving of their downfalls. The viewer does not get off either as Fulci inflicts his gruesome set pieces on anyone watching in a manner that suggests he wants disgust more than any other emotion. Fulci also delivers his trademark eyeball torture; this time in the form of a razor blade being sliced down the centre of an eye. Nasty. The feature ends on a shot of a crying child before switching to a wide shot of New York. There is a message in there, somewhere...

Ripper was denied a UK certificate for a number of years due to its violence towards women as well as (the ultimate no-no in the eyes of the BBFC) its nudity and blood..

Although it may be deemed frivolous by some, for this writer the faceless killer's strange quacking and meowing as he attacks women is unsettling. Fulci eventually gives the viewer a reason why this happens yet the Ripper would have perhaps been even more disturbing if there was no logical reason for the noises.

The New York Ripper is not that well associated with VIPCO which is probably due to its release being made late in the firm's history. For British fans, it is better remembered by other firms such as Shameless Entertainment.

The New York Ripper is a depressing time capsule of sorts for the city of Manhattan. The depiction of NYC in this movie, compared to now, feels like we are witnessing a different planet.

Ripper never made it onto the DDP list of banned films or titles that could be prosecuted yet has strong links to the nasties and is included in this section as a result.

SHOGUN ASSASSIN (1980)

Director: Robert Houston, Kenji Misumi

Writers: Kazuo Koike, Goseki Kojima, David Weisman, Robert Houston

Stars: Tomisaburo Wakayama (Lone Wolf), Akihiro Tomikawa (Daigoro), Kayo Matsuo (Supreme Ninja) EDIT

VIPCO Release: 1981

Also Known As: See below.

VIPCO Plot Synopsis: *Astonishingly violent – Shogun Assassin tells the story of Lone Wolf, a powerful and feared "Masterless" samurai who lives a peaceful existence with his wife and his son. When he refuses to swear allegiance to Retsudo, head of the vicious Yagyu Clan, Retsudo orders the death of Lone Wolf's wife Azami. Blinded by rage, Lone Wolf vows to avenge her death, taking his son Daigoro with him on the path of darkness and retribution. Soon Lone Wolf's sword of vengeance is unleashed upon the evil Shogun's sons, ALL WHO GET IN HIS WAY, and ultimately the legendary "Masters of Death"!*

For some, this film will have been first brought to their attention by either VIPCO or the countless episodes of Channel Five cult flick clip show outTHERE in the early noughties. The title is actually two works spliced together. *Lone Wolf and Cub: Sword of Vengeance* and *Lone Wolf and Cub: Baby Cart at the River Styx*. They originate from 1972 from, as the name would suggest, the *Lone Wolf* series. To try and make sense of what is now a far more complicated plot a voiceover is added to clue in the viewer. The movie itself is good enough to warrant praise regardless of the impressive hyper-violence offered up. For a two-into-one film, it feels as if it was meant to be this way all along.

As *Assassin*, this VIPCO release is fondly remembered. It is also a good starting point for those unfamiliar with VIPCO as it resides alongside the likes of *Cannibal Holocaust* (1980) and *Zombie Flesh Eaters* (1979) as 'quintessential VIPCO viewing'. Like the other heavy hitters Michael Lee put out, the firm got into a spot of bother with this one; it became another target of the curtain-twitching moral crusaders of the era. The use of ninjas and weapons linked to them seemed to spur much of the angst. For a time, as trivial as it seems now, the BBFC and UK press were hell-bent on bringing down martial arts flicks or anything that could encourage the British public to try and re-enact ninja activities.

Assassin was cut due to violence although this did not Mike from being raided by the police for supposedly having boxes of uncut tapes in his house! By 1999, however, *Shogun Assassin* was passed uncut. The ninja scandal which had seen

Teenage Mutant Ninja Turtles (1990) renamed as *Teenage Mutant Hero Turtles* had subsided and the tabloids had moved on to pastures new at this point.

The original *Lone Wolf and Cub* films were directed by Misumi, and it is his ability to balance storytelling with violence that allowed *Assassin* director Robert Houston to do such a good job.

The mash up of two flicks actually works well although the finer points are lost. The condensed and revised story does not allow breathing room and more was perhaps scarificed in favour of including the impressive gore pieces. The legacy of this film hinges on the violence and stunning visuals, not drama or well developed characters. Mike would have picked this up for VIPCO for the blood letting alone, he may have not even considered something as vital as plot when he knew he could sell a lot of copies just off the reputation *Shogun Assassin* had for brutality. It is a little surprising that no follow up happened. There were three other *Long Wolf* films that had not been touched, and all had been available for some time before *Assasin* came to be. The success of the first two merged features, in English speaking territories, would have suggested that a sequel was both likely and lucrative. But it was not to be.

VIPCO would continue to revisit *Assassin* a couple of times more through various VHS and DVD releases. All make use, in some form or another, of the brilliant artwork available.

THE SLAYER (1982)

Director: J.S. Cardone

Writers: William R. Ewing, J.S. Cardone

Stars: Sarah Kendall (Kay), Frederick Flynn (Eric), Alan McRae (David), Carl Kraines ('The Slayer')

VIPCO Release: 1992

Also Known As: *Nightmare Island* (disputed)

VIPCO Plot Synopsis: *In the early morning hours of a cold and gloomy day, two young couples awake and begin preparations for a long awaited vacation. None of them anticipate the web of diabolical terror which awaits them on the isolated retreat they have chosen. Only Kay knows the existence of 'The Slayer', and only then in the dark realms of her nightmares. But imagination is about to become reality as the maniacal, inanimate things which inhabit Kay's nightmares are unleashed upon the world...*

More than the guts and gore VIPCO would have had you believe, *The Slayer* is a flick that was potentially ahead of its time.

The use of main character Kay battling her dreams, and the 'are they just fantasies or actually real?' angle, lifts this above the other Video Nasties of the time. The story becomes something of a psychological horror that explores the meaning of dreams and their consequences on those that have them. Or, in this case, Kay and the murders that happen to her friends.

The Slayer was filmed in 1980 and released in 1982 just two years before *A Nightmare on Elm Street* – perhaps *the* movie for dreams and death. It is not exactly the same as *Elm Street*; director J.S. Cardone has said they differ in ways that make Wes Craven's flick a force all of its own.

The Slayer has a vibe that is more akin to a drama film, and Cardone has made the case that his feature is not the slasher that many people have claimed. Indeed, there is an almost soap opera-like quality to the film, brought about by the cast and the harrowing soundtrack by Robert Folk. The composer was at the start of his career when *The Slayer* was shot (1980) and he would go on to craft the music for all the *Police Academy* films (1984-94) and more.

Thankfully J.S. delivers some truly horrific images over the 86 minute (uncut) runtime that offset the more melodramatic aspects. These can be attributed to the titular 'slayer' who was played by Carl Kraines (who would go on to appear in *The Gate* and it's underrated follow-up *Gate II: The Trespassers*); the visually stunning creature kills people in brutal and bloody ways and the practical effects are strong, especially during the fiery end scene.

The bloodshed would see this title banned in the UK until spring 1985 and the version that VIPCO would eventually release had 14 seconds trimmed by the censors. The shoddily transferred DVD release VIPCO did in 2001 was cut free. Thankfully Arrow Video's 2017 Blu-ray edition has a crisp and clean HD transfer that benefits from some strong special features which is more befitting a movie of the calibre of *The Slayer*.

Originally, filming was to take place in Los Angeles before switching to the state of Georgia. More specifically, cameras rolled at Tybee Island in Savannah which is a place perhaps better known for having an atomic bomb lost in its surrounding waters. In 1958, two US Air Force planes collided and the bomb was jettisoned to avoid potential detonation. In the movie, the scenery on the beach often looks inviting and warm which is uncanny considering *The Slayer* was shot in the winter.

The director has since admitted that the ending is deliberately vague to confuse the viewer for those wondering what the hell it actually means.

Critical praise for the movie back in the early eighties was not exactly positive and remained that way until recently. *The Slayer* is now rightly considered one of the better titles from the Video Nasties era. A must-see for the visually impressive effects and a high concept plot.

THE TOOLBOX MURDERS (1978)

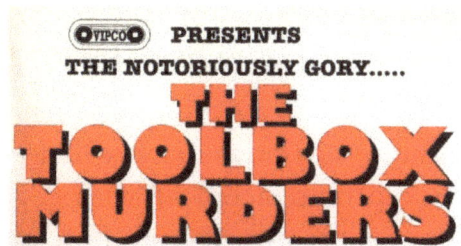

Director: Dennis Donnelly

Writers: Robert Easter, Neva Friedenn, Ann Kindberg

Stars: Cameron Mitchell (Vance), Pamelyn Ferdin (Laurie), Wesley Eure (Kent), Tim Donnelly (Dt. Jamison)

VIPCO Release: 2000

VIPCO Synopsis: *Produced in 1978, The Toolbox Murders made the U.S.A.'s "most disturbing movie list" and was vilified by the nation's media. It was later released in the U.K. – in a gore-filled double bill with Zombie Flesh Eaters – at cinemas across the country. Following its success in the cinema Toolbox was unleashed on video to a huge media backlash, was subsequently banned, and placed on the video nasty list in 1982. It then took almost two decades to gain a certificate.*

Despised on both sides of the pond upon its original release and still lacking the fans it deserves all these decades later *Toolbox* is a little gem of a flick. It tells the story of a hooded killer who commits the most atrocious crimes in American history using a nailgun, drill, and other implements from his toolbox.

When VIPCO obtained the rights to *Toolbox* following the lifting of the ban, cuts were still in place. They can be found during the sequence when the ski mask-wearing loon is chasing a naked woman with a nail gun. Interestingly enough, in 2007 the movie was aired uncut on the UK's Horror Channel (during its brief Zone Horror period) before the BFFC allowed it to be released in uncut form on home video.

The story starts off simply enough, with a man wearing a balaclava forcing his way into people's apartments, then killing them with tools that are readily available. The police then bumble about trying to catch the culprit and think they have their man. They don't, and it is only when the killer's identity is revealed that *Toolbox* becomes a slightly surreal *Psycho*-esque thriller.

Spoiler alert Once the legend that is Cameron Mitchell is exposed as the bloodthirsty handyman, the plot goes into a direction not expected of a film with the title *The Toolbox Murders*. His character – Vance– has taken a young girl (Laurie, played by Pamelyn Ferdin) hostage, gagged her and tied her to a bed. In several scenes, it is revealed that his daughter has died and he plans on making Laurie his surrogate child. Mitchell gives an intense yet surreally heart-wrenching performance as the grieving father. At times, it looks as if his eyes are going to bulge out of his head he is so intense. Ferdin manages a fine performance too, although considering the look on Cameron's face during these scenes she was perhaps not acting and was in genuine fear for her life.

Other actors sadly do not offer anything as entertaining, or over the top, but there is Kelly Nichols who is best known for appearing in countless porno flicks since the seventies. She is nude here, too.

Dennis Donnelly found inspiration for this movie when he saw how successful *The Texas Chain Saw Massacre* (1974) had been. He simply took the concept of 'tool name in title' and changed it to an actual toolbox. This was the only feature film Donnelly directed as all the other works he helmed were for television.

The *Chain Saw Massacre* inspiration for *Toolbox* is somewhat ironic as the director of that film – the late Tobe Hooper – would be responsible for the passable 2004 *Toolbox Murders* remake.

During the United Kingdom's ban on *Toolbox*, VIPCO would sell it uncut as a bootleg in Scandinavia and other territories. Once said ban was removed, the title got a VHS and DVD issue in spring 2000 and the slapdash Screamtime treatment a few years later. Thankfully, 88 Films did a far better job for their DVD and Blu-ray release in 2017.

7

The History of VIPCO (Part IV)

Denmark was very pleased to take my titles, thankfully.

Mike on exporting VIPCO tapes to Denmark and its neighbouring countries.

Mike Lee all but withdrew from the British home video market by the mid-eighties. The Video Nasties scandal had nearly ruined the once rapidly growing firm so, in 1987, Mike tried to drum up interest when he obtained the sci-fi comedy *Hyperspace* (1984) and renamed it *Gremloids*. He posed as one of its characters – Lord Buckethead – at the 1987 General Election, of all things, in a poor attempt to generate publicity. "It still amuses me to this day to recall him in a black cloak with his black 'bucket' helmet on, standing on the podium next to Margaret Thatcher on News at Ten!" a laughing Graham Humphreys said of the matter. Lord Buckethead received a pitiful 131 votes. This particular saga is featured in greater detail later in this book.

Mike also tried his hand at being a producer (while VIPCO 'rested') and he fronted the money for what would become *Spookies* (1986). It was not the success he had hoped for, as the movie had a troubled production and received negative responses from critics and fans upon release. *Spookies* is covered in greater detail, later in this book.

Financially, Mike took a hit during the second half of the eighties; not only were some of his biggest money-makers taken away from him, but he also lost the rights to a number of films having only licensed them for seven years originally.

Some assumed that VIPCO was dead and buried. However, just like the zombies in a Fulci flick, the company and Mike were merely resting before they struck the UK again. In 1992, they were back with a collection of old, edited, favourites… and some new titles. But where had VIPCO been all these years? Between the mid-eighties and early nineties.

VIPCO went to Scandinavia!

Mike licked his wounds from the drubbing he took in Britain, and took advantage of territories (where he still had the rights) which were not as restrictive or edit happy in terms of which videos could be released.

Starting with Denmark, Mike would ship out numerous tapes that would bare the now-iconic STRONG UNCUT or STRONG UNCUT VERSION stickers. Some of the most controversial titles that VIPCO had sold in the United Kingdom would be put out, initially, in Denmark and they would be free of the censorship that blighted them previously. *Cannibal Holocaust*, *The Driller Killer*, and *Zombie Flesh Eaters* thrived and sold well for Mike with other titles also added to the 'VIPCO International Series' that the firm had not sold before in the UK.

These movies, *I Spit on Your Grave* (1978) and *The Texas Chain Saw Massacre* (1974), were just as controversial in Britain as the Nasties VIPCO sold, and faced their own difficulties at some point or another. Again, Denmark – and later on, its neighbouring countries – caused no issues for the features in question, and Mike Lee lined his pockets.

In the nineties, VIPCO's shipments to the Danes also made their way into Sweden and Norway. Not always by legal means, but cult cinema fans in those parts of Scandinavia were a keen bunch.

VIPCO's movies – alongside the early pre-certs and the later 1992/93 wave of titles – were available in many Swedish stores. By the middle of the decade, they would gradually disappear, although another British label (Redemption Films) that specialised in cult and exploitation cinema would be imported and sold instead.

Redemption and VIPCO were viewed by fans as rivals, mostly during the early to late nineties, although Marc Morris who worked for Redemption has stated the firm never saw Lee's label as competition. The quasi-rivalry clearly stretched across the North Sea, despite this opinion.

Norway obtained their VIPCO fill by tape traders importing and selling/swapping the Danish tapes or, by keen fans crossing the border into Sweden and buying the videos there. The dedication shown, and efforts of those wanting VIPCO or Video Nasty titles, must seem like a lot of hard work for the horror fan of today. Nowadays, the unbanned and mostly uncut films are commonly available via file sharing websites or video streaming services.

VIPCO would release/export a couple of titles in other countries during this period too, such as Australia and the Netherlands, but Mike mostly stuck with Scandinavia.

The artwork for many of these releases was either the original pre-cert sleeve with very minor alterations, or new artwork consisting of a key image from the title in question with a design more in keeping with the garish covers of previous VIPCO output.

So, while much of VIPCO's history was based in its native United Kingdom, its neighbours across the North Sea had a hand in keeping them afloat. Denmark and co. helped part of British horror culture to stay alive during this dark period. By the early nineties, however, the term 'Video Nasty' was but a bitter memory; the moral crusaders and press now focussed on other things for the failings of British society. It was because of this that Mike felt the time was right for VIPCO to 'go home' and try its hand, once again, at video distribution in the UK.

8

VIPCO's Style

**Those covers with the gold text, black background and
no image were bloody awful.**

Stephen Brotherstone, co-author of *Scarred for Life vol. 1 and 2*,
on the Screamtime Collection.

People rarely associate 'style' and 'VIPCO' in the same breath, but they do strangely come together and a number of eye-catching – as well as aesthetically-pleasing images – were offered to cult cinema fans. It also has to be conceded, however, that VIPCO inflicted the terrible style of the Screamtime Collection on those same fans.

The earliest VHS and Betamax sleeves would usually consist of the film's original poster, or a couple of stills from the feature, slapped across a primitive one colour backdrop. Some of the imagery was particularly striking, with the likes of *The Evil Force* (1977), *The Bogey Man* (1980) and *The Rise and Fall of Idi Amin* (1981) proving particularly effective.

The 'second wave' of VIPCO output began in 1992 when the firm relaunched in Great Britain. Freelance artist and illustrator Graham Humphreys would design many of the early sleeves in this era, following a phone conversation with Michael Lee. "I had a call from him, and he said he was resurrecting VIPCO. As I hadn't heard from him in a while, I presumed he'd been in prison! He asked if I'd help out with the new packaging." Graham decided to accept the offer; as a freelancer, he didn't know if an offer like that would happen again.

Mike wanted new branding to go with the creation of 'Cult Classics'. "He was confident that his label was familiar enough with cult film fans to warrant branding," remembers Graham. "I reasoned that the packaging should be instantly recognisable and that it proclaimed the new VIPCO branding loudly and clearly."

The new look would feature a smaller version of the original artwork (at the centre of the front cover), surrounded by a blackmail-type note scattered behind it, or a vivid colour border. Above the central image would be the film's title in the feature's best-known font, typically from a previous cinema poster or VHS sleeve. Graham reveals how this 'small poster/large border' design came to be.

"[Mike] still had all the old VIPCO sleeves that had been scanned. The problem with scanning previously printed material was the danger of a moiré pattern; this is a checker-board effect created by clashing print dots – those of the original printed material and those of the new dot matrix. To avoid the problem, you could reduce the size of the image to minimise the dot matrix. This resulted in a generous border. My solution was a collage of the word VIPCO repeated in various sizes and angles with a colour theme that could change according to the genre. It was used on several releases until Michael decided he wanted something simpler and opted for a basic colour."

The new design would feature the 'Cult Classics' logo at the bottom of the cover; a nifty play on the iconic Coca-Cola logo. Graham Humphreys owned up to creating it when asked. "Yes, I did that dodgy logo!" It was Mike's suggestion, and Graham went ahead despite his protests not to. "Michael insisted that the lettering should look like the Coca-Cola logo. I advised against it for potential legal issues, but he was adamant. I don't believe there was any comeback!" the designer remembers.

Beneath the logo was a descriptor signifying what sort of 'classic' the video in question was. More often than not, many in the series were dubbed 'Frightener' and, on occasion, the gimmick was altered to match the nature of the movie. *Night of the Bloody Apes* (1969) was a *Cult Classic: Right 'Nana'* while *Shock Waves* (1977) was *Cult Classics: Video Nazi*. Kudos for the punnery. *Inseminoid* (1981) was given the tabloid headline-sounding *Cult Classics: Monster Bonker*. Ewan Cant says this one always made him laugh. At least *someone* liked that one.

Graham Humphreys also had to redesign the VIPCO logo as Mike did not have a clean or clear enough image of it scanned into the archives!

Over the following years, Mike would alter the layout of the series design several times, with little changes here and there. A bigger overhaul was made in the late nineties/early noughties after Humphreys had departed VIPCO. "I believe he found someone else to churn them out," Graham bluntly recollects. "My working with VIPCO did not last long anyway." As to why, he had this to say, "I can't quite recall. I suspect I wasn't available. As the work was not well paid, often requiring more work than could be covered by the small fees, this was no great loss for me in all honesty." He has not seen Mike Lee since.

Vaults of Horror would arrive in the late nineties; the layout was a black background with the title of the movie in white (in a familiar font) and an image from the feature in the centre. Sometimes it would *just* be the name with the usual logos screaming out (e.g., 'Previously Banned'). More interestingly, the Vault design had a series of computer-generated skulls lined up along the top of the sleeve as if they were looking down the page. They would also have 'blood' dripping down their foreheads.

The Skull-row, for lack of a better term, would become synonymous with VIPCO during this period. This little piece of packaging design would also begin to creep into other VIPCO lines including Cult Classics and the skull-row would be recognised as a VIPCO mascot, of sorts, over the coming years by eagle-eyed fans.

In a supposed effort to save on costs, Mike decided that the last wave of titles his firm was to distribute saw nearly all the colour and flair of past looks disappear. The black background was retained with a shoddy font stretched across most of the front. This was printed in a murky yellow/gold colour that was not pleasing on the eye. The only saving grace was the skull-row, which still looked good but could not compensate for the lack of finesse across the rest of Screamtime's sleeves.

Out of all the styles used by VIPCO, many fans cite the early pre-cert and Cult Classics layouts as their favourite packaging. The eye-catching images and colours retain that exciting feel of the glory days of video rental shops, where VHS sleeves were designed to be as attention-grabbing as possible. Mind you, *The Groove Tube* (1974) is one to forget!

9

The History of VIPCO (Part V)

**I had renewed the rights to many of them [VIPCO titles]
and was off to the races again!**

Mike speaking about the 're-launch' of his firm in the early nineties.

The heat from the Video Recordings Act 1984 had not only died down by the end of the eighties, but had been nearly forgotten by the general public. The Nasties panic had ceased to be, and those who appointed themselves as defenders of the moral faith were busy trying to make themselves look important in other ways. Sadly, we never got to see the proof that the films affected dogs, as claimed by Sir Graham Bright.

The scandal did have a sequel of sorts, in 1993, following the tragic murder of toddler James Bulger by two ten-year-old boys, Robert Thompson and Jon Venables, after they abducted him from a Liverpool area shopping centre. The nation was understandably concerned by this, and the press were up to their old tricks once more. Now, they claimed the murder had taken place after one of the boys (Venables) had purportedly seen *Child's Play 3* (1991) before deciding to kill a child to replicate the film. This is why Thompson and Venables kidnapped and brutally killed James, according to the likes of The Daily Mirror.

This led to the tabloids again claiming that Video Nasties should be banned (despite having already been banned) and even "burned". Other examples of horrors that could encourage the nation's youth to try and kill or maim each other, according to the press, were *Dolls* (1987) and *Dolly Dearest* (1991). Newspapers urged people to boycott or destroy these tapes for the "sake of all our kids" and as a matter of vital "soul searching" following the tragic end that James Bugler met.

Ultimately, the link between *Childs Play 3* and Thompson and Venables was discounted. The investigating police officer – Albert Kirby – concluded that neither child had seen the movie in question, nor its sequels. Psychiatric reports concluded that the boys were too scared to ever watch horrors. Just like with the fabricated 'evidence' of the Video Nasties controversy of the eighties, this complete fiction that *Child's Play 3* was, in part, responsible was left behind as the press moved onto the next witch hunt.

The early nineties was a different time for horror video fans for another reason too. The video rental stores had had their day and were in terminal decline. The boom period was a thing of the past as shops suffered drops in business and began to close outright. Many of the video store wheeler-dealers packed up their suitcases and started shady dealings elsewhere.

Regardless of this downturn in video rentals, and the drop in revenues, Mike Lee started to prepare for a relaunch of VIPCO in this fragile marketplace. He started to re-submit for certification many of the old films in the VIPCO back catalogue hoping that the BBFC, and its director James Ferman, would have softened since they were last submitted to the institute. Mike had believed that every movie would be granted a certificate or have little or no cuts. He was being hopelessly optimistic about this, however. Some titles were still refused classification, and some featured extensive cuts.

This did not put Mike off as he was confident that VIPCO's UK return would be a success, and he struck a new deal with distribution wholesaler S. Gold & Sons to be the sole distributor for VIPCO. This firm had started off with brothers Barrie and Sidney Gold selling vinyl records on a stall outside their father's shop in Barkingside, London in 1963. Eventually, the family opened up a warehouse in Leyton to sell goods in larger quantities following a very successful spell with a market stall in Petticoat Lane Market. Years later, they would be making a deal with VIPCO, a firm that had started in the same year, 1979. As Barrie Gold would explain, "I'd say that in around 1979, I first noticed videos creeping into the market, so Golds looked into dabbling in VHS. Mike Lee was the first person I did business with in terms of video distribution." The deal between the two companies was never inked; it was all done on a handshake. "I had no doubt about his word, and he had no doubts about mine, either." It would stay that way until the end of VIPCO.

The relaunch saw new designs and artwork for the titles that would make up the new line Cult Classics, some of which Graham Humphreys designed. The packaging had less extreme images on the sleeves yet was still just as eye-catching, with bright colours and some impressive artwork. For some videos, the covers looked more like children's films than ever before, which is ironic considering the company were accused of luring kids into buying Nasties back in the early eighties.

Mike, not dwelling on some of his prized flicks being blocked for release, added new horrors to his arsenal. While not as controversial (or even as entertaining as his earlier fare) they kept the cash coming in. Out of the host of new arrivals were highlights such as the Michael Lee produced *Spookies* (1986) which had previously been issued by Palace in the eighties, and Oz flick *Patrick* (1978). There were also some shockingly bad or outright bizarre tapes with the likes of *Zombie Nosh* (1988) and *The Nostril Picker* (1993). Yet, everyone interviewed for this book, from Ewan Cant to Jason Impey, remembers *those* flicks...

Lord Buckethead would re-enter British politics around the time of the re-launch with Lee again donning the ludicrous costume of the *Hyperspace/Gremloids* (1984) character. As if he had not learned his lesson from the 1987 General Election, he took part in the 1992 election and managed to secure even fewer votes. This time he got only 109.

For the rest of the decade, VIPCO would not release too many other titles outside of 1992/93's films. The sales (for some) were good, and Mike was pleased; others massively underperformed which angered him. Any movie that did not 'pull its weight' did not have its rights renewed when they expired; Mike decided to hold on to any that had value in an eventual re-release.

This would happen in 1999 as Mike got ready for the next wave of the VIPCO onslaught. This time, he would exploit a new development in the home video entertainment world. As he had done two decades earlier, with the arrival of VHS, the businessman was going to jump on the growing popularity of something known as DVD.

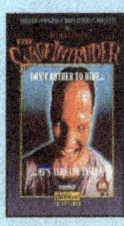 

65

VIPCO would issue many films that were not linked to the Video Nasties scandal, or which did not feature cannibals or zombies. Some were not even horror, as Mike attempted to branch out into other film genres (with limited success). The following reviews cover these other features, and it is quite the mixed bunch. Horror, thriller, action, and more...

A MAN CALLED BLADE (1977)

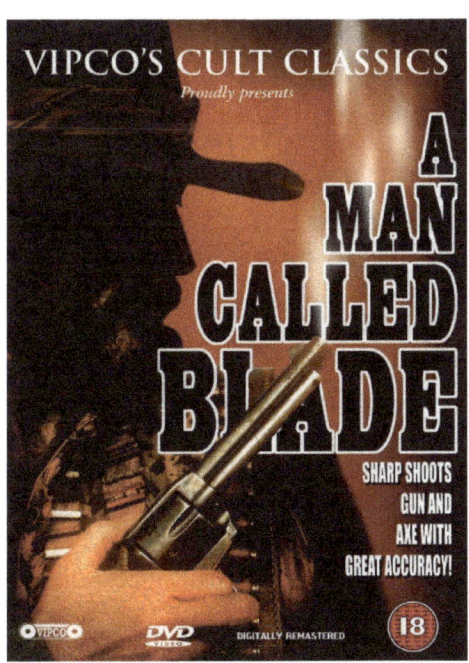

Director: Sergio Martino

Writers: Sergio Martino, Sauro Scavolini

Stars: Maurizio Merli (Blade/Mannaja), John Steiner (Voller), Donald O'Brien (Craven), Sonja Jeannine (Deborah)

VIPCO Release: 2002

Also Known As: *Mannaja*

VIPCO Synopsis: *Blade (Maurizio Merli) is a bounty hunter in the Wild West. Preferring to throw his axe to halt his prey instead of a six-shooter, Blade is also a deadly sharpshooter and is renowned for his prowess and skill. But Blade is no ordinary bounty hunter. As a child, his father was killed by McGowan (Philippe Leroy), a ruthless land developer, and as a grown man, seeks bloody revenge. Aided by Voller (John Steiner), a vicious thug, and a one-handed fugitive (Donald O'Brien), McGowan attempts to snuff out Blade. Even when he is nearly blinded, Blade manages to carve out a cache of stone axes as well as blasting away with his Colt- terminating with extreme prejudice. What remains is an extremely violent and visually stylish Spaghetti Western.*

A Man Called Blade is a typical Sergio Martino movie that runs at a cracking pace. Martino, who is also known for some excellent gialli such as All the Colours of the Dark and Torso, as well as graphic horror Mountain of the Cannibal God, aims true with this pasta western. Slide on your cowboy boots, don the Stetson, spin your spurs and load your Winchester for some frenetic western action.

Italian heavyweight Sergio Martino graces VIPCO's catalogue of titles again. This time, he helms a Spaghetti Western – a film genre that had been popular for over a decade by the time of *A Man Called Blade*'s release.

This movie would follow a similar formula to the hits of previous years when movies such as *A Fistful of Dollars* rode the horse into the ground, as it were, although *A Man Called Blade* came as the subgenre was witnessing a decline in production. Martino's work follows all the tropes that are expected yet, refreshingly, has some elements that mark it out from its contemporaries. The titular Blade has a compelling backstory that is teased out and leads to a revelation about him, and another key character, whilst Martino allows a softer side to be shown in his characters' personalities; some Spaghetti Westerns concentrate too hard on shoot outs and blood splatters.

The feature also has some very good stunt work. Mannaja taking on his rivals in a large mudhole in the middle of the small mining town is exciting to watch; more so, with the knowledge that actor Maurizio Merli did his own stunts. In fact, he did much of his own stunt work throughout the whole feature. Towards the end, he is seen buried up to his neck in a cave. He was in the action up to his neck, too.

John Steiner is a standout as the main villain, Voller. Supposedly cast by Martino for his hard-faced baddie looks, he certainly hits the nail on the head and cuts an imposing figure. One particularly memorable scene sees him sat at a table, in a saloon, with his savage dogs nearby. Steiner was a British actor who found fame in Italian cinema, which led to him appearing in several features now considered cult classics of B movie cinema: *White Fang* (1973), *Salon Kitty* (1976) and *Tenebrae* (1982).

As mentioned above, an intriguing and dark backstory that involves Mannaja and McGowan (Philippe Leroy) is proffered, with the revelation coming at just the right time for maximum impact. It is a plot strand that helps distinguish *A Man Called Blade* from its contemporaries. It will not be revealed here for the sake of not spoiling things, but its inclusion has led a number of critics over the decades to claim this is a spaghetti western with a difference.

Martino would follow this movie up with another title that would become part of the VIPCO catalogue – *Mountain of the Cannibal God* (as reviewed in this very book!). That was a title subjected to many cuts when released. However, *A Man Called Blade* escaped the blade (ahem) of the BBFC and only several seconds were removed in light of the BBFC's no-no on 'animal cruelty' (a horse falling). Sold on DVD by Mike in late 2002, this spaghetti western is yet to be re-issued in the UK on DVD or Blu-ray. Surely, it is a matter of time before 88 Films or Arrow Video change this. It had previously been seen on VHS, in the United Kingdom, courtesy of VTC in 1982.

A TIME TO DIE (1979)

Directors: Matt Cimber, Joe Tornatore

Writers: Matt Cimber, John F. Goff, Willy Russell (as William Russell)

Stars: Edward Albert (Rogan), Rex Harrison (Van Outen), Rod Taylor (Jack), Raf Vallone (Genco)

VIPCO Release: 1982

Also Known As: *Mario Puzo's Story Revenge, Seven Graves for Rogan, Seven Lives for Rogan*

VIPCO Synopsis: *While working with the underground movement in the South of France just before the end of II, Michael Rogan was taken prisoner along with his young pregnant wife and other members of his team.*

Six sadistic interrogators torture his wife and then murder her along with his friends. Rogan is shot and left for dead, but the liberating Americans find him and he recovers.

Rogan now sets out on a trail of vengeance which takes him across all Europe, to the lowest form of life in Munich and into the highest echelons of German Politics.

A tremendous adventure film which will make your hands sweat and tear at the emotions.

Based on Mario 'The Godfather' Puzo's *Six Graves to Munich* (1967) novel, the feature film does not stick strictly to the source material yet is a worthwhile watch regardless. Made many years after other, more successful film adaptations of the late Puzo's work, the renamed *A Time To Die* has been all but forgotten. Its release was delayed by a few years and the story had rewrites in places. Also, despite claims to the contrary, much of the shooting took place in the Netherlands, not Germany, as the onscreen graphics and plot would have you believe.

Those matters having been mentioned, *A Time to Die* is a potboiler of a revenge saga. Lead character Rogan (Albert) sulks and stalks through the feature hunting down the Nazis that executed his family. Indeed, the scene in which this happens is fairly dramatic and harrowing, although a solid way to open the movie. But the plot soon leads to Rogan – having somehow survived being shot point-blank in the back of the head – seeking out those that did the deed, many years later. The drama is left behind for a gritty, brooding vigilante aesthetic. It jars with the powerful opening moments, but not for long.

Rogan tracks down (rather easily) his former tormentors and kills them in brutal ways. Things plod along at an acceptable level with proceedings only getting really exciting when Rogan locks two of the Nazis in a booby-trapped car trunk, then drives off into the night, taunting them as they suffocate to death. There is also a ludicrous moment when he kills one villain with an explosives-filled chess piece!

Matt Cimber (Thomas Vitale Ottaviano) directs with sufficient capability although it is a far cry from his hauntingly chilling *The Witch Who Came from the Sea* (1976), a title that was lumped with the Video Nasties in the eighties. Perhaps he worked within the limits of a screenplay based on a Puzo novel, and the overall film suffered for it? Actor turned part-time director Joe Tornatore was hired to write and direct additional scenes in an effort to spice things up a little. This is why the film was not released until three years later, in 1982.

Rex Harrison co-stars in a part that saw him get star billing in many countries, and his photo graces posters and home video sleeves accordingly. The veteran actor had been active for over 50 years when this movie was shot in 1979.

Albert is passable although he doesn't say a word for the first 20 minutes of the runtime. In fact, he is silent for most of the feature, as he is seen broodingly watching his former captors, or staring pensively into the distance, across many scenes.

A Time to Die only graced VIPCO's slate of titles once in the firm's history, on VHS. It was given a UK DVD release in 2010 by Video International. It has been made available on disc in multiple other countries, too.

When I acquired *A Time to Die* on VHS for inclusion in this book, the copy I received had an index card that been used back in the early to mid-eighties by a nameless rental shop that owned the tape. I have included the card in *Vaults of Horror* to offer a fun little slice of a bygone era; an era when we trooped down to our local video stores and perused the shelves for hour upon end. Also, this is first-hand proof that VIPCO titles were *not* all Video Nasties; they *were* welcome on rental shelves. From June 1983 to October 1986, the tape had been hired out over two dozen times.

TITLE. A TIME TO DIE   PUR./REN. _SWV._

CLASSIFICATION: _A A._   AUDIENCE: ____

LIBRARY NUMBER: _AA 091_   COPY NUMBER: ____

CLUB NUMBER	HIRE DATE	DUE BACK	RETURN DATE
025	29.6 83	30.6 83	✓
104	16. 7. 83	17. 7. 83	✓
081	23.7.83	24.7.83	✓
186	1.9.83	2.9.83	—
183	19.9.83	20.9.83	✓
224	1.12.83	2.12.83	✓
383	16.12.83	17.12.83	✓
310	4.1.84	5.1.84	✓
400	15.1.84	16.1.84	✓
464	28.1.84	29.1.84	—
074	21.5.84	22.5.84	✓
547	22.5.84	23.5.84	✓

CLUB NUMBER	HIRE DATE	DUE BACK	RETURN DATE
500	24.6.84	25.6.84	✓
460	28.7.84	29.7.84	✓
555.	26.10.84	27.10.84.	✓
742.	5.1.85.	6.1.85.	✓
758.	10.1.85	11.1.85.	✓
868.	7.2.85	8.2.85.	✓
858.	23.3.85.	24.3.85	P.
624.	29.7.85	30.7.85	R5
582	16-8-85	17.8.85	✓
1089	5.10.85	6.10.85	✓
902	7.10.85	8.10.85	SM.
986-	22-1-86	23-1-86	SM
018.	31.7.86	1.8.86	R
1440	9.10.86	10.10.86	SM
636-	10.10.86	11.10.86	R

AND NOW THE SCREAMING STARTS! (1973)

Director: Roy Ward Baker

Writer: Roger Marshall

Stars: Stephanie Beacham (Catherine), Ian Ogilvy (Charles), Herbert Lom (Henry), Peter Cushing (Dr Pope)

VIPCO Release: 2002

Also Known As: *Bride of Fengriffen, Fengriffen, Now the Screaming Starts*

VIPCO Synopsis: *When Catherine (Stephanie Beacham) marries Charles Fengriffen (Ian Ogilvy) and moves into the family's old mansion, they are unaware that they are to be the victims of a horrifying curse. Immediately upon moving into the house, they are tormented by a strange life-like portrait, odd servants and a disembodied hand with a creepy crawling intention to see them both dead.*

The King of Horror, Peter Cushing, stars as a doctor who delves into the horrendous Fengriffen curse. This is a horror film in the classic mould – bizzarre, shocking, chilling and terrifying. When the screaming starts, it never stops!

Based on the book *Fengriffen* by David Case, this flick is one of the rare non-anthology horrors that Amicus Studios would produce. The title, *Fengriffen*, does not make one think of a horror movie so this could explain the more drastic title of *And Now the Screaming Starts* being used instead, although this is a slightly frivolous name in itself.

Despite having a solid cast of names that are forever linked with British and horror cinema, this is a feature that concentrates too much on dialogue and not the potential frights to be had. The appearances of Peter Cushing, Patrick Magee, Stephanie Beacham, and Hebert Lom in the same film could have been something really special, but the result is something of a misfire; again, due to the over-reliance on dialogue. Cushing and Magee briefly share a scene; it is too short, but it is fantastic to witness the two horror heavyweights together.

The plot is fairly familiar to anyone with a passing knowledge of British horror of this era. It involves Catherine (Beacham) in her new marital home as she begins to see and hear strange things! Naturally, everyone tells her it is all in her head, but the creepy woodsman (Geoffrey Whitehead) knows more than he's letting on. Her 'delusions' are proven to be real, and they relate to a horrible crime that her husband's ancestor carried out.

As mentioned, the runtime is filled with scenes that have lots of talk, talk, talk, and while this is not totally bad, it does lead to proceedings becoming so pre-occupied with exposition that the story often fails to get on point. When the plot does finally deliver, its payoff it is rewarding although expected. The occasional moments of horror will remind the viewer that this is an Amicus production but the most horrific moment is when, via flashback, we witness the woodsman's young wife being raped by grandad Fengriffen.

For more information on the features director, Roy Ward Baker, see this book's review of *Asylum* (1972).

VIPCO sold *And Now the Screaming Starts!* on DVD in 2002. The transfer is not terrible considering some of the transfers VIPCO brought out. With this, and the release of *Asylum* and *Vault of Horror* (1973), the once-mighty Amicus would see some of its former wares made available to old and new viewers alike (thanks to Mike).

ASYLUM (1972)

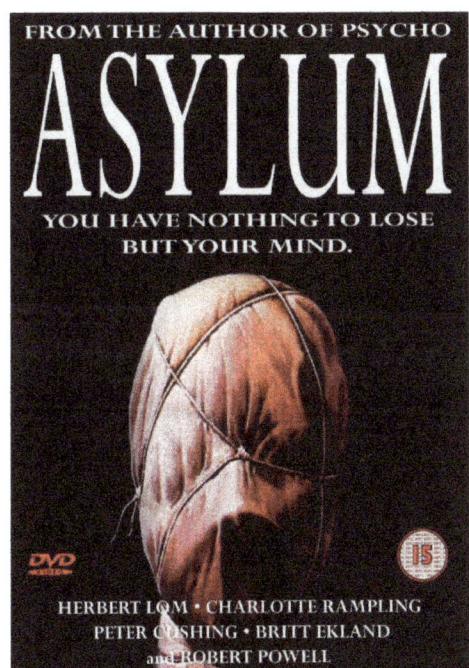

Director: Roy Ward Baker

Writer: Robert Bloch

Stars: Peter Cushing (Smith), Robert Powell (Dr. Martin), Patrick Magee (Dr. Rutherford), Sylvia Syms (Ruth)

VIPCO Release: 1993

Also Known As: *House of Crazies, House on the Strand*

VIPCO Synopsis: *The most bizarre cases of criminal madness possible – all under one roof. Where therapy consists of solitary confinement, kindness and understanding are concepts of the past and the door between the inmates and the outside is kept locked at all times! Welcome to the Asylum where all the loonies run the bin and where once you're in you never get out!*

Asylum was the first of two portmanteau films from the iconic Amicus that VIPCO would release; the other being *Vaults of Horror* (1973). Amicus was a British studio that often specialised in 'portmanteau'/horror anthologies; features that had episodic stories within a 'wraparound' plot to contextualise what the viewer had seen. Although the firm did try its hand at other genres, it is its horror anthology output that it is best remembered for.

Roy Ward Baker was the director. Over his career, he worked with Amicus and Hammer amongst others, and was responsible for classic horror films including *Quatermass and the Pit* (1967), *Scars of Dracula* (1970), and *Vault of Horror* (1973). In terms of output quality, *Asylum* is a solid effort although is often overlooked in favour of his Hammer contributions.

Interestingly, this feature was based on stories written by Robert Bloch – the man responsible for the seminal 1959 novel *Psycho*. The American would pen numerous books and short stories, as well as write for various TV shows and movies. By this point in his career, Bloch had worked on several Amicus films; in *Asylum*, his creative pen would detail the stories of the inmates who relate matters to Robert Powell's Dr. Martin.

The tales themselves vary in quality, all of them predictable. Some benefit from this, as the viewer will enjoy the anticipation of what is clear to all (except the characters on screen).

The first story, titled *Frozen Fear*, sees love-rat husband Walter (Richard Todd) excitedly show his wife Ruth (Sylvia Syms) the new chest freezer he has bought her. The cynic in any horror fan will automatically know this means someone is going to be killed and their corpse stored in the same chest freezer. Indeed, this happens moments later as Walter murders his other half, chops up her body, and places it in his new white good.

The second and third instalments are not as strong; however, they do feature the biggest stars of *Asylum*. A deteriorating Peter Cushing lends his distinguished-as-always presence to *The Weird Tailor*, where he plays a client of a financially struggling tailor (Barry Morse) who makes a suit from a strange, sparkling material. *Lucy Comes to Stay*, on the other hand, co-stars seventies sex symbol Britt Ekland as a trouble-causing friend of the mentally disturbed Barbara (Charlotte Rampling), taking great delight in trying to unravel her pal's fragile state of mind. But there is a twist...

All the plots have twists, in fact. As often found in the genre, it is as if the director and writer know what people expect, and throw in an absurd swerve ending to try to pull the rug from under the viewer's feet. In *Asylum*, the twists miss the mark, but credit must be given to the effort made for the feature's ending. It incorporates the fourth tale, *Mannikins of Horror*, which breaks away from the norm of an inmate remembering a past misdeed, and takes place in the present with the gullible Dr. Martin.

VIPCO sold this Amicus portmanteau on two occasions; on VHS and DVD in 2000, and re-released as part of the Screamtime series of DVDs in late 2003.

THE BIG RACKET (1976)

Director: Enzo G. Castellari

Writers: Arduino Maiuri, Massimo De Rita, Gene Luotto, Enzo G. Castellari

Stars: Fabio Testi (Nico Palmieri), Vincent Gardenia (Pepe), Orso Maria Guerrini (Gianni Rossetti), Renzo Palmer (Giulti)

VIPCO Release: 2003

Also Known As: *Big Violence, Outlaws '77, The Great Blackmail*

VIPCO Plot Synopsis: *Nico Palmieri is a police inspector who battles against hoodlums who terrorise an Italian town and extort cash from the locals. With the threat of horrific brutality, no*

74

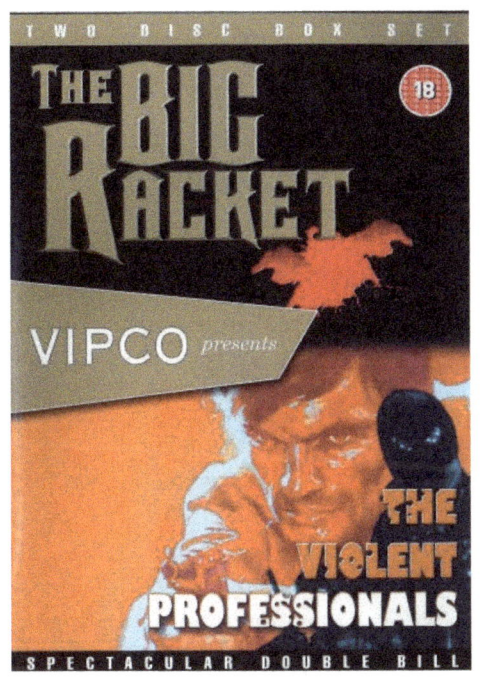

one dares to act except a restaurant owner who approaches Palmieri and sings like a canary. As a result, his young daughter is raped. Discovering that the terrorism is related to drug dealers, Palmieri is forbidden to continue investigating his case by his superiors so he goes it alone. Palmieri recruits men who have become victims of the crooks and the film ends with a bloody massacre. Bullets fly and blood spatters the screen.

This is arguably the best of the Castellari titles that Michael Lee signed up for VIPCO. Gritty, hard-boiled, and with moments of genuine tension, *The Big Racket* is impressive. It is also, potentially, one of VIPCO's best titles, which is not saying much if one considers *Zombie Flesh Eaters II* and *Brain Fix* but, that aside, *The Big Racket* is strong.

The movie starts off with an act of violence and things escalate from there. Shops being trashed, people being knifed/shot/beaten up, raped; shoot outs and explosions all fill out the runtime. Most of these are shot unflinchingly as Enzo really gets the camera 'in there' and revels in the violence like true Italian exploitation cinema is wont to do.

There is controversy, too. Early on, a young girl is raped by the thugs and is shot in a manner that makes the viewer feel like a Peeping Tom. Castellari alternates between close-up shots of the rape and long-distance ones from behind some crates, which feels as if one minute you are being forced to witness the defilement and – the next – put at arm's length to take in the grim scene as a whole. The BBFC, not so surprisingly, cut this sequence.

Fabio Testi is a strong lead actor as Palmieri, if a little too clean-shaven for a rough-and-ready hero in an Italian crime caper. He is such a smooth-looking bastard that there is not a hair out of place or a scratch on him when the crook gang huddle around his car and *flip* it down the side of a cliff, and he suffers a broken neck and leg. Testi, no doubt, was a shrewd piece of casting having already been a star in the likes of *What Have You Done to Solange?* (1972) and *The Inheritance* (1976).

It has to be said that the plot is predictable, with many developments easy to anticipate well before they happen. It is obvious that Enzo is not trying to reinvent the wheel… just make an entertaining movie. He succeeds!

Originally rejected by the BBFC for release in early 1977, VIPCO would give *The Big Racket* the UK release it had been denied for so long in early 2003 on VHS and DVD. There was one condition attached, however. Fourteen seconds were cut from the rape scene, as the BBFC felt the footage would 'harm' the viewer and society. The movie would be packaged with Sergio Martino's *The Violent Professionals* as a 'VIPCO presents' two-disc set in summer 2005.

BLOOD CAMP THATCHER (1982)

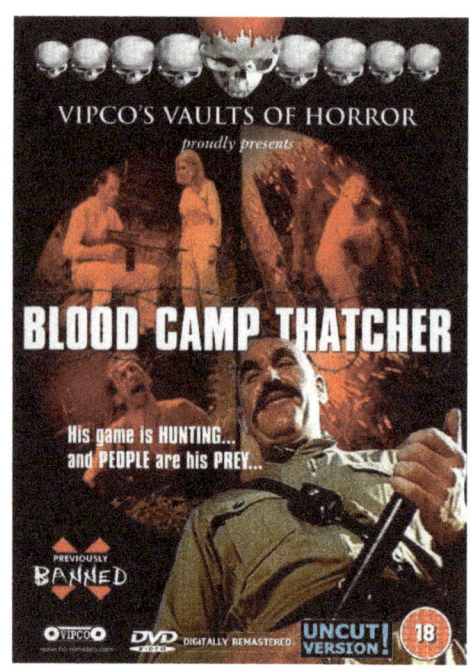

Director: Brian Trenchard-Smith

Writers: George Schenck, Robert Williams, David Lawrence, Neill Hicks, Jon George

Stars: Olivia Hussey (Chris), Steve Railsback (Paul), Michael Craig (Thatcher), Carmen Duncan (Jennifer)

VIPCO Release: 1993

Also Known As: *Escape 2000, Slaughter Game, Turkey Shoot*

VIPCO Plot Synopsis: *In a faceless and clinical landscape of the future where every living soul is a potential enemy of the State, a degenerate hierarchy – ruling by terror and intimidation – wields absolute and ultimate power over life and death. The State has become master; the protesters, deviates. The unfortunates who end up at notorious Camp 17 have little to look forward to. Behind the electrified fences a band of sadistic guards – teasing, taunting, dispensing cruelty at the crack of a whip – make survival a living hell. The cold-blooded commandant Thatcher, and his devious cronies, live a life of two pleasures: one of the flesh, the other organising regular Turkey Shoots – it is the only possible escape. With a head start, selected prisoners are allowed to run beyond the camp's boundaries to the hills and apparent freedom whilst Thatcher and his evil menagerie scheme to devise fascinating and gruesome deaths for their 'turkeys'. As the hunt begins so does the ultimate nightmare.*

Better known by its original title – *Turkey Shoot* – Michael Lee decided to change the name of this Ozploitation flick to *Blood Camp Thatcher*. He believed having the word turkey in the title would invite people to dismiss it as a 'turkey' (a dud), and that flagging up the main character as Thatcher would tap into people's perceptions about Margaret Thatcher, former Prime Minister and Conservative Party leader.

Whatever the name, Trenchard-Smith's flick is, at times, brutal and gruelling to watch. In the decades since its release, people have decried it as trash and devoid of merit. While it is easy to acknowledge these points of view, *Thatcher* is not *that* tasteless. There seems to be some effort at social and political commentary throughout (such as using real riot footage taken from newsreels for the opening titles) and the depiction of individuals in power as abusive, disgusting, and despicable people.

An example of this abuse of power is when Hussey's character is forcibly taken from her place of work and placed in the titular 'blood camp' for merely looking at someone with a slither of power the wrong way.

The plot also brings to mind George Orwell's *1984* as well as several other dystopian works. The manner in which the 'social deviants' are hunted down by the 'VIP's' has a vibe of *The Most Dangerous Game* (by Richard Connell, 1924), a story that featured a man releasing human captives so he could hunt them. Although that film, admittedly, did not feature bazookas and napalm.

Literary, social, or deeper meanings aside, this is pretty much Ozploitation through and through. The excessive violence, the gratuitous nudity, the bonkers script, and the varied level of acting performances account for the other 95% of *Thatcher*. The direction is of an acceptable level throughout, and Trenchard-Smith really amps up the film (and his directing) for the blood-soaked and explosion-filled final act.

Half of the movie's funding failed to materialise, just as filming began, with the shortfall chased through gambling by the producers (as mentioned in the Ozploitation documentary *Not Quite Hollywood*) – and the violence was relied on to make up for the new budgetary constraints.

There is also a giant werewolf/man monster 'thing' (described simply as 'a freak') character that gives the movie a slightly silly tinge to it. Its inclusion is as daft as the explanation given.

Thank goodness that Oz acting legend Roger Ward is here as prison guard Ritter, and his first scene sees him making a poor woman prisoner recite some sort of pledge while he pretends to punch and slap her in an effort to scare her. He gets bored of this and starts beating the crap out of her for real. Ward looks like he is having a real blast during the whole feature. He also appears in the 2014 remake.

Hitting UK cinemas in 1983, as *Turkey Shoot*, the feature would be cut by six minutes, removing footage from several of the more grisly moments. A decade later, when VIPCO got its hands on the film and changed the name, the cuts remained. A decade after *that*, in 2003, an uncut version would get a release from VIPCO on DVD. Strangely, by the end of that year, the film would be released again, by a different firm, under its original title. It is now available to stream via Shudder UK.

In the excellent documentary, *Not Quite Hollywood* (2008) by Mark Hartley, which explores the history of Ozploitation, many of the cast and crew appear and express their regrets about *Turkey Shoot*; many agree with the negative criticisms it received. Oh dear, a movie must be in trouble when those associated with it cannot even defend it.

Brian Trenchard-Smith would go onto direct some other well-known titles in Australian cinema in the following years including *BMX Bandits* (1983, starring a young Nicole Kidman) and *Dead End Drive-In* (1986). By the mid-nineties he was directing American horror sequels *Night of the Demons 2* (1994), *Leprechaun 3* (1995), and *Leprechaun 4: In Space* (1996), amongst others.

Turkey Shoot was remade in 2014 and released in some countries under the name *The Elimination Game*. It, like the original, was also critically mangled.

BRAIN FIX (1993)

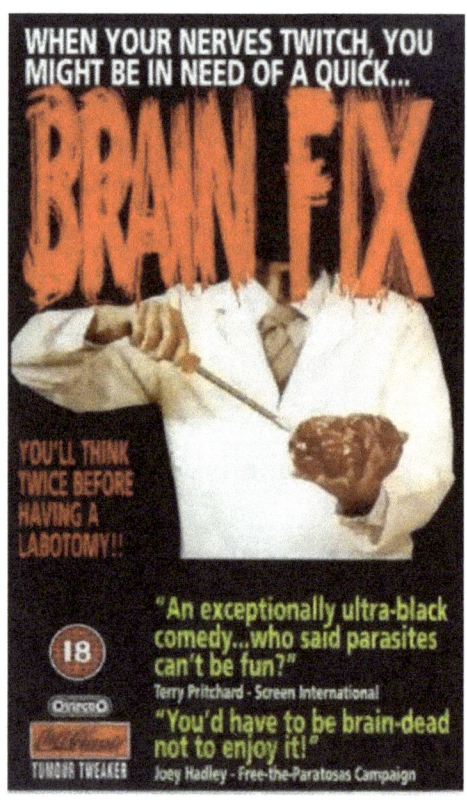

WHEN YOUR NERVES TWITCH, YOU MIGHT BE IN NEED OF A QUICK...

BRAIN FIX

YOU'LL THINK TWICE BEFORE HAVING A LABOTOMY!!

"An exceptionally ultra-black comedy...who said parasites can't be fun?"
Terry Pritchard - Screen International

"You'd have to be brain-dead not to enjoy it!"
Joey Hadley - Free-the-Paratosas Campaign

Directors: Scott J. Wallace, Jay Amin

Writers: Jay Amin (story), Ted Chalmers, Tracy Charlton.

Stars: Charles Coplin (Jeff), Jack Savage (Dr. Feud), Kristin Dean Boswell (Molly), Kim Hyde (Nurse Braun).

VIPCO Release: 1993.

VIPCO Plot Synopsis: *Black-listed Dr Feud believes he has found a cure for acute schizophrenia by implanting living parasites into his patients' brains. When son Jeff witnesses his father at work he is appalled. He and apparently-normal patient Molly, whom he loves, are next on the treatment schedule...*

Starting with a shot of static on a television screen, *Brain Fix* may have been a better film if it had stayed like this for the entirety of its runtime. A horror comedy that doesn't do either very well, *Brain Fix* is, at times, painful to sit through. It is certainly one of the movies that people may struggle to remember VIPCO releasing.

The problem is that, at times, the story switches between humour and horror without any rhyme or reason. In one of the first scenes, a patient named Norm is seen talking to the camera as if he is on a video dating service (for the Tinder generation, Google it). This is followed up by Dr. Feud appearing on a very low-rent-looking chat show parody to discuss his methods of treating people while the TV host mugs at the camera to the sounds of canned laughter. Later on, the scenes in which Feud inserts parasites into his unwilling victims are treated in a similar light-hearted manner, despite the fact that what is happening is quite disturbing. Indeed, that sequence (and a couple of similar ones) happen to have a David Cronenberg-like vibe to them.

The leech-like parasites are placed into people via the back of the neck in a bloody manner. This is somehow supposed to help treat patients, although Jeff later finds out the process does more harm than good. He is seen pulling the organisms out of the backs of peoples' necks in an effort to save them. If shot correctly, this element of the story could have been highly effective.

The rest of the plot struggles to make any sense. An unintentional laugh is caused when Jeff arrives at the hospital to stay a few days with his father, who tells him he will share a room with one of the patients! This is so he can 'see how things are run' according to his deadly serious dad.

Credit must be given to the actors involved; at least some of them were capable of doing what was asked of them. Coplin is likeable as the naïve, wet-behind-the-ears

Jeff. His on-screen father is equally effective, with Jack Savage being the sinister doctor who is up to no good. Richard Arvay deserves a mention as the stereotypical nutjob, Norm, who goes as far as dressing in drag.

It seems there was no budget for the feature, with the 'hospital' appearing to be somebody's hallway and spare bedroom. The set of the spoof talk show is no better; it is nothing more than 'Talk Now' written on a grey wall with a couple of chairs in front of it. The only special effects of note are the parasitical creatures; they look like fake dog poo, covered in red syrup.

This was the first and last film directed by Scott J. Wallace. He seems to have gone on to enjoy greater fortune as an editor on numerous big hit US TV shows – *The X-Files* (for 7 episodes) and sitcom *The Middle* being just two of them. Although it is not listed on IMDb, the executive producer – Jay Amin – also co-directed. Amin has no other credits to his name.

The end credits finish with 'This is dedicated to all parasitical creatures throughout the world.' Nuff said.

For a VIPCO title, it is easy to see why *Brain Fix* has been forgotten. It is not as notorious or infamous as some of the movies they were putting out around this time, and it had no name talent that could attract genre fans. Plus, unfortunately, it is dire to watch.

Unlike many other features released by VIPCO, throughout the company's history, *Brain Fix* would be issued only once.

THE BRONX WARRIORS (1982)

Director: Enzo G. Castellari

Writers: Dardano Sacchetti, Elisa Briganti as Elisa Livia Briganti, Antone Pagan, Enzo G. Castellari

Stars: Vic Morrow (Hammer), Mark Gregory (Trash), Christopher Connelly (Hot Dog), Fred Williamson (The Ogre)

VIPCO Release: 2003

Also Known As: *1990: The Bronx Warriors, The Riffs – We Are the Force*

VIPCO Plot Synopsis: *When the Bronx is officially declared a High Risk District, the Authorities give up any attempts to enforce the law. From that moment on, The Riders reign – but their mortal enemies, The Zombies, The Tigers and The Scavengers, do not go quietly into the night.*

They are all the scum of the earth, your worst nightmare come true. Their names speak volumes for violence: Hammer, Ogre, Hot Dog, Ice and Trash. For them killing is second nature and death means nothing.

The catacombs in the bowels of the Bronx reek with the stench of carnage and carrion. The Disinfectors are burning and gassing the last remnants of New York's social outcasts to build the "City of the Future". The acrid smell of fear and hate tears at the nostrils as the murdering Warrior Gangs of the Bronx unite to defend their homeland, sewer by sewer. Theirs is a war of brutality with a unique prize: TO THE VICTOR GOES THE BRONX...

Over the decades, this movie has often been labelled as a rip off of several more popular films of the early eighties. *Mad Max* (1979), *The Warriors* (1979), and *Escape From New York* (1981) are the most prevalent, and it is easy to see their influence when viewing *Bronx Warriors*.

The idea that 'any attempts to enforce the law' leads to the Bronx becoming a more lawless and dangerous environment is what brings about the *Escape From New York* comparisons, while the reliance on motorcycles and wearing leather is *Mad Max* territory. But it is Walter Hill's classic *The Warriors* that is clearly the biggest inspiration for director Enzo G. Castellari, and writer Dardano Sacchetti. Most of the story is taken from *The Warriors*, especially Trash and his gang travelling through the Bronx and encountering various rival gangs along the way.

Just because *Bronx Warriors* is a rip off doesn't mean it is bad. Admittedly, it does have its weaknesses – namely the dialogue and Mark Gregory's acting – but for the most part, it is enjoyable. The director manages to capture several fight scenes in an exciting manner, especially the ending when there is an all-out war between the gangs, and which incorporates flamethrowers!

But… the weak points do colour the viewer's experience. The script is so bad that, at times, it is laughable. There is one exchange on a beach between Trash and Anne (Stefania Girolami Goodwin), daughter of director Castellari) that is so painful, it is a mercy when it ends. In turn, inexperienced Gregory is so wooden in his delivery that the lines come across more excruciatingly than ever!

Gregory gets a large bulk of the screen time as the star of the feature. He looks the part, there is no denying that, and was cast after his girlfriend sent in his photo. (IMDb only has him listed as appearing in a 1979 movie named *Rainbow*, pre-dating this story.) As a 17-year-old, at the time, this was an early acting role, and it shows. His performance is typically bland and monotonous.

Gregory would go on to have starring roles in several other action movies before disappearing from the industry in 1990. Hardcore fan of *Bronx Warriors* – Lance Manley – has spent years trying to find Gregory, with no luck. You can read about his incredible efforts to find Trash at bronxwarriors.co.uk.

Elsewhere within the cast, there are some faces that will be recognisable to genre fans. Veteran actor Vic Morrow manages to look like a legit badass as Hammer, stalking the streets killing people in a manner reminiscent of Robert Ginty in *The Exterminator* (1980). Tragically, Morrow would die on the set of his next feature *Twilight Zone: The Movie* (1983) when a stunt involving a helicopter went horribly wrong. Everybody's favourite self-devouring cannibal, George Eastman, pops up, too.

Bronx Warriors had cuts when it was first released in the United Kingdom that would be waived for VIPCO's VHS and DVD release two decades later. The firm would also re-release the movie along with its sequel *Bronx Warriors 2/Escape From the Bronx* in a two-disc DVD set entitled 'VIPCO presents' in 2005. The film, and its sequel, were later released by Shameless.

BRONX WARRIORS 2 (1983)

Director: Enzo G. Castellari

Writers: Tito Carpi, Enzo G. Castellari

Stars: Mark Gregory (Trash), Henry Silva (Wrangler), Giancarlo Prete as Timothy Brent (Strike), Ennio Girolami as Thomas Moore (President Clark)

VIPCO Release: 2003

Also Known As: *Escape From the Bronx, Escape 2000, The Riffs II – Escape From the Bronx*

VIPCO Plot Synopsis: *New York City is undergoing a major facelift, and the GC Corporation, the company being the revamp, wants to oust the 'rats' in the Bronx – including self-made warriors Trash and Toblerone – and move them to the new city. Only their operation, led by cantankerous ex-prison warden Wrangler, uses a bit of unnecessary force and the warriors aren't too happy about it. So, with the help of underground warrior Strike, they decide to kidnap the President of GC, Clark so that they'll stop the operation.*

Bringing back memories of the ending of *The Bronx Warriors* (1982) this sequel begins with someone being torched with a flamethrower. In fact, flamethrowers appear *a lot* in this movie. That exciting end sequence from the original clearly made an impact on not just the viewer, but the director Enzo G. Castellari as well.

The actual title for this movie is *Escape from the Bronx,* a title that brings to mind those *Escape from New York* rip off comparisons (again) although no one is attempting any escape from the condemned Bronx here. Much of the feature takes place in either sewers or crumbling buildings. Those who remain in the Bronx will not allow the big nasty corporation to demolish their… erm… lovely home. The help of one person unites them all: Trash!

Despite ending the original film victorious, with his biker friends and the new love-of-his-life, Anne, Trash is solo here and still played by the buff Mark Gregory. Heroic to a fault, he is now compelled to seek vengeance when his parents are killed by the 'Disinfectors' (the henchmen of the evil corp). This is an early challenge for Gregory in terms of acting. Considering his sub-par performance in the first entry, it is a shock that Castellari lingers in for a close up when Trash finds his parents dead. Gregory manages to widen his eyes a little, and forces some tears to well up, but he really looks more like a man who's been told his football team has lost the promotion play-offs; not someone stood in front of the corpses of his parents.

Luckily for the viewer, the cast has a few solid actors in its ranks. Paolo Malco is the snide and nasty corporate suit, Hoffman. The cult film veteran looks and acts like a villain from an episode of *The A-Team* with obvious glee. Ennio Girolami, brother of Mr. Castellari, is the president of the very generic sounding General Construction Corporation. Henry Silva and Giancarlo Prete (aka Timothy Brent) seem to be competing for the most over-the-top and macho performance of the feature. Regardless of who wins this competition, both are a riot to watch.

Of course, things come to a head between the united underground warriors and the generic baddies for the final act. Enzo again unleashes an exciting battle that will wake the viewer up. Gregory shines here and puts to good use that physique he is so fond of showing off.

This movie may be best known to some as *Escape 2000* which was featured as the fifth episode of season seven of *Mystery Science Theater 3000 (MST3K)* in 1996. The movie received the usual treatment from the show, as could be expected.

Bronx Warriors 2 was released by VIPCO several months after they issued the first *Warriors* flick. Unlike *that* title's decent-by-VIPCO-standards DVD transfer, part two is more in keeping with the firm's more standard transfer quality reputation.

Former staff member Jay Slater says he obtained *Warriors I & II* for VIPCO and considers that to be the highlight of his time with Mike Lee's company.

The synopsis on the back of the box treats the potential buyer to a VIPCO 'review' of *Bronx Warriors 2*. It is reproduced below, exactly as it appeared all those years ago with the same grammar and spelling errors. The enthusiasm almost knocks you off your feet...

OUR REVIEW: Superfast-paced and insanely entertaining, BRONX WARRIORS 2 is practically non-stop action, with lots of Castellari's glorious slow-mo, and an unbelievably high body count and level of violence. Bodies are flung from explosions, faces are destroyed by shotgun blows. Henry silva is the villain malisimo, our favourite Classic Silva moment: "No sugar idiot! How many times do I have to tell you?! It makes me CRAZY!!" The theme score is cracking and hits home all through the set pieces. It's definitely not high art, but it has a great-looking, hard as nails hero, and easy-to-hate hissable loathsome villains.More action, more special effects, more BRONX! Oh the joy! We give it 10 out of 10!!!

THE DEADLY SPAWN (1983)

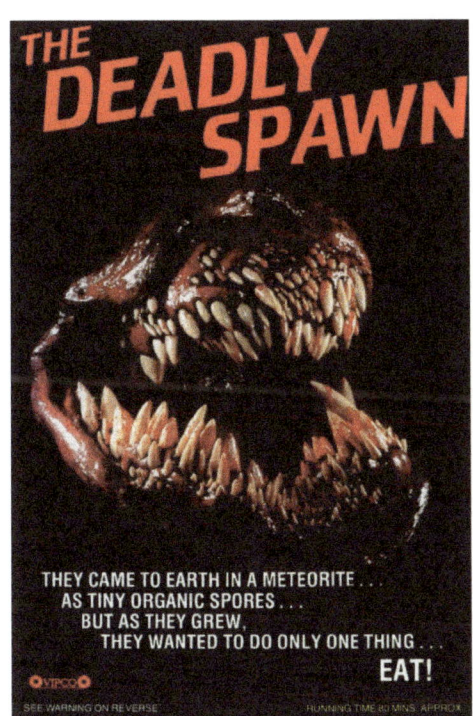

Director: Douglas McKeown

Writers: Ted A. Bohus, John Dods, Douglas McKeown

Stars: Charles George Hildebrant (Charles), Richard Lee Porter (Frankie), Jean Tafler (Ellen), Tom DeFranco (Pete)

VIPCO Release: 1983

Also Known As: *Return of the Aliens: The Deadly Spawn, Return of the Alien's Deadly Spawn, The Alien's Deadly Spawn*

VIPCO Plot Synopsis: *In a remote part of New England, two teenagers on a camping trip see what looks like a meteorite fall from the sky and land nearby. Investigating, they discover the Deadly Spawn – a toothsome alien being that quickly disposes of them before setting off in search of more food. Soon it has found a hiding place in a nearby town, where its terror is fully unleashed upon the unwary inhabitants...*

This film seems to be one of VIPCO's favourites. First released by the company in the pre-cert era of spring 1983, it would see various reissues until the end of the company's existence.

It is, perhaps, a movie that mirrors VIPCO's ethos: made quickly and cheaply with lasting longevity. *The Deadly Spawn* appears to have been made on a tiny budget (which it was), but the cast and crew get the job done with what little they have. The filming locations are primarily contained to a single house, and the actors look as if they are wearing whatever they dressed in – that day – for shooting. The money that the production had, seems to have been mostly spent on the titular deadly spawn.

The alien creatures do look impressive which, of course, VIPCO splashed suitably over the packaging of its various releases. Well, apart from the Screamtime version. A cross between a large phallus and a xenomorph from *Alien* (1979), they are undoubtedly the feature's biggest asset. McKeown, meanwhile, makes sure he builds the viewer's anticipation before they are revealed. The first several times they are on screen they are shown in the shadows or as a silhouette; half-an-hour in, he finally brings the spawn from out of the darkness. Elsewhere, the effects are good too, with one unfortunate woman's face being ripped off by one of the creatures.

Acting-wise, the cast do a commendable job considering their amateur status (barring James L. Brewster). Young Charles, George Hildebrant, is the most enthusiastic of the bunch; his character brings about the downfall of the aliens. Hildebrant would not act again after this movie. In fact, many of the actors here would not act again. Several of the crew appeared on screen during the end sequence outside the house.

While the action on-screen struggles to lift things above the level expected of a feature like this, McKeown does manage to create a tense ending with the main characters trapped in the attic with the spawn.

One of the writers, John Dods, would go on to do special effects on *Spookies* (1986) – the movie that 'Mr. VIPCO' – Michael Lee – produced.

When VIPCO gave *The Deadly Spawn* a VHS reissue in the early nineties, with artwork by Graham Humphreys, the sleeve also bore the message 'They meet you, they greet you, then they eat you.' What Mike meant by this is a mystery, unless he imagined a sequence in which the spawn introduce themselves, shake hands with everyone, then proceed to eat their victims. The skull that features on this artwork is also lifted directly from VIPCO's own Cult Classics release of *Eaten Alive!* (1980) which was also from the early nineties.

DECEPTION (1975)

Director: Maximilian Schell

Writers: Maximilian Schell, Friedrich Durrenmatt

Stars: Jon Voight (Walter), Martin Ritt (Hans), Jacqueline Bisset (Anna), Robert Shaw (Gastmann)

VIPCO Release: 1982

Also Known As: *End of the Game, Getting Away with Murder, Murder on the Bridge*

VIPCO Synopsis: *"Deception" is a cold-blooded game of murder. It starts shortly after World War II in Istanbul with a bet between two young Swiss. The game is to murder – just for fun – and avoid getting caught! Thirty years later the game is still being played. It has become more complicated, with many people now being used as pawns in this bizarre game of chess. The deceptions in Istanbul, Munich, Rome, Lausanne and Berne are refined to the point where murder is done and another pawn in the game is set up as the killer. And so the game continues!*

This crime thriller starts with a woman on a bridge being punched in the face. She then falls into the water below and drowns. The story jumps forward 30 years with no immediate mention of the murder, and it is not until much later into the runtime that we find out why it happened. Sadly, the VIPCO plot synopsis spoils this as Mike (it is assumed he drafted it) divulges that the woman drowning is part of a strange 'game', between friends turned rivals, to commit crimes and avoid detection. And, yes, I am aware that this entry started with a spoiler of what happens in *Deception*!

The feature as a whole is a slow-burner, and does not heat up much once the viewer is let in on 'the game' and the arrival of Robert Shaw's villainous Gastmann. Shaw, who also appeared as the iconic Quint in J*aws* – the same year as *Deception* was released – is intense and his presence lifts the scenes he acts in. The actor personally did not enjoy making this movie and never received payment for it!

Martin Ritt and Jon Voight are also strong characters and help elevate the feature with great performances. Ritt was a respected director, and occasional actor, by this point of his long career and his acting here is that of a world-weary old man that likes his food and the sporadic wisecrack or two. Voight has an unintentionally dodgy German accent and mad-eyed stare. Donald Sutherland plays a corpse in a scene that lasts seconds but it was enough, in Mike's eyes, to earn him a mention on the VIPCO sleeve.

There is a genuinely funny scene when people are at the graveside of a coffin about to be lowered into the ground during a funeral. It begins to rain, which quickly becomes a downpour. Mourners at the funeral unashamedly cut short the paying of their respects to the deceased by running inside as quickly as possible, nearly falling over each other in the process.

Deception was a much longer film than the version on this tape. It ran over 15 minutes longer when at cinemas although this longer version has not been made available in the decades since. The VIPCO version contains some of the scenes from those missing 15 minutes, but this only bumps up the runtime slightly and offers nothing of great value to the plot.

The story was based on a novella named *The Judge and His Hangman* from 1950 by Friedrich Durrenmatt. The author also had a hand in the screenplay alongside *Deception's* director Schell. *The Judge and His Hangman* had been made into several features and television films before this 1975 adaptation.

This movie was one of the few movies directed by the legendary Maximilian Schell. While this is an acceptable effort, and has a direction style that holds the viewer's attention, Schell would spend most of his career acting and winning lasting praise for his performances.

Ennio Morricone provided the score for *Deception* and, as is the case with Morricone's work, it definitely enhances the viewer's experience.

This title has received little attention in the decades since this VIPCO release with its sole outing, on any disc-based home video format, happening in 2011 on Blu-ray, in Germany.

EMANUELLE IN PRISON (1983)

Director: Bruno Mattei as Gilbert Roussel

Writer: Claudio Fragasso

Stars: Laura Gemser (Emanuelle), Ursula Flores (Albina), Gabriele Tinti (Henderson), Pierangelo Pozzato (Blade)

VIPCO Release: 2003

Also Known As: *A Bunch of Bastards, Blade Violent, Women's Prison Massacre*

VIPCO Plot Synopsis: *Investigative reporter Emanuelle finds herself locked up in an all woman penitentiary run by a ruthless warden and her brutally sadistic guards. Vowing to exact revenge upon the corrupt politician who set her up, Emanuelle must first survive the daily torture and attempts at her life by grotesque prison bully Albina.*

Into this powder keg of sex and violence comes four bloodthirsty death row inmates led by "Crazy Boy" Henderson. Blasting their way to a prison takeover, this quartet of psychotic criminals takes advantage of the all-female situation, only to find they have bitten off more than they can chew. With the police launching an all-out assault upon the rampaging inmates, Emanuelle battles to stay alive amidst the bloodshed and depravity...and the most horrifying game of Russian Roulette ever seen!

Directed by Bruno Mattei (as Gilbert Roussel) but cited by Laura Gemser as being helmed by writer Claudio Fragasso, this is – either way – as trashy and smutty a film as can be expected when either of these men are involved.

As it was made at the same time as *Violence in a Woman's Prison* (1982), many of the cast from that WIP flick are put to use in this one. Gemser, Tinti, Flores, Maria Romano, and a few others, are all part of the cast. Some even play near-identical characters, just with different names. Many of the costumes are the same and the same location is used. Those familiar with the people involved, the genre, and its trappings, will know what to expect.

Not beating about the bush (no pun intended) Mattei gets to the naff softcore lesbian action within ten minutes, followed quickly by the usual violence when the same lesbians get roughed up. It is all done with a zeal that adds to the absurd campiness; much of the sex and violence makes this movie feel more like a longer episode of British primetime drama *Bad Girls*. (*Bad Girls* was also set in an all-women's prison where female inmates tried to either make love or murder each other, with bent guards and the occasional male sexual interaction.) Perhaps the scriptwriters of that show were fans of Women in Prison films?

Regardless, Mattei not only lives up to the genre's clichés, he seems to add to them and expand on them. If the women are not seen longing for each other, then they are lunging for each other instead, with questionable dialogue from Fragasso's script bringing some unwanted humour during the film's more 'serious' moments. "I'd like to bite your nipples off!" one character shouts early on. Later, Gemser screams at another female inmate, "You *bastard*, I'll kill ya!"

Things get more exploitative when a group of violent male prisoners is kept in the all-female jail following some frivolous reason. Then they overpower those *in* power and run rampant. This results in more trash and lurid sex, which Bruno shoots in a way that only he can. Admittedly, this is entertaining.

The male actors bring intensity to their scenes and truly come across as vile pieces of shit. They molest, torture, and violate the female prisoners. Their actions progressively become more and more dangerous with a disturbing scene where Emanuelle is raped, and the girls are forced to play Russian Roulette. Indeed, scenes like this show that Mattei did have talent… given the right ingredients.

The women get their revenge in a quite extraordinary manner thanks to one female inmate. She embeds a razor blade into a champagne bottle cork, and inserts it into her vagina. When she seduces one of the men, and he starts to have sex with her, he meets a grisly and sharp demise. Thanks, Bruno.

Although under-utilised in the previous feature (*Violence in a Woman's Prison*) Ursula Flores is given more screen time on this occasion. As the wild-eyed, wig-wearing Albina, she seems to be 'top bitch' and makes life miserable for Emanuelle. She is so over-the-top, at times, that she unintentionally becomes a caricature whilst giving the most memorable performance.

Emanuelle in Prison was coupled with made-at-the-same-time *Violence in a Woman's Prison* in a two-disc set by VIPCO in summer 2005, having already been released as a standalone title in June 2003.

THE EVIL FORCE (1977)

Director: Evan Lee

Writers: Ray Atherton, Keith Burns, Miklos Gyulai, Steve Singer

Stars: James Habif (Prof. Cantrell), J. Arthur Craig (Detective Wexler), Robert Clark (Sean), Doug Senior (Dirk)

VIPCO Release: 1983

Also Known As: *Hollywood Meatcleaver Massacre, Meatcleaver Massacre, Morak*

VIPCO Synopsis: *Armed with sharpened knives and meat cleavers, four crazed killers butcher an entire family. The master of the house – a professor of the supernatural – survives, though deep in a coma, and calls upon "MERAK", a demon of the occult to revenge the wretched horror brought upon his family.*

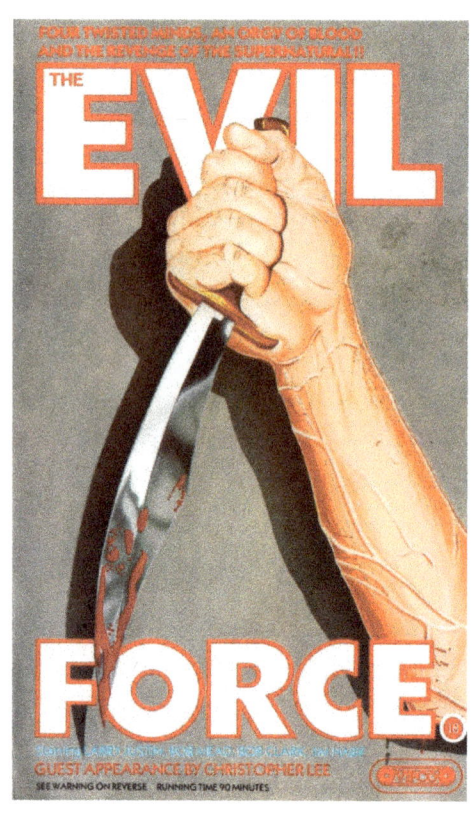

This terrifying force is immediately felt by the savage murderers and one by one they are destroyed in a gruesome manner, it will fill your heart with fear and stay imbedded in your mind forever!!

Christopher Lee appears, at the start, to warn us about what we are to see, and then briefly talks about human souls leaving the body, as well as the supernatural and spirits. Old Chris appears again, at the end, with similar waffle. Both these segments seem irrelevant to the main bulk of the story that happens in-between, though. There is a good reason for that… they *are* irrelevant.

Christopher Lee filmed these scenes for another, unconnected, and unknown movie that fell-through. The scenes were subsequently added to *The Evil Force* without the actor's knowledge and he was not happy. Lawyers got involved at one point before Lee decided to let the matter drop. The addition of a star of the calibre of Lee was no doubt an effort to lure in potential viewers through star power.

The film itself is passable at times and less so at others. The efforts made to stress the importance of Professor Cantrell's work, and the meaning it will have to the rest of the plot, later on, are let down by the events following the savage murder of his family. In fact, the slaughter of the family is the highlight of the feature; it manages a level of tension and drama that the rest of the film cannot muster.

When the Professor manages to unleash the wrath of the demon Morak, the rest of the runtime concerns itself with this revenge. The film suffers here, unfortunately, as the death scenes hop from genre to genre. It gives proceedings a muddled feel; director Evan Lee disregards whatever he may have worked towards, for what he seemingly feels will work for the next zany murder. When one of the killers is attacked in the middle of a desert by cactuses, you can't help but laugh.

Some of the acting is dire and bogs the movie down further. The titular *Evil Force* could very well be the particularly wooden acting of J. Arthur Craig as Detective Wexler. This is, thankfully, his only film role but those who witness it will likely never forget it.

The film was released in some markets as *Meatcleaver Massacre*, which is misleading as there are no meat cleavers to be seen. This may be the reason why VIPCO released it under the less inaccurate name of *The Evil Force*. The sleeve, a shot of an arm clenching a dangerous-looking knife, is simple yet highly eye-catching. VIPCO sold it on VHS one last time in 1993. It is, at time of writing, available on YouTube as *Hollywood Meatcleaver Massacre*.

GOD TOLD ME TO (1976)

Director: Larry Cohen

Writer: Larry Cohen

Stars: Tony Lo Bianco (Detective Nicholas), Deborah Raffin (Casey), Sylvia Sydney (Elizabeth), Sandy Dennis (Martha)

VIPCO Release: 2004

Also Known As: *Demon*

VIPCO Synopsis: *A rooftop sniper guns down 14 pedestrians on the streets of New York City. A mild-mannered dad takes a shotgun and blows away his wife and children.*

A cop goes on a sudden shooting spree at the St. Patrick's Day Parade. Each of these unlikely killers makes the same dying confession: "God told me to."

Now a repressed Catholic NYPD detective must uncover a netherworld of deranged faith, alien insemination and his own unholy connection to a homicidal messiah with a perverse plan for the soul of mankind. This is the critically acclaimed cult classic written, produced and directed by Larry Cohen that remains one of the most disturbing and though-provoking horror films of our time: God Told Me To.

Mike mistakenly writes in the synopsis that this Cohen film is 'though-provoking' and while it is clearly a typo, the intention of the statement remains the same. This *is* a *thought*-provoking horror movie.

God and religion are always delicate and tricky subjects to tackle; Cohen instead takes them on in a blunt and brutal manner. He felt that – in the bible – God is actually a very violent 'being' and looked to convey this in a film. The choosing of another sensitive aspect of religion – people committing crimes after God 'speaks to' them – further compounds matters.

As the story unfolds, space aliens and abduction are inserted and they take the feature into a slightly silly yet still rewarding direction. The budget limitations that Cohen faced in making this feature are present during some of the alien sequences as stock footage from 1970's British sci-fi television programme *Space: 1999* is used in place of creating new special effects. It is the lack of budget that can also explain why some of the killings are blood-free.

Cohen is a name synonymous with cult and B movie cinema, and the American created a stir just a couple of years earlier with *It's Alive* (1974). *God Told Me To* is quite the contrast to that outing, but this would go towards Cohen's growing reputation of being edgy; a director who could deliver a movie that is exciting as well as terrifying. In the decades since, Larry Cohen is rightly seen as a trailblazer of cult movies.

Tony Lo Bianco is a good lead actor as Detective Nicholas, playing a role that would not be a million miles away from the many others he portrayed during his lengthy career in crime television. Veteran actors of the 'Golden Age of Hollywood' – Sandy Dennis (Martha), Sam Levene (Everett) and Harry Bellaver (Cookie) – have supporting roles. Richard Lynch appears as a psychic hermaphrodite and tackles this 'tricky' character with his usual zeal. Young comedian Andy Kaufman is a police officer in the St Patrick's Day Parade scene, in what was one of his first film roles. Kaufman would go on to be a big name in US sitcom *Taxi* (1978-83), as well as a controversial figure off-screen.

The only time this feature has been available in the UK is via VIPCO's Screamtime Collection in 2004, as well as a two-disc set that would see *God Told Me To* strangely packaged with *Pranks* (1982). Here's hoping a firm like 88 Films, 101 Films, or Arrow Video re-issue it on Blu-ray soon! This is a movie that still packs a punch and should be made available again on home video in Britain. It is available on YouTube to stream.

GREMLOIDS (1984)

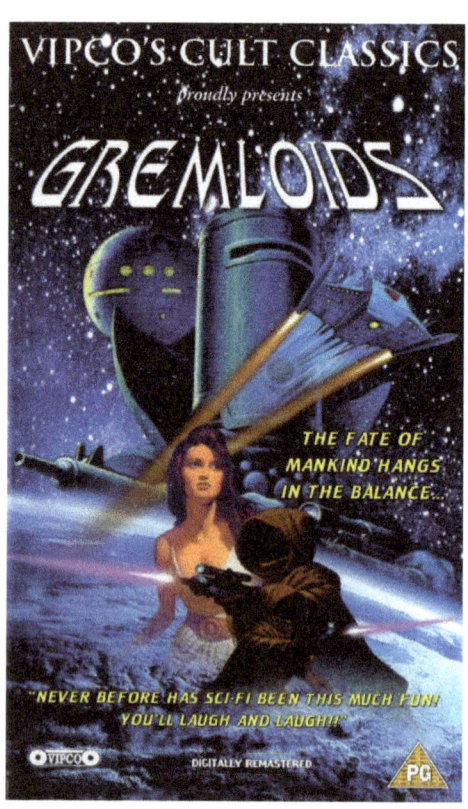

Director: Todd Durham

Writers: Todd Durham

Stars: Paula Poundstone (Karen), Chris Elliot (Hopper), Robert Bloodworth (Lord Buckethead), Barry Cooper (voice of Lord Buckethead)

VIPCO Release: 1987

Also Known As: *Gremlords, Hyperspace*

VIPCO Synopsis: *Not long ago in a galaxy too close for comfort, the rebel alliance intercepted some secret transmissions from imperial leader, Lord Buckethead. Buckethead and his alien cohorts mistakenly traced the transmissions to the planet Earth, where they found a peculiar and frustrating new resistance at work…*

Now the fate of mankind is in the hands of a pest control expert, a geriatric superhero and a speech-impedimented alien with a coal-scuttle for a head in this outrageous comedy in the tradition of 'Spaceballs'.

This film has a unique place in cinema, as well as VIPCO, history *and* in the domain of politics. Firstly, the director is Todd Durham, a man who (decades after *Gremloids*) would create the big money CGI kids' movie franchise *Hotel Transylvania*. Strange to think that the man that gave us Lord Buckethead would then spawn, as of 2019, a billion-dollar cash cow.

As for its place in VIPCO's history, *Gremloids* is even more strange. Following the dark days of the post-Video Nasties scandal, Mike was struggling to keep his firm going. Several big sellers were now banned or heavily cut, and he dabbled in exporting tapes of some of his newly-banned wares to Scandinavia. Yet, this was not enough. He would acquire *Gremloids* during this period, believing this sci-fi comedy could help attract a more casual and family-friendly audience to compensate for the lost Nasty crowd (albeit temporarily). He invested a lot in trying to make sure people knew of *Gremloids'* release on VHS. Indeed, he came up with what he thought would be a unique and effective way of attracting buyers… Mike got involved in politics!

In 1987, the United Kingdom had a General Election and Mike felt that taking on the persona of *Gremloids'* lead character Lord Buckethead – in order to become Finchley's MP – would be just the right way of raising awareness of said film! The selection of Finchley was no doubt deliberate; it was the constituency of then-Prime Minister Margaret Thatcher. Lord Buckethead, supposedly an evil overlord and destroyer of planets, taking on the Iron Lady would be a 'battle' not to be ignored.

Mike – or should that be Lord Buckethead – had some interesting policies. He pledged to demolish the city of Birmingham, for example. The good people of Finchley were unconvinced though; only 131 people voted for him. Still, the sight of Mike/Buckethead raising a clenched fist as his pitiful result was read out, live on BBC television, is surreal and can be found on YouTube decades later. Fast forward five years, and Lord Buckethead opposed Margaret Thatcher's successor (John Major) at a General Election. In an effort to win the constituency of Huntingdon, 107 people voted for Mike and the Gremloids Party this time.

As an aside, Lord Buckethead would 'return' to British politics in 2017, although not related to Mike this time.

Despite its meaning to VIPCO and politics, *Gremloids* is not a brilliant film. The opening sequence looks promising enough as *Star Wars*-esque opening text crawls on-screen, proclaiming that this is 'Episode IV: The Last Resort'. This is accompanied by music that sounds an awful lot like John Williams' classic score for *Star Wars*. For all intents and purposes, this looks like it could be a spoof that will riff on the source material down to the finer points. Sadly, it doesn't last.

The movie gradually dispels *Star Wars* elements in favour of mediocre jokes and occasional sight gags. The only real reminder it is a *Star Wars*/sci-fi parody is the continued presence of Lord Buckethead and his evil, little alien sidekicks that cause havoc. Clearly a Darth Vader knock-off, this villain stomps around deserts and buildings with an extra-long coal scuttle on his head instead of a helmet and mask. Barry Cooper, who provides the voice of Buckethead, sounds *a little* like Darth Vader.

Out of the small cast, there is one face that will be recognisable to viewers: Chris Elliot. The comedian was at the start of his career when *Gremloids* was made; he was working behind the scenes and appearing on screen for *Late Night with David*

Letterman at the time. Elliot is likeable in the role, which is just as well… there are not many other characters to invest in.

The sci-fi spoof had been released several times over the lifetime of VIPCO, but it should be noted that Mike deliberately tried to make the first two releases appear as though they were not from VIPCO. Much like his choice of a non-horror title, Mike decided that he would issue the VHS on the 'SGS' label to attract movie fans that might have been put off if VIPCO had been anywhere on the packaging. SGS, as a name, can be attributed to S. Gold & Sons. *Gremloids* would be sold as a 'non-VIPCO' tape in 1987, and again in 1992, before ultimately finding an actual VIPCO name-bearing DVD and VHS re-issue in 2002, as a 'VIPCO Cult Classic'.

KING FRAT (1979)

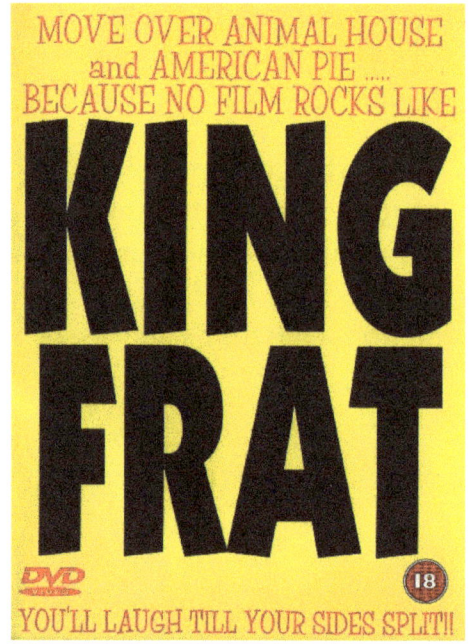

Director: Ken Wiederhorn

Writer: Ron Kurz as Mark Jackson

Stars: John DiSanti (J.J.), Robert Small (Kevin), San Chandler (Chief Latrine), Charles Pitt (Fred)

VIPCO Release: See main text

Also Known As: *Campus King, Delta House, King F***in' Frat*

Five Star Entertainment Plot Synopsis: *You won't believe the riotous, X-rated antics of 'fat, funny and flatulent' John DiSanti and the rest of the Pi Kappa Delta crew in this outrageous comedy! These guys are corpse stealing, substance abusing, pigging out, full mooning, womanising Gods!*

One of the several non-horror and non-action flicks VIPCO was to release, *King Frat* was first put on VHS in the spring of 1982 during the pre-cert days of home video. Like a turd that just won't flush, *King Frat* would return to video shop shelves again and again thanks to VIPCO's (or probably Mike Lee's) apparent fondness for the lowbrow comedy.

This is a movie that was clearly inspired by the recent frat comedy *Animal House* (1978), a film that had a lot of talent involved and which made a lot of money on a relatively small budget. Pale imitations followed in an effort to try to get a piece of the action. Some succeeded, some failed. *King Frat* is in a category all of its own.

Taking what worked for *Animal House,* director Ken Wiederhorn multiplies it by ten and throws it all at the viewer. The college frat gags, the crass behaviour, nudity, and toilet humour overwhelm proceedings while the flimsy plot takes a backseat. The cast all give over the top and utterly obnoxious performances that only add to the schoolboy humour level of the script.

The movie can be encapsulated in the opening credits sequence. While an annoyingly catchy song plays (called *King Frat* and performed by Penny Alemian), lead frat boy J.J. and the rest of the boys are shown driving the streets of the middle-class area where their frat house is located. Their vehicle is a hearse which is filled to breaking point with beer cans and kegs. They shout sexist slurs at women, yell inaudible banter or scream 'YEAH!' every other sentence as well as moon (for quite a long time) most people they pass. They eventually drive past the elderly Dean of their college and moon him; he has a heart attack at the sight of their naked hairy arses. The lads keep on driving and laughing as he lies in the road and dies.

The rest of the film has several other plot points that it 'sort of' pays attention to, in-between the fart gags and drinking beer. The new Dean wants to clean up the Delta House with the aid of some preppy types, the boys visit a massage parlour (of course they do), a bumbling cop investigates the Deltas for stealing a statue with a large penis, and there is a 'much anticipated' fart contest.

It is the fart contest that gets much of the attention in the first half of *King Frat* with J.J. taking his training seriously by doing farting exercises. The viewer would be forgiven for thinking this would be the major story of the movie, with J.J. coming up trumps (pun intended) in a rousing finale of him literally blowing away the competition. Instead, the payoff happens less than halfway through the film, which means the other underwritten storylines briefly return for little or no payoff. At least we get the image of a dog farting so hard it launches itself off the floor and flies across a room, right?

Out of all the actors on screen, John DiSanti is the only actor who seems to be genuinely enjoying himself. As the titular *King Frat,* he barges through one scene to the next, while shouting and being a slob. He is essentially the movie's main asset, which is a strange asset admittedly; some posters of the film display him on a grimy toilet while flipping the bird. In some ways, that image sums up *King Frat* on most levels.

The director of this frat house flick is Ken Wiederhorn, a man whose debut feature was another eventual VIPCO release; *Shock Waves* (1977).

In 2000, following the success of *American Pie* (1999), *King Frat* would be released on DVD by a firm named Five Star Entertainment. This company was, in fact, owned by Michael Lee, the owner of VIPCO. Despite its cheap bright yellow sleeve, the layout is similar to that of most VIPCO titles, and it's distributed by SGS Home Video, aka Golds (who did many VIPCO releases). The disc even comes with the same trailers that would be found on the Vaults of Horror and Screamtime DVDs. Mike's salesman hype is in full force claiming, 'You'll laugh till your sides split!!' You won't.

MIDNIGHT (1982)

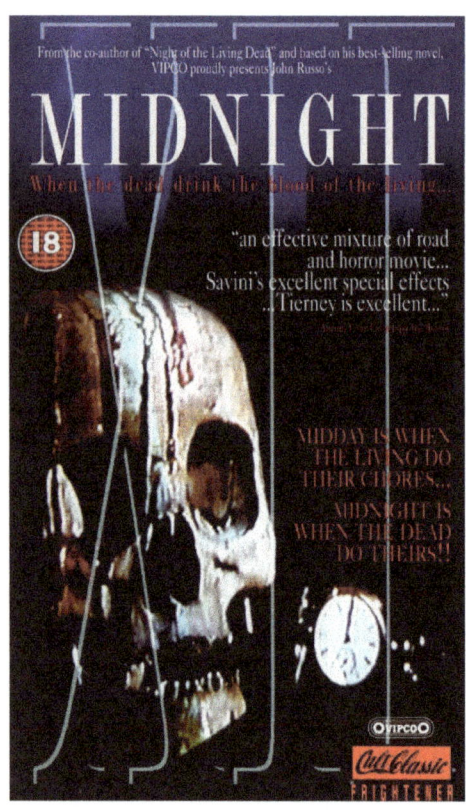

Director: John A. Russo as John Russo

Writer: John Russo

Stars: Melanie Verlin (Nancy), Lawrence Tierney (Bert), Bob Johnson (Rev. Carrington), John Amplas (Abraham)

VIPCO Release: 1993

Also Known As: *Backwoods Massacre, John Russo's Midnight*

VIPCO Synopsis: *Fleeing the drunken fumblings of her leching stepfather, a young girl hitch hikes south into American redneck country, and stumbles straight into a string of horrific Satanic slayings...*

Locked in a cage and forced to wait her turn, she prays... the sacrifice is scheduled for MIDNIGHT... and she's next on the menu.

From the best selling novel by the co-author of NIGHT OF THE LIVING DEAD, VIPCO proudly presents the cult splatter classic MIDNIGHT.

Starring Lawrence Tierney and John Amplas, and with special make-up by Tom Savini, MIDNIGHT is released in its UNCUT UK video form.

The people behind *Midnight* (and their exploits in horror cinema before and since this movie) are far more interesting than the feature itself. This does not mean *Midnight* is a badly-made film – it is put together with a level of competence – just that it is rather dull.

The opening credits reveal some well-known names of cult cinema, including (limited) special effects by Tom Savini, a man responsible for doing similar on countless, better-remembered horrors such as *Dawn of the Dead* (1978) and *Maniac* (1980), amongst others. There are also 'additional stills' by Bill Hinzman, an actor who famously played the 'graveyard zombie' that staggered into horror history in *Night of the Living Dead* (1968) before eventually directing/writing/producing and starring in *Zombie Nosh* (see this book's review of *that* title in the Zombie section).

John Russo was the writer and director of *Midnight*. He had also been a part of *Night of the Living Dead* and had come up with the basic idea for *NotLD's* plot, as well as performing scriptwriting duties. Subsequently – having revolutionised the zombie genre with George Romero – he wrote novels that became the basis for other films, *Midnight* being one such work.

He would perform screenwriting/directing duties on some of the feature films based on his own work as well. Unfortunately, this does not make for a better viewing experience in the case of this effort. A typical premise unfolds: some teens stumble upon a bunch of backwoods weirdos that are part of a bloodthirsty cult. Frustratingly, the wacko clan is not given enough attention and what could have been an asset (a group of oddballs in horror movies usually generate something exciting) is not capitalised on.

This is mostly down to Russo's overreliance on developing the relationships that the hapless teens have, before they end up in a spot of bother. Well over half the runtime is dedicated to this and while welcome in some areas (drunken stepfather Bert), it is not in others (Nancy going for a nice stroll in a forest). It is actually Bert, a morally repugnant character, that is the only saving grace at times. Played perfectly by veteran actor Lawrence Tierney, he slurs and bumbles his way through some scenes and pervs on his stepdaughter Nancy. "I just want to see what you look like naked!" he tells her, as he sways around her bedroom trying to 'cuddle' her. Bizarrely, he ends up the hero of *Midnight* by the end of the feature.

John Amplas is part of the loony gang, in a role that takes advantage of his youthful looks. Amplas is the star of Romero's modernist vampire flick *Martin* (1978), and this fact will be in many viewers' heads as they start lamenting how they could have been watching the brilliant Romero work instead of *Midnight*.

Russo would direct and write *Midnight 2,* in 1993, which is marginally better than the original. He also announced in 2017 that he was helming a remake of his original feature, although little has been heard since.

Midnight is a relatively tame offering compared to some of the other titles VIPCO sold. Never 'officially' classed as a Nasty, it was deemed by the DDP – under Section 3 of its notorious list - that those selling it would have copies confiscated and possibly destroyed. The version sold by VIPCO is technically uncut as Mike states in the synopsis (a VHS edition of the cinema version had never previously been sold), but there *was* some footage removed although this was not mandated by the BBFC; Mike thought this would allow him to state the video was uncut.

Midnight would never again grace the shelves of collectors, through VIPCO, after its 1993 VHS release. Arrow Video would re-release the movie in the UK on DVD in 2011 but, at the time of writing, no Blu-ray has been issued.

THE MUTILATOR (1984)

Director: Buddy Cooper, John Douglass ('co-director')

Writer: Buddy Cooper

Stars: Matt Mitler (Ed .Jnr), Jack Chatham (Big Ed), Bill Hitchcock (Ralph), Ruth Martinez (Pam)

VIPCO Release: 1993

Also Known As: *Fall Break*

BY PICK...
BY AXE...
BY CHAINSAW...

BYE BYE!!!

THE MUTILATOR

18

"Vivid. Vile. A virtuoso horror flic."

"Relentlessly Gory...a steel stomach is required. the Grisliest film I've seen in years"

"VIPCO proves once again that in the horror department, they have the cutting edge."

VIPCO Synopsis: *This spine-tingling chiller is the harrowing tale of the high-school students whose dream vacation of a fun-filled holiday at the beach becomes a nightmare when they are stalked by The Mutilator.*

Ed, a likeable high school student, busily discusses vacation plans with his friends when he recieves a message from his father asking that he close up the summer house at the beach. While his friends feel that it's the perfect opportunity for a vacation Ed is uneasy about the request, as his father has never quite forgiven him for the accidental shooting of his mother.

When the group arrives at the summer house they discover Ed's father's collection of bizarre weapons. To add to their anxieties there is the ever-present feeling they that are being watched. Suddenly, Ed's house guests begin to meet bizarre deaths, each one more grisly than the next, but The Mutilator is saving the best for last... the best for Ed.

What good son wouldn't clean his father's guns for his birthday? This is how *The Mutilator* opens, with a child – Ed Jr – eagerly cleaning his daddy's gun collection and making a birthday cake. Tragedy strikes as one firearm, that is unknowingly loaded, blasts Ed's mother to death by accident. Despite the absurd nature of the opening scene, the shotgun blast is a powerful moment. A bit of morbid humour arises as the shocked father returns home to the horror, and ends up having a birthday toast with his dead wife.

After this, the movie mostly feels like some hokey eighties teen comedy – instead of the hokey eighties teen slasher that it actually is – although this eventually changes.

Grown-up Ed and his friends talk about going to his dad's beach condo after Ed is asked to take care of the summer home. Everyone thinks it is a good idea to go party there, although Ed has to be convinced… "I got a bad feeling about this," he groans. No shit.

Once at the beach condo, the viewer is shown an establishing shot of its garage and we see someone hiding in there! Ed's bad feeling was right! Certain hunting weapons that are meant to be adorning the walls of the condo are mysteriously missing, too. It is only a matter of time before the hide and seek nutter targets the hapless teens with these gruesome tools.

When the typical slasher flick violence does happen, it does so with a genuinely impressive level of skill. The synth-heavy score helps to create jarring unease as the believable gore effects splatter across the screen. The viewer can also easily anticipate how the feature will finish. Which is not necessarily a bad thing. The direction, cinematography and score help elevate proceedings, and the end credits feature outtakes from the movie, which is a nice touch.

VIPCO first released *The Mutilator* in 1993 with 26 seconds of cuts, and the logo 'VIPCO PREMIER' featuring in the top left-hand corner of the VHS sleeve. When reprints were made, Mike very crudely attempted to obscure the word 'premier' by scribbling over it in white. The silhouette of a man holding an axe above his head also features but, strangely, has the image of Llewelyn Thomas' face covered in blood from the artwork for *The Bogeyman* (1980). When the slightly less cut 'Extreme Version' was released on DVD by the firm in 2000, the scribbled-out logo and Thomas' face had wisely been removed. Mike made sure to get *The Mutilator* onto the Screamtime line a few years later.

THE NEW BARBARIANS (1983)

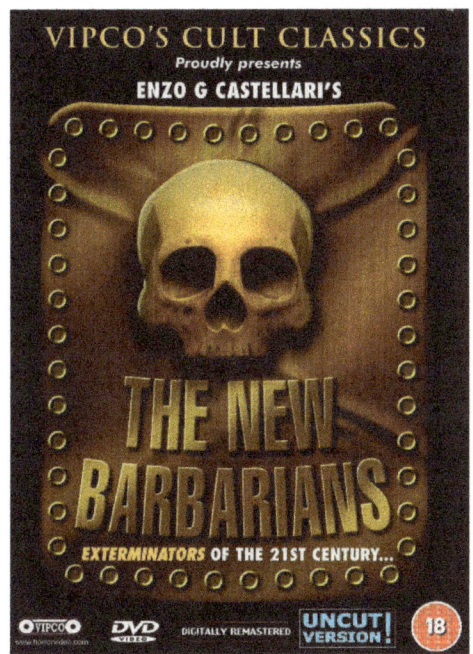

Director: Enzo G. Castellari

Writers: Tito Carpi, Enzo G. Castellari as Enzo Girolami

Stars: Giancarlo Prete as Timothy Brent (Scorpion), Fred Williamson (Nadir), Anna Kanakis (Alma), George Eastman (One)

VIPCO Release: 2003

Also Known As: *2019: The Barbarians of the Future, Metropolis 2000, Warriors of the Wasteland*

VIPCO Plot Synopsis: *It's the year 2019, fifteen years after the world was devastated by a nuclear war. It is a land where gangs of human predators travel in packs like wolves, where junkyards are filled with the dying remnants of society, and an army of carnivorous escaped military prisoners threaten a fragile sliver of civilization. The only hope of the few remaining survivors is to reach a distant land from where radio signals, indicating the presence of human life, are being emitted...*

Sandwiched between the release of *The Bronx Warriors* (1982) and *Escape from the Bronx* (1983), in its native Italy, this similarly-themed flick from Castalleri is perhaps the weakest of the three movies. Starting with what is clearly a shoddily made mini cityscape being 'destroyed' by a nuclear bomb, *The New Barbarians* plods along.

The plot is reminiscent of *Mad Max 2* (1981) – amazingly so – although the scuzzy and post-apocalyptic landscape of *The New Barbarians* pales in comparison. Instead, lead character Scorpion, and his pals, survive in a world that seems to be picturesque country hills or a bleak looking quarry. Most of the characters sport immaculate clothing, with Scorpion's rivals – the Templars – having spotless white outfits (and the biggest shoulder pads to have appeared on film).

The leader of the obligatory group of villains is the one and only George Eastman. His snarling performance as the evil One, and on-screen partnership with Shadow

(Ennio Girolami, benefiting from his director brother's nepotism again), borders on campy Scooby Doo baddie-levels of nastiness. Despite the unintended silliness of Eastman's role, it is central to the most memorable and shocking scene in the entire feature.

One, and his goons, take the heroic Scorpion prisoner and rack him up to be tortured or killed. One has different ideas, though, as he removes the back of Scorpion's pants and has him forcibly bent over. He then briefly anally rapes him. This is no doubt the director's effort to show the viewer just how vile and sinister One is but, if anything, it is so out of place it will have the viewer wondering what the hell Enzo was thinking. Eastman has acted out *worse* things on screen.

Come the end of *The New Barbarians,* there is some sort of ironic justice at work when Scorpion and One are in a car chase. The hero's car is 'equipped' with a giant corkscrew which is whirled into the back of the rapist's vehicle and pierces the metal exterior; the metal appendage then appears to go right up the backside of Eastman. He understandably crashes his vehicle which then explodes.

The cast has the usual faces for an Enzo G. Castellari movie. Giancarlo Prete, Fred Williamson, George Eastman, Ennio Girolami and Massimo Vanni are the regular players with the notable addition of the cutesy brat from *House by the Cemetery* – Giovanni Frezza. There is also an additional uncredited cast member: the cheesy sound effects. They are used so often that they are more common than the lines spoken by the cast. After a while, they become annoying.

Considering the expected rugged appearance of a hero in a movie set in a dystopian/post-apocalyptic future, Prete is rather lame. If anything, he looks like a middle-aged school headmaster on 'dress down day'. The stunning Anna Kanakis (Alma) cannot resist his bland style, though, and has sex within moments of meeting him. Pass the knitwear...

The New Barbarians was only released once by VIPCO, on DVD as part of the Cult Classics line with some seriously nifty artwork.

Like *Bronx Warriors 2*, this Castellari flick gets a blushing review from VIPCO on the back cover. In this one, the reader is told that the film kicks ass and is great, without a hint of irony. There is even a recommendation to 'buy it' which is perhaps the most honest part of the review: just buy the bloody thing. See below for more (as always spelling and grammar mistakes remain)...

Our Review: Again more BRONX!! Enzo directs again a fantasy ambientad in the apocalyptic world, style of MAD MAX. We tell you this film kicks ass ! Watch it and fall into the fantasy of living in a post-nuke wasteland! This film is great for so many reasons , but above all it's thoroughly entertaining with an unmatched cast. A brilliant action movie from start to finish. But it, get some cheap beer, and watch it with some friends for a great time! 10 out of 10.

THE NOSTRIL PICKER (1993)

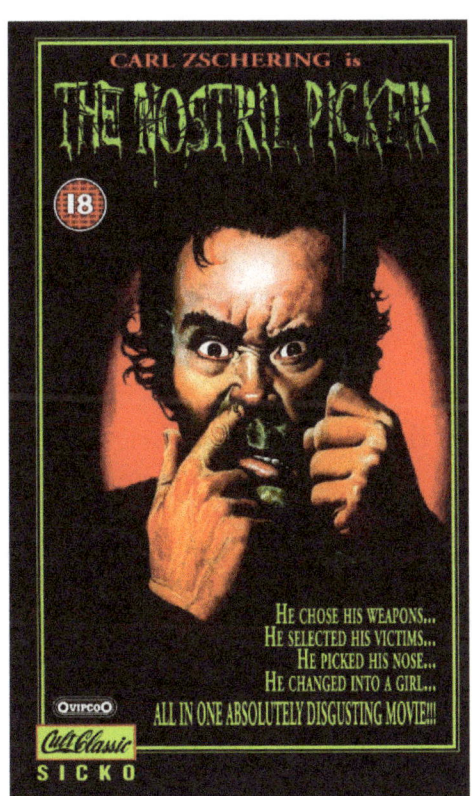

Director: Mark Nowicki

Writer: Steven Hodge

Stars: Carl Zschering (Joe), Ann Flood (Jo), Horace Grimm (hobo), Steven Andrews (Transvestite prostitute), Brian Faes (Dt. Johnson)

VIPCO Release: 1993

Also Known As: *The Changer*

VIPCO Plot Synopsis: *He chose his weapons... he selected his victims... he picked his nose... he changed into a girl... all in one absolutely disgusting movie!!!*

A fine example of Michael Lee making a movie appear to be something it is not with a name change and eye-catching VHS sleeve; Mark Nowicki's only film was originally released as *The Changer*. How it became *The Nostril Picker* can be attributed to two brief moments in which lead character Joe is seen to have a quick poke up his shnozz. It is certainly a good job Joe was not on screen rubbing his backside, otherwise we would have ended up with *The Arse Scratcher...*

It would have been in keeping with the feature's theme though, which is that of a lowbrow comedy plus horror elements thrown in. A measure of deadpan humour is on display too. Joe turning into the pretty and popular schoolgirl Jo is more often than not depicted as the male Joe walking down school hallways, hanging out in the locker room, and taking classes as his ordinary, scruffy and deranged looking self, and is played completely straight. But the joke is that everyone sees and hears him as a petite teen girl.

Joe is played superbly by the awkward-looking Carl Zschering in what would be his only acting credit. Whether it be him sat in a squalid apartment with his blow-up sex doll, or rubbing his crotch (now *there* is a film title) while staring at girls when stood in the middle of school, his facial expressions and down-at-heel body language adds to the absurd nature of the character.

It is easy to forget that this is meant to be a horror as the plot concentrates on the funnier side of the story. But when horror does rear its head it is done so in a gory fashion. When Joe has tricked schoolgirls into thinking he is one of them – leading to him being asked to 'babysit' with them – he takes advantage then changes back into the creepy man he is, and violently kills them. He partakes in a little bit of cannibalism as well.

Nowicki's direction is standard, and not insulting, although he would leave directing behind after the movie. In the decades since, he has worked as a colourist for film and TV alike. The biggest project he did this work on was *The X Files*, for which he worked on over 200 episodes.

The Nostril Picker was first part of VIPCO's Cult Classics line up then Vaults of Horror before finally making its way to the cheapie Screamtime Collection. When Mike originally sold this title, he did so without legally gaining the rights. Nowicki was not best pleased when he found this out, after the fact. Eventually the two sides came to an agreement and VIPCO could continue to sell *The Nostril Picker*.

The Nostril Picker has since slipped into relative obscurity, a common thing with some of VIPCO's releases. Oddly, everyone I interviewed in the name of research for this book could cite *Picker* as a VIPCO release; they remembered the bizarre name and original artwork.

It has recently resurfaced on Amazon Prime Video in the UK under its original title *The Changer*.

PATRICK (1978)

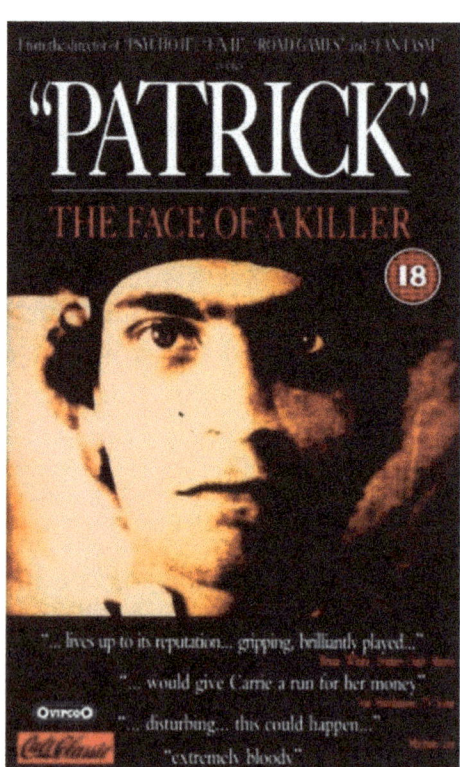

Director: Richard Franklin

Writer: Everett De Roche

Stars: Susan Penhaligon (Kathy), Julia Blake (Matron), Robert Helpmann (Dr. Roget), Robert Thompson (Patrick)

VIPCO Release: 1993

Also Known As: *Coma, Patrick – Amazing Experience*

VIPCO Plot Synopsis: *To all intents and purposes PATRICK is dead to the world. Since his mother and her lover died in a bizarre but unfortunate electrical "accident", poor poor Patrick has been so traumatised, his brain's just curled up inside and left his body for dead. Patrick's a good boy. He's obedient. He doesn't complain about the hospital food. He doesn't make the nurses life tough. But after all, he is only 170 pounds of limp, pallid flesh hanging off a* comatose brain... OR IS HE??

There is a myth surrounding this film that Robert Thompson (Patrick) never blinks once during the runtime. This is clearly wrong, as Thompson blinks within ten seconds of appearing on screen. It is only once Patrick suffers his trauma that he remains in a wide-eyed coma for the rest of the film.

As well as staring into space, Patrick spits too. It's laughable at first – explained as a 'nervous reflex' – but strangely becomes a vital part of the story as things progress.

Made in an era of Australian cinema that produced the seminal *Mad Max* (1979), *Patrick* is a curio of Oz film that has remained underappreciated since it was first unleashed on the world in autumn 1978. It's a shame because *Patrick* tries to be different from other horrors from this time and is – at times – intelligent and insightful, with care given to exploring the deeper theories on what people experience in comas, or when they have suffered mental distress. At one point, the villainous-like Matron proclaims, "Disease, like god, can move in mysterious ways" and that is the case with the psychosis of the titular Patrick.

There are some 'issues' with the story, though. The way in which Kathy seems to be falling for Patrick, the reasons behind the seemingly brain-dead patient being kept alive, and the eventual metamorphosis of Kathy, all stretch credibility. But a movie about a man in a coma playing mind games on people, and killing them, is bound to have credibility issues, so this is forgivable.

The story is a slow burner. After an initial burst of excitement in the opening scene, the plot settles at an even pace as Kathy starts her new job at the hospital and is assigned to oversee the patient in room 15 (Patrick); flings arise, while she tries to come to terms with a divorce from her husband. Hints as to Patrick's capabilities are dropped throughout until, finally, he communicates with Kathy psychically. Using a typewriter. The pace only picks up when Kathy is fired for potentially ruining the Matron's plans for Patrick, and the bed-ridden lover unleashes telekinetic hell on everyone.

Depending on what part of the world you were in at the time of *Patrick's* release, you will have either seen the Australian version which had music by Brian May, or the European market version which had cast-offs from, believe it or not, Goblin.

Although Thompson plays the character the feature is named after, and Penhaligon gets the most screen time as Kathy, it is Julia Blake that gives the star performance as the dastardly Matron. From the very first moment she appears in *Patrick,* she is instantly entertaining; scenes without her lack any real interest. Helpmann as the new age Doctor Roget acts as if he should be one of the patients; he is that manic and hammy.

The picture's director, Richard Franklin, does a decent enough job although he allows things to get boring shortly after Patrick is seen receiving electric shock treatment. It is not until the closing moments that the tension and excitement get ratcheted up. Franklin would go on to direct several other movies including the excellent *Road Games* (1981) and the decent *Psycho II* (1983).

Patrick must have had its fans at the time as an unofficial sequel titled *Patrick Still Lives* (1980) was subsequently released; it would be the final film of Italian director Mario Landi. *Patrick Still Lives* has no real link to the original and is inadequate as a film on its own merits. A dire remake of *Patrick* by Mark Hartley would surface in 2013, starring Charles Dance and Rachel Griffiths.

Released by VIPCO as a 'Cult Chiller', the usual hyperbole-filled video sleeve is replaced here with a somewhat sombre and sedate cover of Patrick's face. Well, sombre for VIPCO. There is a completely frivolous quote stating '...disturbing...this could happen'. The bold claim in question is credited as coming from... VIPCO owner Michael Lee!

Patrick has also been released on DVD in the UK, in 2004 and 2007, and on Blu-ray in other countries. Streaming service Shudder currently carries the film.

PROZZIE (1983)

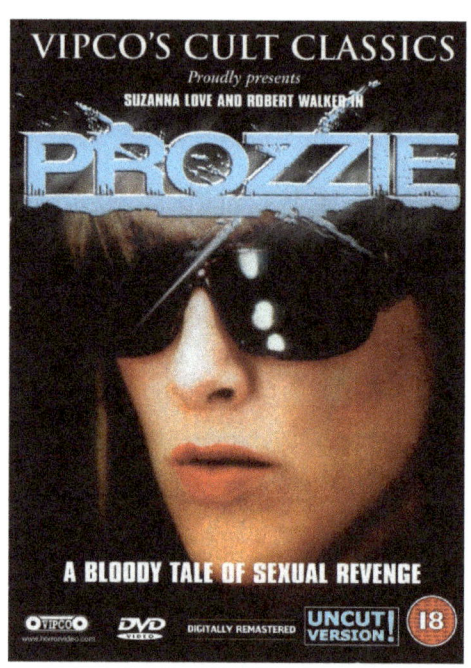

Director: Ullli Lommel

Writers: John P Marsh, Ron Norman, Ulli Lommel

Stars: Suzanna Love (Olivia), Robert Walker Jr. as Robert Walker (Mike), Ulli Lommel (Detective), Jeff Winchester (Richard)

VIPCO Release: 1983

Also Known As: *Beyond the Bridge, Double Jeopardy, Faces of Fear, Olivia* (original title)

VIPCO Plot Synopsis: *Through the keyhole begins a game that results in the violent death of a prostitute, watched helplessly by her daughter. The story continues when the daughter, now a prostitute herself, suffers psychological aliments that make her seek revenge on those she makes contact with by repeating the events she witnessed the night her mother was killed.*

Although it was released by VIPCO under its original title of *Double Jeopardy* (in the pre-cert era of British home video), Ulli Lommel's work would get a re-release in the early nineties with a different and more attention-grabbing title: *Prozzie*. Credit to Michael Lee for doing this because it is as *Prozzie* that this movie has become best known. Even a 2016 Blu-ray/DVD release from cult experts 88 Films used this delightful-sounding name over the original; it even the features the actual name of *Olivia*.

The VIPCO plot write-up on the back of the release is quite restrained, which is something of a shock after the eye-catching effort given to later releases. Of course, it mentions the prostitution and murder aspects to proceedings, but not in the usual crude way for a VIPCO 'review'. The synopsis also makes no mention of the dramatic plot and location shift halfway through *Prozzie*, when the viewer is whisked away to the picturesque Lake Havasu City in Arizona.

This is another strange and eerie entry into the series of films from then-husband and wife combo Ulli Lommel and Suzanna Love. By this point, they had already made *The Bogey Man* (1980) together, and the duo came up with the idea for *Prozzie* while they were supposedly preparing for the dire *Bogey Man II*, having stumbled upon the original London Bridge in Arizona. The bridge had been in the state since 1971 after it was bought by businessman Robert P. McCulloch in 1967. Quite how finding this landmark in an unexpected part of the world led to a story about a woman with a split personality killing people remains unclear.

At first, the plot bears similarities to Lommel's video nasty *The Bogey Man*. The use of a child witnessing the death of a parent during a violent sexual encounter occurs in both works although with different outcomes. *The Bogey Man* goes for surreal and supernatural, while *Prozzie* opts for gritty and everyday in its approach to the resultant story.

In terms of acting quality, there is little to go on. The cast is very limited with Love and Walker Jr. taking up much of the screen time. Walker Jr. (who would also appear in Lommel's *The Devonsville Terror* in the same year) is a long way from his glory days of the sixties. As for Love, this is not her finest performance and her efforts at a cockney accent are grim. She is still stunning to look at, and Lommel filmed her nude for some scenes. Love claimed she would drink vodka in order to tolerate these moments. The marriage did not last. Oddly, Love likes *Prozzie* and her performance in it, despite her need for alcohol to get through filming.

Ulli Lommel is a talented director; his 1973 work *The Tenderness of the Wolves* is a powerful piece of cinema. However, he quickly went down the route of silly and gory horror films and he never replicated the artistic high of *Wolves*. There is nothing wrong with 'silly and gory horror', of course, but if you were to compare *Wolves* to *Prozzie* (made just ten years apart) the drop in quality is glaring. Lommel stuck with horror by this period of his career as he felt the genre was always going to be a money-maker. He was right.

PSYCHIC KILLER (1975)

Director: Ray Danton as Raymond Danton

Writers: Mikel Angel, Greydon Clark, Ray Danton

Stars: Jim Hutton (Arnold Masters), Paul Burke (Lt. Morgan), Julie Adams (Dr. Scott), Aldo Ray (Lt Anderson)

VIPCO Release: 1980

Also Known As: *Killer Force, The Kirlian Effect, The Kirlian Force*

VIPCO Plot Synopsis: *Wrongly accused of murdering the doctor who refused to treat his ailing mother, young Arnold is placed in a mental institution under the care and supervision of Dr. Laura Scott. Whilst there, he is taught the secrets of 'out of body travel' by a fellow inmate. Freed when the real killer is found, Arnold swears revenge on those who committed him. Using his*

103

new-found psychic powers, Arnold eliminates those he hates in a brutal and bloody reign of terror, which leaves detectives Morgan and Anderson faced with a killer they can't even see...

For a mid-seventies psychological thriller, that feels like mid-seventies TV fare, and which is directed by a man known for directing mid-seventies TV shows, *Psychic Killer* is a strange part of VIPCO's history.

Released very early in the distributor's history (in 1980 on VHS and Betamax), during the 'pre-cert era', it was released again in 1992 with 14 seconds cut then released uncut on DVD in summer 2000, and finally – *yet again* – several years later as part of the no thrills Screamtime Collection. Michael Lee must have loved *Psychic Killer* because it certainly is not a movie that warrants so many re-releases. Maybe he purchased lifetime rights to it and wanted his money's worth? This film would have seemed drab when it was first released in the mid-seventies; decades later, it is woeful.

The director of this feature was Ray Danton; a decade's long TV actor who first went behind the camera in 1972 with *Deathmaster*. With *Psychic Killer* it feels like he has taken TV directing methods and applied them to a motion picture. The pacing feels like it belongs to a drab crime drama serial, as opposed to the whacky feature it is used in. Danton also co-wrote the script which explains some of the substandard dialogue. It is no surprise that Danton would move into television work after this, and he was responsible for dozens of episodes across several popular series of the seventies and eighties, with *Quincy M.E.*, *Tales of the Unexpected* and *Cagney & Lacey* being some of the hits he worked on

There are some interesting elements at work here that suffer from a director who does not know how to get the best from them. The idea that lead character Masters can only psychically kill people by essentially stopping his heart while in a coma-like trance, then 'leaving his body', lends itself to a rather impressive way that Lt. Morgan stumbles upon to try and stop the killer.

The film takes on an exploitation feel during one scene when a busty young woman is having a shower. Danton makes sure the viewer sees plenty of her sensually cleaning her breasts before the 'psychic killer' strikes. As she is being killed, in a manner that defies description, the director also makes sure we see her slashed boobs shoved right into the camera for good measure. It is also this shot which was cut by the BBFC for the 1992 reissue.

The titular murderer is played by Jim Hutton. His acting here borders on comical which undermines the fact he is trying to be deadly serious. Once likened to James Stewart, Hutton by this point in his career had stuck to television work. *Psychic Killer* was his last film role as he died in 1979 at the age of 45 due to liver cancer. His son is Best Supporting Actor Oscar winner Timothy Hutton.

The movie would make its Blu-ray debut in 2016 thanks to Vinegar Syndrome. It is also available to stream on Amazon Prime.

RATS: NIGHT OF TERROR (1984)

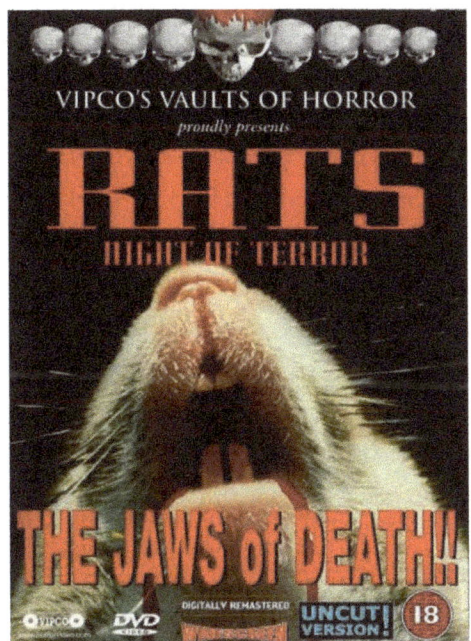

Director: Bruno Mattei as Vincent Dawn

Writers: Claudio Fragasso, Herve Piccini, Bruno Mattei

Stars: Ottaviano Dell'Acqua as Richard Raymond (Kurt), Henry Luciani (Duke), Geretta Geretta as Janna Ryann (Chocolate), Massimo Vanni as Alex McBride (Taurus)

VIPCO Release: 2002

Also Known As: *Blood Kill, Rats, Rats of Manhattan*

VIPCO Plot Synopsis: *One hundred years after a nuclear war has devastated the planet, society has been reborn into two factions; the underground society and the scavengers above in the wastelands. A group of scavengers on bikes come across a town infested with flesh eating rats, and soon the gore is spilling everywhere! Ferocious in their demonic intent they devour human flesh and all that they can get their teeth into... the flesh eating RATS are here!!*

The dynamic duo of Bruno Mattei and Claudio Fragasso once again grace VIPCO fans with their presence in a hokey yet passable dystopian flick about killer rats.

The movie begins with a voiceover telling the viewer that a nuclear war from 2015 has seen Earth, as everyone knows it, come to an end. The age of 'After the Bomb' has begun.

Survivors live underground but some of the population grow tired of the structure they must follow and return to the surface. Those still underground are apparently sophisticated and hate those who live up top. So far, so good, but it is soon pretty clear that the post-apocalyptic world they inhabit is some scrubland and a quarry, plus the odd abandoned building.

Another *Mad Max 2* (1981) rip off, Mattei and Fragasso create a feature that is campy and over-the-top, instead of a gruelling dystopian saga. Proceedings concentrate on the gang of survivors or, more precisely, descendants of the survivors looting buildings and fighting rivals. Then there are the rats.

Admittedly, some of them look like dirty little critters, but more often than not they spend their time sniffing around or cleaning themselves when on camera. They do not seem like much of a threat. This is a problem when the premise of the film is that they are meant to be threatening and menacing. When rats are obviously thrown onto actors, in an effort to make it appear they are being attacked, it causes unintentional humour.

The vibe this film has is that of *Beneath the Planet of the Apes* (1970) meets *Mad Max 2* meets *The Bronx Warriors* (1982). In Germany, *Rats* was actually released as a sequel to *Bronx Warriors* in a blatant cash-in on a more popular film.

There are several notable names within the cast that help *Rats* to be passable. Ottavaino Dell'Acqua is a rugged bastard and the typical gusty leader of the gang. Henry Luicani is solid as the bullish and arrogant Duke. Geretta Geretta and Massimo Vanni are other genre names featured.

Rats was marketed by VIPCO as 'uncut', which is questionable since the movie had never been cut to begin with.

VIPCO nearly did not release this Mattei flick for reasons revealed by the firm's very own Jay Slater. "I remember [Lee] called me when we had the rights for Bruno Mattei's *Rats: Nights of Terror*. He was not happy as he had read user reviews on websites that weren't good and had changed his mind." Jay argued that Mike should not back out. "I told him it being bad is part of the Mattei package; that people expect it, and it hasn't been released on DVD, plus it's technically sufficient, gory and entertaining." Clearly Mike saw sense after this discussion.

Rats: Night of Terror had not been released in the UK since the 2002 VIPCO VHS/DVD but, while writing this book, 88 Films revealed they would be issuing it on Blu-ray in November 2018.

Despite its flaws, *Rats* is not a complete write off and if you are in the right frame of mind can be entertaining in a peculiar way. It is worth viewing for the madcap ending alone...

THE RISE AND FALL OF IDI AMIN (1981)

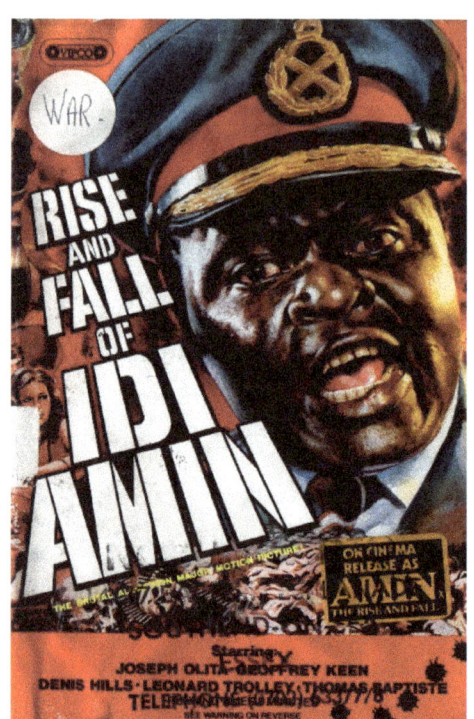

Director: Sharad Patel (also producer)

Writer: Wade Huie

Stars: Joseph Olita (Idi Amin), Thomas Baptiste (Dr Oloya), Ann Wanjuga (Mrs Olaya), Leonard Trolley (Bob Astles)

VIPCO Release: 1981

Also Known As: *Amin: The Rise and Fall*

VIPCO Plot Synopsis: *Idi Amin seized power in Uganda on January 25th, 1971. During the following eight years, his reign of terror led to the death of half a million people and the near ruin of a nation. Through imprisonment, torture, murder and rape he drove his country into a state of terror and poverty. Within two or three months of assuming power, Amin had built up his own terror army and secret police - the notorious State Research Bureau. He murdered most of the former*

Ugandan army, imprisoned and killed opposing intellectuals and students, abolished the freedom of speech and the press. The Rise and Fall of Idi Amin follows these events until his descent into megalomania and madness.

This was one of only a few movies that VIPCO released which the firm's owner actually liked. Mike was quite pleased he got to release *Amin* in what would turn out to be its only UK home video release.

Why this was one of Mike's favourites is not quite clear; it certainly isn't one of the most controversial or better-remembered titles from the VIPCO vault.

Idi Amin was the president of Uganda from 1971 until 1979. During his lifetime and stay in power, Amin is believed to have ordered the deaths of nearly 500,000 people. The reasons were multi-fold: he thought they were a threat to his power, they were Kenyans, they owned businesses he wanted to give to his friends, or he doubted their dedication to him. He is also rumoured to have eaten the flesh of some of his victims in an ultimate sign of power, and had heads of some kept in his freezer. That's why mums go to Iceland. Amin was eventually overthrown and went into hiding in Saudi Arabia until his death in 2003 due to kidney failure.

This film came out shortly after Amin fled from Uganda, and (for the most part), tries to be a serious political tale; at other times, it borders on being a violent exploitation movie. It is a combo that does not work. When the viewer is shown Amin and his various associates arguing about ways to strengthen his power, or kill off a rival, the scenes become repetitive and dull. The murders and bloodshed, meanwhile, feel as if they belong to a different feature altogether.

The movie starts well, though, with a stern male voiceover telling us how Uganda and Amin came to be, while photos of the man throughout his life are shown. The way this is edited, coupled with the haunting score by Christopher Gunning, ready the viewer for what could be a great film. That illusion does not last long.

The only consistently good thing within this feature is the performance of lead actor, Joseph Olita, who was a relatively unknown Kenyan actor. Olita does bear an uncanny resemblance to Idi Amin and gives a performance that is, at times, fierce, and comical at others (the real Amin was said to be dim although this has been labelled as a ploy to trick people into underestimating him). Olita seems to be having the most fun when he is in bed with several young women at once; "Women love me because I am never too tired," he explains later on, with obvious glee. Olita rightly received praise for his acting here and, again, when he reprised the role in *Mississippi Masala* (1991). Despite the success, he went on to have an unremarkable acting career which he ultimately left behind. After trying various other ways to make a living afterwards, none of them with much success, he died aged 70 in June 2014 after attending his mother's funeral.

It should be pointed out that the terrifying image of Olita 'shouting', on the VHS cover is taken from a rather brief and not very terrifying scene in which Amin is on the phone. For the sake of a good poster, most releases had the phone covered or removed. Still, it looks good.

The direction is nothing outstanding but Sharad Patel does put good effort into the moments of violence that are peppered throughout. The comparisons to exploitation rear their head, though, as he indulges killing and rape with some unflinching direction. A woman kills herself rather than being raped (Olita's facial expression as this happens is genuinely funny), the notorious 'heads in the freezer' scene is shot in such a matter-of-fact manner it makes the thing even more ludicrous than it already is, and the visual style in which a bishop is shot in the head would make even the most hardened grindhouse director jealous.

Patel would not direct again after this, and he would instead concentrate on being a film producer. His output is more than a little surprising after *Amin*. The cult eighties comedy *Bachelor Party* (1984) and its belated sequel in 2008 are exec produced by him, as well as live action versions of *The Jungle Book* (1994) and *Pinocchio* (1996, as *The Adventures of Pinocchio*).

The movie ends with a serious block of text on the screen detailing the number of dead victims of Amin, and that the feature is 'dedicated to them'. After seeing the depiction of how some of those victims met their fates, filmed in a manner that has no sensitivity to the loss of life that actually happened during the dictator's reign, this dedication feels very misplaced.

SHOCK WAVES (1977)

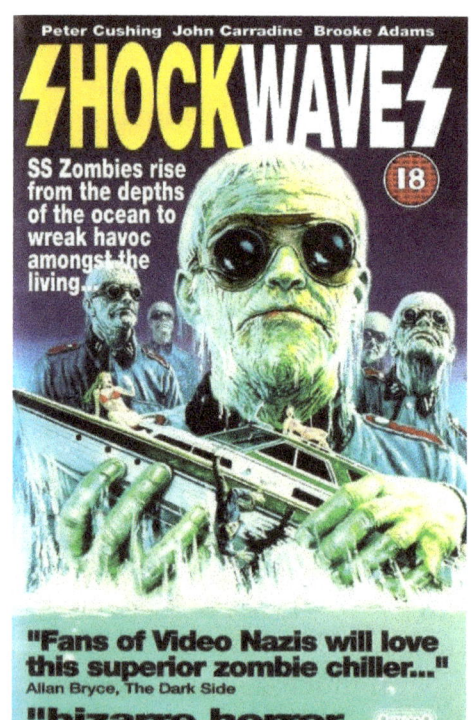

Director: Ken Wiederhorn

Writers: John Harrison as John Kent Harrison, Ken Pre (uncredited), Ken Wiederhorn

Stars: John Carradine (Cpt. Morris), Peter Cushing (Commander), Brook Adams (Rose), Fred Buch (Chuck)

VIPCO Release: 1993

Also Known As: *Almost Human, Death Corps, The Undead Commando*

VIPCO Plot Synopsis: *In 1945, during the final death throes of the Third Reich, a crack division of SS Shock Troops went down aboard their ship... They had supposedly drowned beneath several fathoms of ocean... But there was one thing about them the world didn't know... they couldn't die — they had never been alive in the first place. Genetically-engineered and adaptable to battle conditions anywhere — even under water — these were the Gestapo outfits known as the Death Corps, pathological murderers and criminals with an innate desire for violence, unpredictable and uncontrollable — lethal weapons in themselves...*

Nazisploitation makes an appearance in the catalogue of films to be distributed by VIPCO via *Shock Waves*. It is watered down (pun not intended) for a flick of that particular sub-genre, though, as there is no concentration camp or horny lady Nazi officer in sight. Instead, the viewer gets a dull film that has a strained plot.

The initial idea that there is a specially created group of 'Super Nazis' that cannot be stopped or killed could have lent itself to something special. Picture said Über Nazi's being shot, stabbed, and blown up, only to silently march on. Instead, very little is seen of them and, if they do appear on camera, they are filmed from a distance, wading through thigh-high water. Thrilling.

The story is needlessly full of dialogue and exposition – well beyond the point that it remains informative – and eventually becomes boring. Even when a group of tourists become shipwrecked, and find themselves on a tropical island, the narrative concerns itself with their exploration of the island (for long periods); viewers will quickly yearn for the arrival of the Nazi dead.

John Carradine has joint top billing with Cushing, but does not appear for long. Thank goodness for the arrival of Peter Cushing. The screen legend looks very thin and worn down here, he must have still been waiting on that money Morecombe and Wise owed him. Cushing immediately lifts the film.

Released on VHS twice by VIPCO (1993 and 2001) the transfer to video is bad. It is terrible, even by VIPCO standards. Thankfully, the firm never reissued this on DVD where the picture quality would have been even more dire. *Shock Waves* has, in fact, never received a UK DVD or Blu-ray release in the decades since; it is available to rent via streaming service Amazon Prime.

Funnily, the 1993 video tape version put out by VIPCO is described as a 'Video Nazi'.

This was the first full-length film of director Ken Wiederhorn, a man who would also give the world *King Frat* (1979) and direct several episodes of *Freddy's Nightmares - A Nightmare on Elm Street: The Series*, as well as the underrated *Return of the Living Dead II* (1988).

SUICIDE (2001)

Director: Raoul W. Heimrich, Yvonne Wunschel

Writers: Yvonne Wunschel

Stars: Dmitri Alexandrov as Dmitri Alexander, Yvonne de Bark, Markus H. Eberhard, Ralph Polinski as Raplh Polinslki

VIPCO Release: See main review

Also Known As: *FinalCut.com*

Shock Cinema Synopsis: *We have the rights to a few minutes fame even if they are our last so believe the two filmmakers we follow in "Suicide".*

They don't wish to question why people want to immortalise their suicidal deaths, they just offer an opportunity to become the focus of attention at least once in their lives...

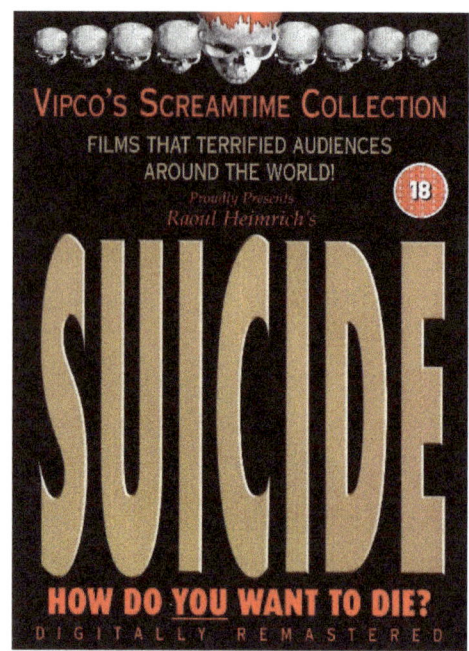

As the filmmakers become torn between sympathy for their customers and greed for the money they are being paid, how far will they go? By filming the events are they becoming accomplices to the deaths? And by watching, how drawn do we become?

"Suicide" exploits the camera in an ultra-real way and challenges our emotions more and more with each episode, an experience shared by the cast and crew during production, every scene was shot in one take, this had to be enough because the actors and crew were so moved that they couldn't bear trying it a second time...

Suicide is a movie that some may think is strange to include within this book. It was not one of VIPCO's best-known releases, nor did many people buy it. The majority of people that did were not impressed, and in the years since, the few people that have managed to watch it have not been impressed either.

Made on a budget as thin as a shoestring, this German production was picked up by Michael Lee in 2002. Fearing the 'snuff' nature of the film would attract bad press to VIPCO, the decision was made to change the distributor's name on the packaging to 'Shock Cinema'. Mike clearly had no problems about changing names later on, he would eventually re-release *Suicide* as part of the dreaded VIPCO Screamtime Collection.

This is perhaps one of the worst sellers in VIPCO history and Mike has expressed his deep dissatisfaction with it, when being interviewed for this book, and in *The Untold Story*. He believes it did not sell because it was a movie devoid of merit, although this view is applicable to most titles – from Mike's perspective – if they did not sell stacks of copies. This also explains why he would dump *Suicide* onto the Screamtime line; he did this with many movies he did not like.

Criticism is warranted. The plot does not concern itself with much outside the premise of 'these people record others committing suicide'. Many characters do not even have names; they just appear to be another suicide to be captured on camera. The ending can be predicted, too, although this is one of the more interesting moments of *Suicide*. Other criticisms are that there is very little gore or bloodshed, considering the subject matter, and many of the deaths involve methods of suicide that should lead to gore and bloodshed!

Despite the above, this writer thinks it is a commendable effort. Some of the onscreen suicides have power due to the manner in which they are shot, and the actors play everything seriously. One scene depicts a hopeless junkie deliberately overdosing in a public park, with the camera lingering on him as he slowly succumbs to death. The opening sequence of a man going to commit suicide by jumping to his death from the top floor of an abandoned building is also solid, especially when he changes his mind and runs away but falls through a gaping hole in the floor and dies anyway. What a shitter.

The movie is shot in a way that feels as if it is a snuff; it is not known if the viewer is meant to think it is real, or know it's merely a facsimile of one. The snuff vibe does lend itself to the grim junkie-in-the-park suicide scene, though. It might also be why Mike got cold feet on releasing it via VIPCO, leading to the advent of Shock Cinema and an over-the-top press release (written by poor Jay Slater) which hypes the touchy subject matter and the way in which it was shot. Thanks to the kind efforts of Jay, as well as Marc Morris, the actual press release has been included within this book.

As can be seen by the Shock Cinema DVD synopsis, Mike also tried to ram home the message of how disturbing a feature *Suicide* was (well, at least in his head). The reference to the crew trying to shoot scenes in one take – because of how 'moved' they were – is more than likely due to the fact this was shot with one camera; as a result, any edits to link together multiple takes would have been obvious. The front of the sleeve informs the potential buyer that the film is the 'uncut UK premiere' of *Suicide* which implies the movie had been cut in some form in the past in Britain. It has always been available uncut, although the directors had allegedly made cuts to their feature before releasing it.

Suicide has remained relatively obscure in the years since but is on YouTube thanks to Troma (who also issued it on DVD in the States) as well as being on Amazon Prime Video. The picture is, of course, subtitled in English.

A curio in terms of VIPCO history has made this movie worthy of inclusion in this book. Mike never really dealt with ultra-low budget indie flicks, especially ones that were not in English, but he did with this German pseudo-snuff movie. He would end up regretting doing so, but his 'mistake' (at least to some fans) provided a brief glimpse into a potential new direction for his ailing firm.

Jay Slater PR on behalf of Shock Cinema Proudly Presents a Raoul W Heimrich Film

SUICIDE

The most shocking film ever

Balancing on the edge of a rooftop, a man decides against tumbling to his doom and panicking darts into the gloom of an abandoned warehouse – eight stories above a mosaic of jagged brickwork and rusted pipes. He falls through a hole to have his body broken and mutilated below. A young junkie has had enough of his heroin addiction and injects himself through the penis with a lethal concoction – all shot in real time – until he breathes his last. One injects air into an artery and another, with a shotgun, blows his brains out. Someone jumps in front of a speeding lorry to be pulverised and a terminally ill patient pumps antifreeze into his heart...

The horror film of 2003 is here.

These devastating acts of self-destruction are only some of the visual horrors committed to celluloid in *Suicide* – a film that will shock and genuinely upset most viewers. *Suicide* is fascinating and disturbing, not just because of its authentic images of graphic death, but for tackling sensitive social issues. *Suicide* is not only of interest to those who want to be stunned by its visual portrayal of death but also debates euthanasia and questions the soaring UK suicide rate.

This is a world premiere VHS/DVD release and is fortunate to be completely uncut certificate 18. Not since legendary movies such as *Executions*, *Faces of Death*, *Snuff* and *Cannibal Holocaust* have authorities been shocked by a film and its impact on the British public.

When recently screened at a Japanese film festival, *Suicide* had patrons vomiting in the aisles and is said to have influenced people with suicidal tendencies think twice before killing themselves. Now, make up your own mind but prepare for a film that will stay with you forever.

Released nationwide on 17 March 2003 priced £17.99 on DVD and £15.99 on VHS

How do you want to die?

For more details, review copies and press interviews, please contact Jay Slater PR on 0208 686 0432 and/or email jayslaterPR@hotmail.com

VAULT OF HORROR (1973)

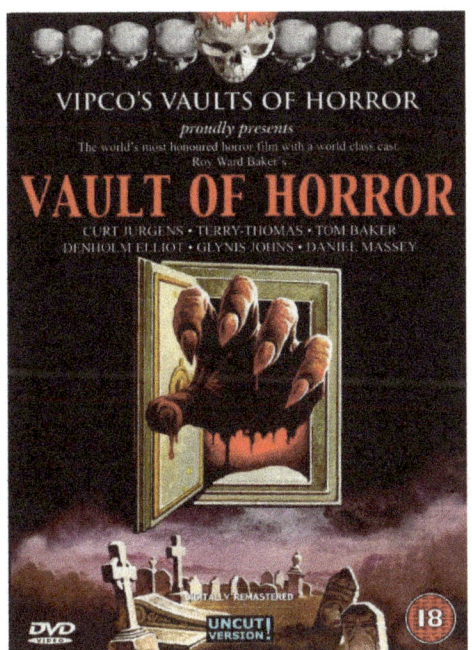

Director: Roy Ward Barker

Writers: Milton Subotsky, Al Feldstein (based on stories written by), William M. Gaines as Bill Gaines (based on stories written by)

Stars: Tom Baker (Moore), Terry-Thomas (Critchit), Denholm Elliot (Diltant), Curt Jurgens (Sebastian)

VIPCO Release: 1993

Also Known As: *Further Tales from the Crypt, Tales from the Crypt II, The Vault of Horror*

VIPCO Synopsis: *From Roy Ward Barker – 'the Grand Old Man' of British Horror, comes a collection of stories that will reach out and grip you in a vice of fear.*

Based on the spine-chilling comic-books "Vault of Horror" & "Tales from the Crypt" and featuring a sensationally star-studded cast, these are the tales of five hapless men huddled together in a vault beneath the Thames, each awaiting the fulfilment of their own prophetic nightmares.

See Curt Jurgens as a murderous magician with a few rope-tricks up his sleeve; Tom Baker (Dr Who) as a blood-drained brother biting off more than he can chew. Watch in horror as the crypt opens up to reveal an encyclopaedia of death from which no-one can escape alive...

With the sleeve synopsis ending "...opens up to reveal an encyclopaedia of death..." Mike Lee came up with quite a unique boast into this horror movie's prowess. While *Vault of Horror* is not an encyclopaedia of death, it has several stories and a bizarre wraparound narrative tale which makes for a fun and frivolous horror.

The cast of well-known actors contribute to the feature's worth. Tom Baker is on hand, just before he started he iconic run as *Doctor Who* in 1974, plus gap-toothed comedy veteran Terry-Thomas, and the always reliable Denholm Elliot, to name but a few. Some of these actors have sadly passed away in the decades since, and watching *Vault of Horror* in the 21st century is a reminder of a bygone era of British cinema.

The titular vault is the setting for the wraparound story. The opening credits see several men enter the elevator of a high rise, only for it to stop unexpectedly at the mysterious vault. Within it are a table with food and drink. They all seem confused about the scenario they find themselves in, but quite happily sit down, have a drink, and are keen to listen to each other's stories about their recurring dreams of strange deaths.

There are five stories in total, each one focussing on one of the stars of the movie. They range from a village of secret vampires to deadly insurance scams to Indian magic gone wrong. These are all based on Tales from the Crypt comics barring the second story (The Neat Job) which is from Shock SuspenStories. Out of the five, the most entertaining are Midnight Mess and The Neat Job.

Over the decades, there have been different cuts of this feature, although VIPCO – gasp – actually released *Vault of Horror* uncut! This thankfully means that those who bought the VHS or DVD were able to see the inventive yet macabre ending of Midnight Mess in full.

The artwork used on VIPCO's 1993 video release is a sight to behold, and was slightly altered for the 2001 DVD. Sadly, it was dropped in 2003 when the film was reissued as part of the budget Screamtime Collection. In some markets, *Vault of Horror* was renamed *Tales from the Crypt II*, trying to capitalise on the success of *Tales from the Crypt* (1972) which was another horror anthology by Amicus.

VIOLENCE IN A WOMAN'S PRISON (1982)

Director: Bruno Mattei as Vincent Dawn

Writers: Claudio Fragasso as Oliver Lefait, Ambrogio Molteni as Palmambrogio Molteni

Stars: Laura Gemser (Emanuelle), Gabriele Tinti (Dr. Moran), Lorraine De Selle (Warden), Ursula Flores (Consuelo), Maria Romano (Kitty)

VIPCO Release: 2003

Also Known As: *Caged Women, Chicks in Chains, Emanuelle in Hell, Women's Penitentiary 4*

VIPCO Plot Synopsis: *Laura Gemser plays yet another Emanuelle, a reporter who goes to prison on trumped up charges to expose the corruption within the prison and to secure a scoop about the bad conditions run by sadistic warden Lorraine De Selle. She is exposed, locked up in a cell together with hundreds of hungry dirty rats and eventually manages to escape with nice doctor Gabriele Tainti. In the prison she sees all of the torture and sex that the female inmates are exposed to.*

Supposedly shot at the same time as *Emanuelle in Prison* (aka *Women's Prison Massacre*) (1983) this movie would be released at the same time as that title, via VIPCO, in June 2003 on DVD. They would even be packaged together in what would be one of the few two-disc sets that the company would offer.

For those who are unfamiliar, *Emanuelle* was a notorious and somewhat smutty film series based on a 1959 French novel in which the author, Emmanuelle Arsan, details her sexual exploits and fantasies. The first movie came in 1974 and was a hit for the nudity and its softcore porn. A run of sequels quickly followed and unofficial sequels or cash-ins were on the scene too. In 1975, *Black Emanuelle* (directed by Bitto Albertini aka Albert Thomas) would see Laura Gemser play the role for the first time, an actress who would go on to appear in many movies as Emanuelle (now spelt differently to the original films for legal reasons).

By the time of this Bruno Mattei flick, Gemser had played the sultry character seven times in the past and mostly with director Joe D'Amato. Not noted for being a brilliant actress, Gemser is best remembered for her stunning looks which all the films were quick to exploit. Mattei clearly understood this; he had her strip down naked within the first eight minutes of *Violence...* and several more times throughout.

This has the added bonus – for exploitation fans – of being an Emanuelle film set in a women's prison. The viewer is not only treated to Mattei doing an *Emanuelle/Emmanuelle* flick, but also shown the delights of prison exploitation, aka Women in Prison/WiP genre cinema. This is a type of movie that embellishes the potentially violent and sexually volatile nature of an all-woman jail for maximum shock and titillation. The subgenre was enjoying a boom period at the time *Violence...* was made, and Mattei was never one to miss a fad to exploit.

A sure-fire success then? Not quite. The film is rather tame for the genre(s) it inhabits, especially in light of who was writing and directing. There are the anticipated lesbian romps, and the typical nasty acts of violence, but for patches things are rather dull. The lead character – Laura Gemser – does not put forward an entertaining performance, which only adds to the problems. Her facial expressions are often that of complete indifference or boredom. She does manage to act, late into the runtime, when she is covered in rats though.

The plot is flimsy with Emanuelle going undercover to expose brutality by prison staff. When her ruse is exposed, the warden of the prison (played by Lorraine De Selle wearing the biggest pair of glasses you will ever see) decides to teach Emanuelle a lesson by... beating her up and torturing her! Not the smartest of moves considering the journalist's planned article.

The addition of male prisoners, in the film, is ludicrous and leads to a somewhat frivolous scene. While the men are stood outside, watching one of the female prisoners showing off her breasts, a male inmate becomes irate. He campily walks around scolding the men, saying that they do not need women because they did not mind having sex with him beforehand. This underwritten gay stock character aggravates the perving men so much that they jump him in a moment that looks like they are either beating him up or actually raping him. He dies of his injuries in a melodramatic fashion shortly afterwards.

On the VIPCO packaging, the title was spelled as *Violence in a Woman's Prison* when the on-screen title reads *Violence in a Women's Prison*. This is mentioned for any of the pedants reading this book who notice 'these sorts of things'. I clearly did.

Speaking of the packaging, Michael Lee treats us to another 'honest' review of the movie. Anyone picking this off the shelf in an HMV, MVC, or Music Zone back in 2003 must have been blown away by what they read:

Extremely kinky as expected with Mattei [credited as his usual "Vincent Dawn"] managing to stage a somewhat bizarre art rape-scene which looks like something from a Tinto Brass movie, where the warden and her lover gets horny while watching a girl being raped and beaten up by the male inmates (oh yes, there are male inmates here too!) Lorraine De Selle is great as the evil warden and there's another loud great soundtrack by Luigi Ceccarelli. A fabulous WIP prison from one of Italy's sleaze masters, Mattei.

THE VIOLENT PROFESSIONALS (1973)

Director: Sergio Martino

Writer: Ernesto Gastaldi

Stars: Luc Merenda (Giorgio), Richard Conte (Padulo), Martine Brochard (Maria), Silvano Tranquilli (Gianni)

VIPCO Release: 2003

Also Known As: *Death is on My Side, The Italian Connection, Milan Trembles: The Police Want Justice*

VIPCO Plot Synopsis: *A highly praised Italian crime thriller from Sergio Martino about a tough, smooth-guy cop who goes undercover as a wheels man to infiltrate a ring of cop-killin' bank robbers. It's great stuff with a bit more plot complications than the usual pasta-cop outings with some stunning chase sequences thrown in to boot!*

Starting off quite moribund, with an opening sequence following a car driving around town, this movie quickly lives up to the word 'violent' which makes up part of its title. A pair of convicts, being transported on a train, brutally shoot and murder all their prison guards and make a daring escape. Rousing stuff.

Just after this, the same escapees force a car on a country road to stop. They kill the male driver and speed off… except… the driver's young daughter is still in the car. They are in two minds to kill her; one con shouts for her to be shot, while the one with the gun seems hesitant. When he finally pulls the trigger, Martino cuts to the very next scene wonderfully, swerving the viewer at such a heightened moment. Then, with a single shot of the interior of the car in the scene after this, he lets the viewer have the full impact of how violent these men really are. The girl's blood-covered hand is shown on the back seat. They have killed a child. A powerful act whenever depicted in film.

Martino sets the bar high early on for the bloodshed and acts of violence, with more to come. Despite the escalating mayhem, he somehow manages to retain a high level of quality and even tops it on occasion.

There are two absolutely astounding bank robbery and car chase scenes in the second half of the feature. The first car chase results in a crash that was innovative for the time thanks to excellent camera work. For the second robbery, Martino decides to further highlight the gang's merciless ways when a heavily pregnant female hostage is blasted in the stomach with a gun.

The star is Luc Merenda as Lt. Giorgio, a bona fide manly-man, who 'plays by his own rules', and who is a handsome bastard of a cop.

Lia Tanzi appears as a prostitute in the pocket of Giorgio. She is no doubt intended to be eye candy but she also brings a little comic relief to proceedings with her animated facial expressions. She would go on to be cast in other Sergio Martino works, *The Visitor* (1974), and *The Suspicious Death of a Minor* (1975), as well as that of his brother (Luciano) with *Erotic Exploits of a Sexy Seducer* (1977). The cast also benefits from the presence of Silvano Tranquilli, who worked with the likes of VIPCO favourites Umberto Lenzi and Enzo G. Castellari.

In the canon of features that VIPCO released, *The Violent Professionals* is certainly one of the better titles chosen. It had a standalone VHS and DVD release before being reissued in 2005 as part of a two-film set with Castellari's *The Big Racket* (1976). Considering *Professionals* and *Racket* are both brilliant movies, the two-disc set is great value for money if you can find it.

11

The History of VIPCO (Part VI)

The tapes were still cheap to do, so I didn't stop them outright at first.

Mike on why VIPCO continued to sell VHS alongside DVD in the early noughties.

As the dreaded Y2K Millennium Bug was gearing up to ruin the world, VIPCO were readying to ruin Britain's youth… all over again. Well, not quite. The firm was actually resubmitting movies that had previously been banned, or heavily cut, in the hope that they may finally be able to sell them again.

The director of the BBFC, James Ferman, had retired in 1999. Almost straight away, censorship and classification in the United Kingdom changed; Ferman's hard-line stance on certain features was now a thing of the past – and the best example of this would be *The Exorcist* (1973) which finally got a VHS release many years after Ferman overruled a BBFC decision to grant the film a certificate for home video. Not only had Ferman imposed his own views on the features he was meant to assess open-mindedly, but he forced his opinions and decisions on his co-workers too, with former staff speaking out in the years since of how they would follow what he told them.

The fact Mike still had the rights to many of VIPCO's back catalogue – films which had faced stern BBFC sanctions in the past – meant he could put them forward again, more confident that they would *now* be passed. He had also obtained the distribution rights to some controversial Video Nasties which had not previously be released in the UK by his company. *Zombie Creeping Flesh,* amongst others, graced the VIPCO Vaults for the first time. In turn, he also acquired several *more* Lucio Fulci flicks, giving his firm a very pro-Lucio reputation.

Of course, Mike had become a big fan of the godfather of gore following his first viewing of *Zombie Flesh Eaters* (1979), a film that had previously been the firm's first horror title, and the biggest seller in its history. Mike had also released other titles by Fulci at this point, including the *Gates of Hell* trilogy during the early nineties, as well as *The New York Ripper* (1982) in Denmark. Mike even joked that the BBFC would sigh in despair whenever he had submitted a Fulci flick in the eighties. Now, he hoped, things would be different.

Mike felt vindicated during this era of eased censorship, believing it showed he knew better than the BBFC the entire time. The

INCLUDES MATERIAL BANNED SINCE 1983!!

packaging for VIPCO's titles would often be more over-the-top than usual, with slogans such as 'BANNED SINCE 1983' stamped on them.

Some non-horror titles were picked up during this time too, although they were mainly in keeping with VIPCO's exploitation-happy image. For the most part, though, Mike stuck with the old faithful horror genre, and christened the 1999-2002 series of titles 'VIPCO's Vaults of Horror'. The sleeve design for the titles was standardised to give the new label an identity, with the now-iconic bloody skulls lined along the top of the cover, against a black backdrop, with part of the film's original poster front and centre. There would also be the attention-grabbing exclamation of the movie having been banned previously, or it now being uncut.

Another trick was up Mike's sleeve for his turn of the century blitz on the shelves of home entertainment stores. He made the decision that VIPCO's new line-up would see selected titles released on a relatively new technology and format known as DVD. The power of this movie-on-a-disc and the superior image and audio over the commonplace VHS was only fully known by a minority of fans during this time. Those in the know had forked out big money for the pricey new DVD players, and the discs to watch on them were of a high price too.

The decision to adopt DVD so early by VIPCO was due to Mike's past as a staff member at Laskys. Having worked within home electronics two decades earlier, and having kept an eye on developments in that industry ever since, Mike sought to recreate the success that VHS had delivered for VIPCO.

So, now, Mike was going to exploit DVD to tie in with the onslaught he had planned. A 'Digitally Remastered' graphic was added to sleeves to appeal to anyone with a DVD player; the use of this new medium was also a way for Lee to get fans who already owned prior edition films into buying a new 'better' version of, say, *The Burning* (1981). Many a punter would have gone for a DVD to replace their worn down and played-to-death VHS tape of *Shogun Assassin* (1980). Easy money, right?

Well, that was the theory. Mike failed to do one thing that was fairly vital in relation to selling DVDs, and marketing a film as 'Digitally Remastered'. That vital thing was actually to remaster the movie, digitally. The new releases were not.

In the research for this book, Mike admitted that he did not actually do anything with the original prints of films, when he transferred them to DVD. That's because he was in a rush to get them out on shelves. Somewhat sheepishly, he acknowledged that he did not fully respect the opportunities the DVD format afforded him and customers. This is why, years after this misstep, when cult cinema fans in the UK hear the name 'VIPCO', they think 'shoddy DVD transfers'.

When Jay Slater was asked about the DVDs, he had the following to say: "I can totally understand the reception! The discs were full price yet were nothing compared to the competition. I told Mike about this at the time, and he didn't fully understand DVD and thought the additional cost of remastering a film as needless."

The picture and sound quality on these discs were appalling. They were very clearly lifted straight from the master tape (which itself was usually in a dire condition) and not cleaned up or digitally remastered. The fact the packaging claimed it was, when VIPCO knew full well it wasn't, was misleading. DVDs were still carrying a hefty price premium during this time because of their supposed superiority over videotape, which included the bonus of being able to have extra content with special features on the disc to complement the film. VIPCO had essentially no extras save for the always laughable boast of 'interactive menus' and trailers for *Psychic Killer* and *Shogun Assassin* that would be on nearly all VIPCO DVDs.

Mike continued to sell movies on tape during this period; he realised that VHS was still – for a few more years anyway – the home entertainment format king in the United Kingdom.

There is an alternative opinion on the sub-par discs. "Yes, the transfers were horrible but, in reality, I didn't know what I was missing," says Arrow Video's Ewan Cant. "I was just a kid trying to see some mad-looking horror film; I didn't have a clue about picture quality."

Mike's desire was to strengthen his firm during the early noughties, but the ill will caused by the lacklustre DVD releases had soured things in the minds of many a fan. Marc Morris is of the belief that Mike had no respect for horror, and its fans alike; his lack of care for his DVDs was proof he was 'only in it for the money'.

Mike Lee suffered another misstep when he failed to renew the rights on his biggest seller *Zombie Flesh Eaters*. It meant someone else, Stonevision, cleaned up when they gave that former Nasty its UK DVD debut. Indeed, the title which had made VIPCO a mint was now out of the vault (as it were) leaving Mike to scramble for a replacement. That is why he would obtain *Zombi 3* and *After Death*, only to rename them *Zombie Flesh Eaters 2* and *3* respectively. He thought the value was in the *name*, which could possibly be true, although he failed to realise that it was the *movie* itself that had made *ZFE* such a hit. The new arrivals became VIPCO DVDs with very similar artwork.

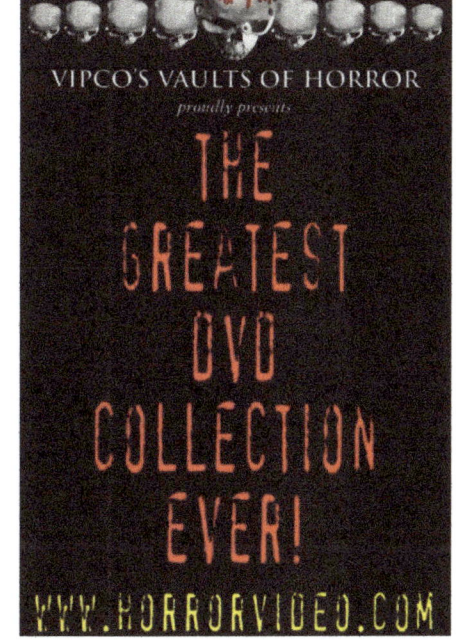

One good bit of forward planning Mike did, was to set up the horrorvideo.com website. It was admittedly rudimentary, but many websites of this era were. It helped open up a new revenue stream and allowed for extra sales.

DVDs had begun as an attempt to bring VIPCO into the 21st century, and give the impression of the firm being a trendsetter, but they became a tipping point for the company. The reputation for selling controversial horror, and catering to hardcore gore fans, was now being replaced with perceptions of a company struggling to adapt to change, and cutting corners. The next few years would only enhance these sentiments...

12
The Genres of VIPCO

Horror is the cinema genre most associated with VIPCO. While it did not start out with horror, and was never strictly limited to it, most of the company's output was of this type. Even though owner Mike Lee hated horror. Money talks.

Other film styles also graced the tapes of VIPCO. Exploitation cinema was a fit for the company, for example, and many of the most controversial works of that genre would receive their first British release thanks to VIPCO. A couple of low-brow comedies also cropped up over the years, not that many fans can recall them. In the very early days of the enterprise, softcore porn was also offered; until then, it could only be viewed in dodgy movie houses whilst wearing a raincoat.

As history shows, VIPCO never went for arthouse films although the hipster flicks *Andy Warhol's Dracula* (1974) and *Flesh for Frankenstein* (1973) are pretentious attempts at this (or harrowing dramas or chick flicks, depending on your perspective, (unless, perversely, you think *Prozzie* is one such movie)). VIPCO – or should that be Mike – stuck to what they knew, and what sold the most.

As the years went on, the various subgenres that were not horror or exploitation were to vanish from VIPCO's countless re-releases. Mike cut his losses whenever he saw underperformance; he knew where the money was, and that his creation had a reputation for the more controversial offerings.

It would have been strange, and likely a bad idea, if by the early nineties – when the company re-emerged in the British marketplace – Mike had obtained mainstream drama or family-friendly fodder. Undoubtedly, a fresh VIPCO-owned brand would have been created, but bargain bin sleeve designs plus shoddy audio and video would have no doubt remained. Production values are something that fans of horror can overlook; whether someone wanting to watch a good rom-com would do the same is debatable.

Admittedly, there were some efforts to get a slice of the pie from other genres. *A Time to Die* (thriller), *King Frat* (teen comedy), *Tim* (Australian drama starring a young Mel Gibson), and *The Rise and Fall of Idi Amin* (exploitation masquerading as political biopic), along with several other releases, were non-horror features that Mike felt he had to release. He either thought they would sell well, or he simply enjoyed them personally.

As many of the features covered in this book illustrate, horror was the lifeblood of VIPCO – despite what its owner may have felt.

13

The History of VIPCO (Part VII)

I had this new line – Screamtime – on DVD. I sold loads of them!

Mike on his memories of the Screamtime Collection.

A new line of VIPCO re-releases started in 2002, and would go on to make up the bulk of the company's output for the rest of its history. The Screamtime series was introduced with a handful of titles, at first, and the catalogue would ultimately go on to include over 40 movies.

Now, typically, concerns and criticisms from consumers of any brand represent something that can be learned from. To restore faith in a product, and to continue to attract new buyers, most businesses look to act quickly to implement changes that reverse or negate any damaging feedback.

For VIPCO, this did not happen.

The abysmal Screamtime DVD releases with their bad transfers and wrong aspect ratios would continue in earnest, from the earliest releases to the last. Titles wrongly labelled as digitally remastered would persist.

The now-notorious Screamtime Collection appeared on the scene with all the grace and appeal of spending a night with Mary Whitehouse. This was a budget line that was aimed at those wanting to sample some horror on DVD without paying a lot for the privilege. To distinguish the collection from his Vaults of Horror, or Cult Classics series, Mike decided that the packaging for the cheapie DVDs would have a unique look. What he came up with made them stand out, alright, just for all the wrong reasons.

The design still causes nightmares among VIPCO fans to this day. The black backdrop of the Vaults of Horror sleeve was retained as well as the iconic tzompantli/bleeding skulls along the top of the design. Laughably, 'Digitally Remastered' was still stamped on the bottom. The rest of the cover was a hideous bronze/bile, yellow, larger-than-life splodge of text of the movie's name. Anyone that remembered the good old days of the over-the-top, gory and colourful image-packed VHS designs, or the beautiful artwork of Graham Humphreys, would have been dismayed with the lack of effort and all-round ugliness of the Screamtime aesthetic.

If this was done because Mike wanted the buyer to know they were about to buy a budget title, then it certainly worked. The price, the look, and the now customary shoddy transfer all amounted to a piss-poor product. Personally, this writer was baffled for many years why VIPCO went this way. Surely, it would not have cost *much* to do things better? Others were just as mystified.

The truth is that Mike went this route with Screamtime because he actually "couldn't be bothered" designing another sleeve for a previous title, or creating one from scratch for something new. He had an extra reason that hinged on his own personal opinion. If Mike did not particularly like a movie which he had the rights to, or which had underperformed in the past, then he decided it would be relegated to the Screamtime Collection for its next VIPCO outing. Screamtime was the don't-give-a-fuck wrapper.

Considering that there are 45 films within the woeful collection, Mike must have disliked an awful lot of movies. In research for this book, he expressed not just dissatisfaction towards some films he sold over the years, but utter disdain for them. Mike's lack of love for the horror genre (save for a couple of works) is something that has never left him despite the successes the genre brought about. With *Death Screams* (1982), he even transferred some of the film reels in the wrong order, such was his 'concern' for the feature.

In a way, this public demotion of his own products, and the lack of care he afforded them, was interpreted by many fans as VIPCO having stopped caring. They had interpreted the scenario correctly.

Maybe if Mike had decided to come clean about his titles not actually being digitally remastered, the sudden dwindling of the fanbase may not have happened, or at least been slowed. By 2004, the home entertainment market had embraced DVD as a medium, and its popularity was soaring. Other companies actually bothered to digitally remaster their films for the new technology. VIPCO not delivering the goods, while other companies did, only quickened the growing ill will.

When speaking to people who worked or still work for the likes of Arrow Video, Vinegar Syndrome, Redemption or Nucleus Films – the same opinion as to Mike's bargain bin approach shines through. *They would never dream of doing it.* The idea that selling a DVD with a bad reputation sat well with Mike shocked many of them; some felt it showed his lack of respect for the horror consumer.

In the early years of the millennium, Mike released other DVDs while quietly abandoning VHS. Some even had – *gasp* – passable sleeve designs. These were mostly action or exploitation features that had colourful photographic, or artwork-filled, front covers; usually the movie's original poster or an altered version. VIPCO even dared to go as far as giving buyers value for money with some of these non-horror DVDs; some would be two-disc affairs, containing similarly themed movies.

By 2005, the once mighty and beloved VIPCO was weakened and being deserted by those it relied upon. But what happened to Michael Lee and VIPCO next was tragic, for a number of reasons…

14

Lucio Fulci: Gates of Hell

It was a Fulci film that put VIPCO on the map in the UK with the release of *ZFE*, and it would be Fulci that VIPCO would turn to again, a number of times, over the years. The firm would release over half a dozen of the Italian director's works – some good and some bad. While a few of those titles are featured elsewhere in this book, I thought it would be the right thing to do to give his famed *Gates of Hell* trilogy a section all of their own.

CITY OF THE LIVING DEAD (1980)

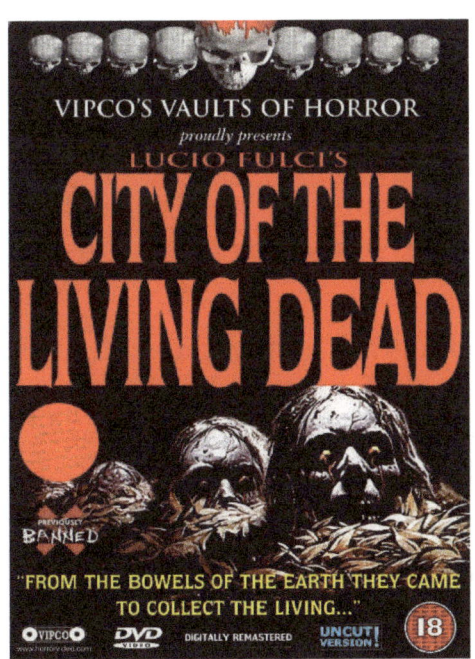

Director: Lucio Fulci

Writers: Dardano Sacchetti, Lucio Fulci

Stars: Catriona MacColl as Katherine MacColl (Mary), Christopher George (Peter), Giovanni Lombardo Radice (Bob), Carlo De Mejo (Gerry)

VIPCO Release: 1992

Also Known As: *A Corpse Hanging on the Bell Rope, Fear in the City of the Living Dead, The Gates of Hell*

VIPCO Plot Synopsis: *The story of a young woman whose horrific visions foretell the opening of the gates of hell under a New England town named Dunwich. When she reveals her fears to a journalist they set out together for Dunwich – H.P. Lovecraft's famous horror setting – where they discover that a zombie army of those burned at the stake centuries ago has reformed to seek horrible revenge on mankind!*

The first of the *Gates of Hell* trilogy (although VIPCO released it a few weeks before the second entry: *The Beyond*), which is often considered a golden period of Lucio Fulci, *City of the Living Dead* is high on visually impressive gore scenes and odd imagery but low on plot or a coherent story. In many ways, it is typical Fulci, a man who once said: "Violence is Italian art". As art is open to interpretation, the director goes for broke with his version in this flick.

At times illogical, and at others irrational, the story often feels like it is only in place to give the director something to pad out the runtime between gory deaths and

127

zombie attacks. At least Fulci does these with his usual zeal and disgusting eye for the macabre. But those wanting a plot that makes sense (or even a proper ending) should know better than to watch a Lucio feature. The priest that hangs himself seems to be the main thread throughout *City*, yet this too is clouded in uncertainty. Why does he kill himself? Does he do it as he has lost faith in God or because he has somehow seen the hell that is about to happen? If it is the foretelling of bloody doom, then did he know he would come back from the dead as part of this damnation?

Moments of implausibility abound. Intrigued journalist Peter, played by George, somehow hearing the muffled screams of a buried-alive Mary (a seemingly dead woman who had experienced visions of a priest hanging himself, and who really should have been embalmed) while honking cars, police sirens and passing planes can all be heard in the cemetery is one example. Another is when one character dismisses a mirror in a bar cracking suddenly in four places as caused by a 'passing truck'. The same character does not seem too concerned when a wall cracks in half, later on; he must have brilliant insurance to be that confident.

The buried alive scene is deserving of more attention as it is one of the most iconic moments of *City*. MacColl gives a dramatic performance as Mary waking to find herself entombed in a coffin. True 'what nightmares are made of' stuff. Fulci's direction is tight and claustrophobic which, of course, lends itself to the scenario. Even the strange blue cinematography adds to the tension despite the fact the inside of the casket should be pitch black. When Peter manages to save Mary by smashing a pickaxe through the roof of the coffin, this too adds to the terror as the would-be hero nearly sends the point of the axe directly through Mary's face. Even when being saved, there is a chance of death. Fulci does not let the viewer off the hook until the very last second.

Other standout moments include the numerous 'brain grabs' (when the undead rip handfuls of brains out of people's skulls), the feckless Bob being drilled in the head, and the genuinely stunning death of a woman who simply throws up her innards. All done with practical effects that hold up well, which is good because Fulci lingers on all the blood and guts for as long as possible.

Of course, *City* would end up being censored in the UK upon cinema and various VHS/Betamax releases in the eighties. VIPCO picked the title up for a Cult Classics VHS release in 1992 before *City* would get an uncut VHS/DVD reissue as part of the Vaults of Horror line.

Lucio also managed to cast some name actors who are now part of cult cinema royalty. When Christopher George appears onscreen, you know it's going to be a fun movie! George had appeared in the likes of *Grizzly* (1976), *Day of the Animals* (1977), and *The Exterminator* (1980) by this point in his career. Sadly, he would pass away due to a heart attack at the age of 52, in November 1983. MacColl brings glamour to the flick as terrified Mary. Despite having issues with Fulci during filming, and only doing *City* for the money, she would go on to star in the other two *Gates of Hell* movies. Giovanni Lombardo Radice plays a role not too different from the one he plays in *House on the Edge of the Park* and also meets a grisly end.

His role was originally meant for Michele Soavi, but the actors were switched with Soavi playing the smaller role of a flesh-hungry zombie.

Fulci does manage to create a strange atmosphere during *City*, part in thanks to an eerie fog/mist and the cinematography of Sergio Salvati that seems to descend over the town of Dunwich (a creation of Lovecraft) whenever something nasty is about to happen. The atmosphere is also delivered thanks to a pulsating score by veteran Lucio collaborator Fabio Frizzi.

For those wondering about the ending, which will not be revealed here for spoiler reasons, and why it is so out of the blue and nonsensical, please do not blame Dardano Sacchetti. The movie had a different ending, but the negative was destroyed by accident due (allegedly) to hot coffee being spilled on it. Whatever the reason behind its demise, a scramble for a new ending happened and what we see in *City* is sadly the best that could be done. Fulci movies have had even dafter endings than what is on show here, so fans of his work will potentially take this explanation with a pinch of salt.

THE BEYOND (1981)

Director: Lucio Fulci

Writers: Dardano Sacchetti, Giorgio Mariuzzo, Lucio Fulci

Stars: Catriona MacColl as Katherine MacColl (Liza), David Warbeck (Dr. McCabe), Cinzia Monreale as Sarah Keller (Emily), Antoine Saint-John (Schweik)

VIPCO Release: 1992

Also Known As: *Seven Doors of Death, Woodoo, L'Aldila, Eibon – Die 7 Tore des Schreckens*

VIPCO Plot Synopsis: *A young woman inherits a decaying hotel on the edge of a Louisiana swamp, unaware that more than fifty years ago it served as the gateway to hell, and that it's horrific evil lives on to this day. Her dream to build a new life for herself becomes a nightmarish fight for survival as horrors straight out of Lovecraft's Book of Eibon lay their own claim to her property, and the souls around her...*

Fulci expert Stephen Thrower calls it "the threshold of the quintessential Lucio Fulci film". Euro Gothic author Jonathan Rigby described it as a movie that pays "only the scantest heed to narrative logic". Both men are talking about the same film; the second entry into the *Gates of Hell* series: *The Beyond*.

As can be gathered, this is a movie that has its fans and critics. Whatever side you fall on, *The Beyond* is undoubtedly Lucio's most iconic work alongside *Zombie Flesh Eaters*. Much like his other movies, such as the first instalment of the *Gates of Hell* trilogy – *City of the Living Dead* – a coherent plot is lacking but, this time, it doesn't matter so much. Fulci controls things with a style that is genuinely impressive. The atmosphere of 1920's Louisiana, the long road shots of Emily, and the hypnagogic-esque ending show a director that is flexing his artistic muscle.

Of course, it is still filled with gore. The trademark Fulci eye-gouging scenes are here (this time more than once). Some unfortunate woman's face is dissolved by acid, there's a throat-ripping *Suspiria* homage, tarantulas tear into a man's face, and there's the still stunning sight of a girl being blasted through the head with a bullet. The exemplary special effects of Germano Natali are superb from start to finish. The BBFC being snip happy, naturally, would censor *The Beyond* as a result of the gore when this title was unleashed on Britain. All the cuts were eventually waived in 2001.

Fulci shows a level of restraint in *The Beyond* that may help explain why some believe it to be his best work. Instead of a rush of gore scenes, that are loosely connected by a nonsensical plot, he allows the story time to breathe. Admittedly, there are still incoherent moments but, for the most part, it has pacing and a structure; the bleak and depressing ending is a way of hammering home the nightmare the characters have found themselves in. The director even takes his time with the bloodshed, drawing out the suffering in the face-melting and tarantula scenes. Dardano Sacchetti and Giorgio Mariuzzo helped Fulci write the movie, so it is perhaps their influences at work.

Gates of Hell veteran Catriona MacColl (here listed as Katherine) stars, and her performance brings a touch of class to proceedings. She seems to have chemistry with her co-star, David Warbeck, who cuts a believable hero (barring the brief moment he is seen trying to reload a gun by attempting to force the bullet down the barrel of his revolver; MacColl corpses at this). Sarah Keller/Cinzia Monreale, as the blind girl, has a strange and eerie essence to her performance. Credit to her for wearing contact lenses that seem as thick as plates in order to appear blind.

Filmed in late 1980, *The Beyond* was recorded in various towns throughout Louisiana. The different filming environments that the geography allows are put to good use by the director and allow the already-mentioned artistic exploration of Lucio. The most iconic building of the feature – the 'Seven Doors Hotel' – is actually Otis House in Fairview-Riverside State Park in Madisonville. It was built in the 1880s, and is open to tourists. One for diehard fans to check out, perhaps.

Grindhouse Releasing gave the movie a limited theatrical release in 1998 which was uncut for the first time in the US, where it had previously been issued as *7 Doors of Death*. Quentin Tarantino is such a fan of *The Beyond*, he got it a DVD release in the States via his Rolling Thunder label.

This movie, for a time, was not going to be directed by Lucio Fulci. Lamberto Bava has claimed he was offered directing duties on *The Beyond* but declined because he 'didn't want to make it'. Which seems as good a reason as any.

The feature already had cuts when it was first released in the UK in 1981 taking the runtime from 87 minutes to 85 minutes. Cuts were made to a mid-eighties VHS release, and remained for the first VIPCO release in 1992. Mike would again release *The Beyond* on VHS and DVD in 2001 with no cuts, then one further time as part of Screamtime. The 1992 VHS, as part of the Cult Classics series, had a gaudy blue sleeve with a large photo of a couple of the zombies (added to the movie upon the insistence of German backers). This is not as bad as the hideous Screamtime Collection sleeve that *The Beyond* would end up with over a decade later.

After VIPCO ceased trading, the short-lived Beyond Terror put out *The Beyond* (recycling VIPCO discs) before the movie got a very worthy release from Arrow Video in 2011, as well as several re-releases in the years since by the firm.

THE HOUSE BY THE CEMETERY (1981)

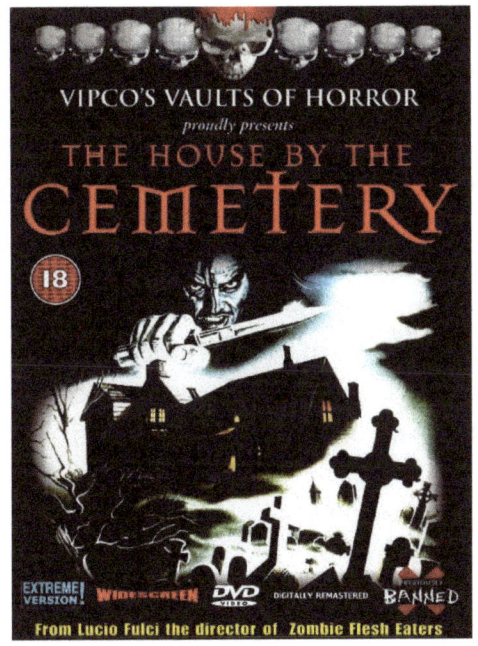

Director: Lucio Fulci

Writers: Elisa Briganti (story), Giorgio Mariuzzo, Dardano Sacchetti, Lucio Fulci

Stars: Catriona MacColl as Katherine MacColl (Lucy), Paolo Malco (Norman), Giovanni Frezza (Bob), Giovanni De Nova (Dr. Freudstein)

VIPCO Release: 1992

Also Known As: *House Outside the Cemetery, House at the Cemetery Wall, The Ripper New York 2* (sic)

VIPCO Plot Synopsis: *A young family move into a forboding New England mansion, unaware that it was once the gruesome residence of Dr Freudstein, a dabbler in bizarre surgical practices. Soon Freudstein – now a classic Fulci zombie – is up to his murderous old tricks again, seeking freshly severed limbs and organs to keep his corrupt, rotting flesh alive!*

Lucio Fulci takes what he learned with *The Beyond* and makes this flick more coherent and slow-burning. Less about going right for the kill straight away, *House by the Cemetery* is about building tension and making the viewer wait for the impending doom of the Boyle family. That having been said, the director does give us a knife through the back of some poor woman's head within two minutes. Classic Fulci.

The conclusion to the *Gates of Hell* trilogy, this is perhaps the most traditional horror out of the three. Fulci concentrates on the Boyle family and their new home while various strange occurrences begin. Norman, the father, is repeatedly told by people he has only just met, that they have actually met before (which he denies). Young Bob befriends a girl named Mae who has a *Shining*-like psychic link with the child. Most strange of all is the boarded-up basement door and the tomb of a deceased Dr Freudstein in the house.

It is the sealed shut door to the basement that Fulci teases and draws out the most. This being a horror movie, no one thinks it might be a good idea to leave the thing shut; instead, the Boyle's manage to open it and all but seal their fates. To confirm this, when they enter the basement/cellar, they are attacked by a large bloodthirsty bat straightaway. Norman's hand is savaged by the winged creature which he manages to stab to death. The fake blood splatters everything, of course! This leads to the most fun within *Cemetery,* with the zombie Dr Freudstein lurking in the cellar. The Dr Frankenstein comparisons are there, but instead of using body parts to create a monster, this doctor uses his victims to enable himself to remain alive, after death.

The Freudstein character is creepy in appearance and demeanour, with the grisly zombie effects of *Zombie Flesh Eaters* (1979) nowhere in sight. Freudstein looks, for lack of a better term, like a chewed-up toffee. He moves slowly, and shuffles, like the typical Fulci undead but at times cries like a child and emits eerie noises. He is an iconic character in the director's canon.

Much has been made about the dead doctor's name: Freudstein. Some believe it ties in with the Frankenstein nature of the character ('stein') as well as, on a deeper level, Sigmund Freud. Taking into consideration that, for decades, many have played down the intelligence of Lucio Fulci films, it is frivolous to look too deeply into the name of one character. Lucio expert Stephen Thrower theorizes in his excellent book on the man, *Beyond Terror,* where the name comes from. Thrower points out that the head of foreign sales at the legendary Titanus International was Michel Freudenstein. The director will have known who Freudenstein was, due to his role in selling Italian movies for international distribution; Thrower believes Freudstein is a play on Freudenstein as a result.

The bleak and cold winter landscape of the New England area of the north-east United States was the shooting location for most of *Cemetery.* Quite the contrast to the humid New Orleans of *The Beyond,* this landscape lends itself to making the final *Gates of Hell* movie stand out even more. An on-screen graphic claims that the Boyles are in 'New Whitby, Massachusetts' but this is a fictional town. Most of the exteriors were shot in Concord, MA, and the titular house is located in Scituate, MA. The Concord Free Public Library is featured, also used in *The Beyond* for the infamous tarantula scene, although the library fails to mention this, decades later in the history section of its website! An oversight, surely?

Catriona MacColl (billed as Katherine) completes her trio of *Gates of Hell* flicks with another performance that lends itself to proceedings. The scene where she is trying to escape Freudstein sees her give a frenzied showing. Giovanni Frezza, who will be recognisable to genre fans for his roles in Fulci's *Manhattan Baby* (1982) and Lamberto Bava's *A Blade in the Dark* (1983), is the blonde-haired boy that is annoyingly cutesy. He was eight-years-old when *Cemetery* was filmed in early 1981. Argento veteran Ania Pieroni plays Ann, who meets a gory fate. Giovanni De Nava shuffles about as Dr Freudstein as well as he can.

It is worth noting that Fulci puts to work a tactic that did so well for him in *City of the Living Dead.* When the undead Doc has little Bob's head forced up against a

132

door – as Norman smashes an axe through it – the tension and dread that Bob will 'get it' brings to mind the dramatic freeing of MacColl's *CotLD* character being rescued from a casket.

The ending is almost as bleak as that of the film before it, *The Beyond*, implying that the events that have taken place were inevitable and the characters cannot escape the house by the cemetery. Indeed, the *Gates of Hell* trilogy ends on a truly depressing note. Lucio's career would never produce the same sort of highs again.

Edited for cinema, and first VHS release, *Cemetery* would be banned by the mid-eighties. It was released again in 1988 with more cuts, and when VIPCO first released it on VHS in the summer of 1992 even *more* footage was taken out. When the firm released it on VHS/DVD in 2001, all the cuts barring half a minute were reinstated. These 30 seconds would finally be waived for Arrow Video in 2009. One sequence remains cut, but it was Fulci himself who did this as he was unhappy with how the finished death looked (estate agent murder scene, for those wondering) and not because of the snip-happy BBFC.

15
The History of VIPCO (Part VIII)

You'd have liked him, Adam. He was a lovely lad.

Mike, on his late son, Adam Lee.

The next couple of years, 2005-2007, would ultimately see the end of VIPCO. What caused its ultimate downfall was not the issues detailed throughout this book, although they would have perhaps contributed. No, it was something beyond the firm's control that ultimately brought about its demise. In fact, it was something that was even beyond the control of owner Mike.

Mike Lee had a son, Adam. In mid-2006, when Adam was in his mid-twenties, he began to experience health problems. Indeed, his condition would worsen as the year went on. Ultimately, tests would reveal that Adam had a brain tumour that was inoperable. Across this exceptionally sad and difficult time, Mike and his ex-wife Susan, Adam's mother, devoted their time and money to help their son.

In May 2007, the battle with the tumour was lost. Adam died at the young age of 24.

During this period, Mike 'took his eye off the ball', in relation to his company. He stopped being quite so hands-on, at first, then let many other aspects of the firm slip into disarray. His business screeched to a halt. Mike found the grief too much to overcome.

For a parent to suffer the tragedy of seeing their child die is something no one should go through. To have it happen in such a painful and drawn-out manner only intensifies the turmoil. Adam's ill health and death hit Mike incredibly hard, right from the moment the Lee family were made aware of what was causing Adam's sickness. When the day came that Adam passed away, Mike was the hardest hit. Although he had neglected his day-to-day life and business during the ordeal, the aftermath would see the neglect worsen.

VIPCO was abandoned as Mike no longer cared; it was not even a distraction for him anymore. It was far from his mind and its closure inevitable. Mike was consumed by the pain and inner turmoil of Adam's loss and, as surreal as this sounds, Mike told people associated with VIPCO to literally 'burn everything'. He wanted nothing more to do with the firm. Barrie Gold tried to talk him out of it, but Mike ignored the pleading and demanded VIPCO be scrubbed out of existence. Barrie had no choice but to honour his friend's wishes – all the VIPCO stock he had, was destroyed. Mike disposed of all the paperwork he had in his office, too.

Mike's own health and wellbeing rapidly deteriorated following this. He became seriously ill but did not care; he withdrew from life and became isolated. As he vanished from public life, VIPCO was no more... after nearly three decades.

16

Nearly VIPCO...

Throughout VIPCO's history, there were a few titles that Mike Lee wanted to release (or had even planned to release) but which fell through. For the most part, Mike picked up whatever movie he wanted, and then released it several times, but here follows some 'near-releases'.

One such film was Wes Craven's exploitation classic *The Last House on the Left* (1972). Mike was a fan of Craven's early work and had publicly and privately expressed his desire to get this one a VIPCO release. One of the reasons why Mike perhaps never got *Last House...* on the VIPCO books was because the controversial home invasion flick was banned in the UK at this point (in the early nineties) and would remain so for some years. It had been banned following the introduction of the Video Recordings Act of 1984, and while other former Nasties would go on to gain (re)releases with cuts during the ensuing 15 years, *Last House...* was still a no-go. The ban was not lifted until 2003, following various court cases and appeals. During all this, VIPCO never got its hands on Craven's classic.

Mike claimed he appreciated the film, and the skills of its director, He was a fan of *The Last House on the Left*, for sure, but he may have also liked the attention a VHS or DVD release would have garnered. Either way, it never happened.

As mentioned by director Jason Impey, in this book's foreword, *Absurd* (1981) was a film that came close to joining the VIPCO catalogue. Jason was the one who suggested this Joe D'Amato 'classic' to Mike. A sequel of sorts to 1980's *Antropophagus, Absurd* also starred George Eastman and is just as gory and nonsensical.

The film was part of the Video Nasties scandal and picked up its predictable ban. Nonetheless, Mike took Jason's recommendation seriously and had started enquiring about rights to the film and submitting it to the BBFC. This was around 2002 when many former Nasties had been re-submitted as bans were being lifted. Mike was hoping for the same with *Absurd*. For reasons only known to Michael Lee, he decided not to pursue classification at this stage, and simply stopped. Maybe he feared the BBFC would refuse to lift the ban and decided it was not worth his time or money? *Absurd* would finally see a UK re-release in early 2017 thanks to 88 Films.

Although Mike had released *Flesh for Frankenstein* and *Andy Warhol's Dracula* in the pre-cert era of VHS, he had planned to re-release them. Privately, he was disappointed when his plans failed to happen. Whilst these movies were given the

VIPCO treatment previously, they are included here due to the fact that Mike was so keen to have them re-issued and it never happened.

17

The History of VIPCO (Part IX)

The reason, the *real* reason, that VIPCO closed is somewhat removed from the decade-long rumours of Mike packing up shop and moving on to some other money-making venture… or having gone bust. What happened, in reality, was more important than the firm closing its doors.

For a company that brought so much entertainment to so many over its existence, the end had nothing to do with the industry it was in. The bad press, the cutting corners, the dire DVD transfers, the bargain bin packaging, competition from downloading and developing streaming services, as well as a lack of new and compelling titles to the line-up, were not responsible either; even though they were enough to a sink a business in their own right, either singularly or as a group.

Simply put, the loss of Mike Lee's firm was nothing compared to the loss of his son. Perhaps those that have long pondered about VIPCO's demise will agree that Mike made the right decision as a mourning father.

Those that wonder if VIPCO will ever return will hopefully agree, too, that the reason behind a return never happening is a warranted and worthy one. In the few years immediately following Adam's passing, Mike, as mentioned, withdrew from life completely. He also neglected his physical health and lost a lot of weight. Mentally, the scars never healed and only deepened as his memory began to suffer due to severe mental illness. Ultimately, Mike was admitted into a care home for the elderly who suffer from such long-term issues. He has been there for several years now. His current situation looks unlikely to change.

That is the reason why there is no VIPCO revival.

Thankfully, Mike is physically healthy again and is getting the best care possible. He has regained an interest in talking to people and is friendly. He is enjoying life again. He still speaks fondly, and often, of Adam.

As mentioned in chapter 15, at the end of VIPCO's run, Mike had little interest in running his firm and destroyed everything to do with it: stock, artwork, paperwork, whatever. Mike has said that, as far as he knows, there is nothing remaining of paperwork or contracts or property – in a legal sense – which state that his firm ever existed and doubts anything will be found.

This problem was proven while writing this book. Throughout much of the period it has taken to write and then find a publisher for the book, I was informed from a very reliable source that one, then two, distributors (who I will not name here), were fighting it out in an effort to obtain the rights to *Spookies*. The lack of any legally binding paper trail that could help these firms put pen to paper with Mike, in order to release *Spookies* on Blu-ray, resulted in a heated battle between them. For a while, it seemed there would be no resolution, yet – after much time and searching – a positive outcome might be in the offing. Watch this space...

18

House of Doom (1989)

In the late 1980s, Italian cinema legends Lucio Fulci and Umberto Lenzi became involved in a project by Italian television channel Reitalia. The aim was for each director to create two horror movies for the channel, each based in (or around) a house with spooky goings-on. Actually, originally, it was to be six films with Lamberto Bava helming the other two entries, although he ultimately withdrew.

Named the *House of Doom* collection, the movies were never transmitted – Reitalia deemed them to be too violent. They have eventually found their way onto VHS and DVD, in various countries around the world, in the decades since. As VIPCO seemed fond of Fulci and Lenzi's work, it is no surprise that the House of Doom titles were released by the firm in 2003. They proved to be quite a mixed bag...

THE SWEET HOUSE OF HORRORS (1980)

Director: Lucio Fulci

Writers: Gigliola Battaglini, Vicenzo Mannino, Lucio Fulci

Stars: Cinzia Monreale (Marcia), Jean-Christophe Bretigniere (Carlo), Lino Salemme (Guido), Lubka Lenzi as Lubka Cibulova (Mary)

VIPCO Release: 2004

Also Known As: *The House of Horrors, The Sweet Home of Horrors*

VIPCO Plot Synopsis: *Sweet House of Horrors gets off to a great start with a masked man breaking into a house and brutally murdering the owners. The story continues after the aunt and uncle of the children whose parents were murdered decide to take care of the children in the same house. Soon the two creepy kids conjure up a supernatural force that brings their parents back. Along with this, a number of strange supernatural occurrences go on inside and out of the house.*

"...when I try to imagine the impossible, I would like to return to childhood. Only children can reach the impossible..." N. Hawthorne. Quote at the start of *Sweet House of Horrors.*

With this feature being only 79 minutes long, it can be assumed the film's length is because director Fulci originally made it for Italian television. The run time would have been bulked up with commercial breaks. That did not happen in the end, which means *Sweet House of Horrors* runs to just *under* what many consider an acceptable time for a full-length feature. To cheat the viewer even more, the first two minutes are opening credits before the movie starts properly.

The 'banned from Italian TV for being too violent' story – the supposed reason why these films were never aired – does not hold water here. Although the movie starts with one very gory opening scene, nothing of note – violence-wise – happens after this. Indeed, in this opening scene, a married couple is brutally killed by a burglar dressed in black. Lucio's love of eyes-being-attacked is on show here when the poor woman is smashed in the face with a meat tenderizer that causes her eyes to squish out of their sockets. It is a great, exciting, and bloody way to kick things off after the long opening credits. Sadly, the rest of the feature is tame in comparison, and it is as if Fulci knows this. Halfway through *Sweet House,* he has the extreme opening scene played again in flashback form. It only serves to remind the viewer how dull the story has become since then.

Later on, there is a moment of sheer lunacy that is so over-the-top it will cause unintended laughs. When the killer burglar is eventually revealed, he runs into the middle of a road where he is attacked by a large dog (that appears from out of nowhere) and then run over by a speeding truck; all in the space of ten seconds. 'Why?' is the question that immediately springs to mind.

The rest of the plot concerns itself with the children of the murdered couple befriending 'fairies' that turn out to be the now omnipresent spirits of their deceased parents. *Sweet House* then feels like a haunted house flick for kids due to the plot shift. The director concentrates on the children playing with the beaming ghosts of mum and dad while attempting to thwart a planned sale/demolition of the family mansion. The spirits manage to save the day and make the kiddies happy while the evil grown-ups are left fuming… like *Scooby-Doo* villains. At times, proceedings feel bland and predictable and, because of this, *Sweet House of Horrors* has all the hallmarks of late-era Lucio Fulci that plagued his final works.

The cast is limited to half a dozen actors with the unlikeable brats getting the most screen time. Thankfully, for cult fans, there is the involvement of Cinzia Monreale (the blind chick from *The Beyond*) and Lino Salemme who is best known for his roles in the likes of *Demons* (1985) and *Delirium* (1987). Salemme has, in the years since, said he did not enjoy making this movie because of Fulci's notorious temper, and the way he was treated during filming. It did not stop him from working with the fiery director again for *Demonia* (1990).

With three more entries into the *House of Doom* series to go, things have not got off to a good start…

THE HOUSE OF CLOCKS (1989)

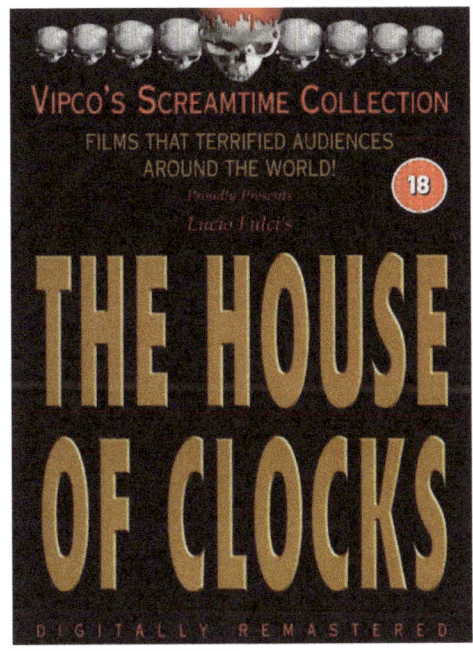

Director: Lucio Fulci

Writers: Gianfranco Clerici, Daniele Stroppa, Lucio Fulci (story)

Stars: Paolo Paoloni (Vittorio), Bettine Milne as Bettina Milne (Sara), Al Cliver (Peter), Karina Huff (Sandra)

VIPCO Release: 2003

Also Known As: *The Clock of Evil, The House of Time*

VIPCO Plot Synopsis: *A gang of ruthless thugs intent on robbery pass upon a seemingly harmless elderly couple, Vittorio and Sara. The simple plan turns into a terrifying nightmare, as Vittorio's antique clock collection mysteriously turns back time. Now the hunters become the hunted and the old couple become a vengeful, malevolent force.*

"...if time turned back, our sins would also have to start anew..." Honore de Balzac. Quote at the start of the feature.

Like *The Sweet House of Horrors*, this is a short affair with the movie clocking in (no pun intended) at just over 80 minutes. Thankfully, it's an altogether more enjoyable experience than the previous Fulci *House of Doom* effort, and has brief flashes of the director's former brilliance.

With a story that starts off looking like it will become another *The Last House on the Left* (1972) home invasion rehash, *Clocks* quickly becomes an Edgar Allen Poe-like tale of quasi-time travel and the uncanny. A well-off elderly couple, that just happen to have a set of corpses in their property, is tricked by a group of youths into coming out of their mansion (the titular *House of Clocks*) and are held hostage. The old duffers do not stand a chance and, along with their one-eyed handyman, are murdered. The plot then turns supernatural as the clocks start going backwards and the deceased come back to life to plague the delinquents.

The movie really comes alive when the gang force their way into the pensioners' home. For a brief moment, there is actual tension as Fulci swerves the viewer by having the handyman appear out of nowhere to save his employers, only for another swerve to happen within moments as a deadly struggle breaks out amongst the characters. Once dead, the victims begin to appear throughout the house and, then, they are somehow alive again. The clocks continuously going backwards are, it is implied, responsible for this, and supposedly the house is travelling back in time. No explanation is given for how and why any of this happens, though. Fulci uses this plot device to allow for some gothic imagery, and developments that give *Clocks* a real sense of creepiness.

The cast is limited to a handful of players with the standout being veteran actor Paolo Paoloni. He comes across as a kindly old toff one moment, and sinister the next, when he batters a small bird with his walking cane. Fulci favourite Al Cliver makes a good effort, too. The rest of the cast are nondescript.

The ending is so out of the blue, it feels as if Lucio must have tacked it on to try and swerve the viewers one last time. You'll have to watch *Clocks* to see what happens. Luckily, the rest of the film is strong enough so that this does not completely ruin the experience.

THE HOUSE OF WITCHCRAFT (1989)

Director: Umberto Lenzi

Writers: Gianfranco Clerici, Daniele Stroppa, Umberto Lenzi

Stars: Andy J. Forest (Luke), Sonia Petrovna (Martha), Marina Giulia Cavalli (Sharon), Paul Muller (Andrew)

VIPCO Release: 2003

Also Known As: *Ghosthouse 4: House of Witches*

VIPCO Plot Synopsis: *A young man dreams a recurring nightmare in which he runs away from someone before he reaches an old house where an ugly old woman boils his head in a big kettle! His girlfriend thinks it's good for him to take a few days off from work and they drive to an old house that belongs to her family. Unbeknownst to her, the house is the one the young man always enters into in his nightmares!*

Umberto Lenzi takes over the ill-fated Italian TV movie series with his first offering: *The House of Witchcraft*. The man responsible for iconic VIPCO releases *Eaten Alive!* (1980) and *Cannibal Ferox* (1981) presents a very different movie here. Unlike his previous output, it lacks the typical Lenzi finesse.

The longest of the four films, at 85 minutes, the feature starts with Luke (Andy J. Forest) running through some woods while seemingly being chased by a pack of howling dogs. He manages to find refuge in a house but, once he enters the kitchen, an old woman is boiling his head in a cauldron! He should not have worried; it turns out 'it was all a dream' and Luke is, in fact, in bed. Phew!

With that cliché out of the way, the first moment of shoddy scripting arrives when Luke's wife, Martha, calmly tells him their marriage is 'a disaster' but she will take him on a retreat to save the union. The way in which this dramatic news is told to Luke is given all the seriousness of her telling him they have run out of coffee. It turns out this major plot development exists simply to deliver the house from Luke's nasty dream onto the screen.

Of course, Luke starts seeing and hearing strange things in the house as Martha begins to sleepwalk across the property's grounds. Cue a blind old man – Mr. Mason – who says the house has a certain 'sorcery over people'. No explanation is given for what is happening, and when some context is attempted – with Mason revealing a woman's body had been found buried within one of the walls, and had been there for 'several centuries' – it feels flimsy and non-credible. With no evidence to support his claim, Mason says he thinks the dead woman was a witch because that 'sort of thing' happened around the time. He later mentions his wife had died in the house, during a fire, which is a plot point that serves no purpose to the story.

Witchcraft is also not much of a horror film with the characters mainly walking around the house and talking for many scenes. A man is stabbed with garden shears (only to fall down an exposed well, seconds later), and a girl is stabbed repeatedly in the chest, and a couple of other typical horror movie moments do crop up, yet they contain minimal gore. If the *House of Doom* series was refused an airing on Italian TV for being too violent, *Witchcraft* certainly is not the guilty party.

As with other titles from the series, this film has very few cast members. Marina Giulia Cavalli (Sharon, old man Mason's niece) is likeable and charismatic. Sonia Petrovna is cold and distant as Luke's haughty wife. Forest's performance as Luke is bland and generic, plus he often looks genuinely confused. There is one point in the movie when (spoiler alert) he hops into bed with Sharon moments after he has just seen his beloved wife being killed. What a saint.

THE HOUSE OF LOST SOULS (1989)

Director: Umberto Lenzi

Writer: Umberto Lenzi

Stars: Stefania Orsola Garello (Carla), Matteo Gazzolo (Massimo), Joseph Alan Johnson (Kevin), Gianluigi Fogacci (Guido)

VIPCO Release: 2003

Also Known As: *The House of Wandering Souls*

VIPCO Plot Synopsis: *Young geologists make the unwise decision to stay in a rundown and abandoned hotel in the middle of nowhere. Unknown to them is the hotel's dodgy past where the landlord had murdered his family and all the guests for good measure! Now, the murders begin-a-new and the geologists are killed in bizarre and extreme ways. Eerie things start to occur as cries of pain are heard, tarantulas arrive, corpses appear, and blood begins to drip from the ceiling!*

The fourth and final film in the *House of Doom* abandoned TV movie series – *House of Lost Souls* – is a sorry end to what had already been an inconsistent collection.

Casting further doubt as to why the series was rejected by television executives, *Souls* rarely shows the 'moment of impact' when something gory does happen. The viewer sees the immediate aftermath (sometimes blood splatters onto the camera lens before this) but, more often than not, Lenzi cuts to the next scene. Considering the lack of restraint he used in his earlier flicks, this is frustrating. Is this a sign of the director mellowing or simply trying to please the television station that was writing the cheques?

Lenzi does allow the gore to take centre stage a couple of times, thankfully. One such moment is when a young boy is decapitated by a washing machine, and his head tumbles around inside its spinning drum in slow motion. But other more brutal killings, such as a man's head being sawn off by a ghost-operated chainsaw, frustratingly remain out of sight.

The story and script by Lenzi are pedestrian and unoriginal, and the plot is by the numbers and predictable. Sadly, unintentional laughs are to be found in the script, with characters saying some truly inane things to each other. When one woman has lucid visions of murder, her boyfriend tells her "(the) doctors said you have a reasonable explanation (for this) ... you're a psychic" as if it is the most rational reason possible. Another female character, after being locked by an unseen force inside a walk-in freezer with dead bodies, is told she imagined it like the time she thought she saw Donald Trump! The end scene contains the line: "I wonder if this will ever be over?" which telegraphs the fact it is not. This is proved, mere seconds later, when – gasp – it is not over.

The cast is annoying and unlikeable. Carla, played by Stefania Orsola Garello, is tolerable, however. Cult movie regular Hal Yamanouchi is worth watching for his retro portrayal of a zombie as he staggers around looking gormless with his arms outstretched in front of him. It feels as if he played his role this way to get laughs. Whether the laughs were for the benefit of the cast and crew, or the viewer, is unclear.

Overall, *House of Lost Souls* manages to take the 'Worst Film in the *House of Doom* Series' title from Lucio Fulci's poor *Sweet House of Horrors*.

When VIPCO picked up the four *House* flicks for UK release, the two Fulci entries were released in late February 2003 with Lenzi's efforts hitting the market in mid-March. They were then released in a boxset as *The House of Doom Collection* in August of that same year. The series has been released on VHS, DVD (as a boxset), and as part of the Screamtime Collection (sold individually).

19

The History of VIPCO (Part X)

It [VIPCO] was a lot of fun, especially during those wild Video Nasty days!!

Mike, on his time running VIPCO.

In the decade-plus since Mike called it a day, VIPCO's presence has remained in the background of the horror home entertainment marketplace. Since then, other firms – big and small – have bought and released many of the features that VIPCO offered in the past.

Some of these companies, naming no names, simply bought the remaining Screamtime stock and changed the packaging, before selling the discs as their own. Anyone who bought them, at the time, will have been very confused when they opened up *House by the Cemetery* to see a DVD with VIPCO printed on its face. More so when the disc itself is playing on their television, and the same shoddy transfer, extras, and interface appear.

Thankfully, other companies were a bit more respectful of fans' desires to purchase former VIPCO titles. Arrow Video is perhaps the biggest example with their series of Blu-rays that came out in 2010-2012; actual (gasp) remastered versions of the films were provided, with a rich selection of outstanding extras plus some stunning packaging. In the years since, Arrow Video has re-released these (minus much of the limited edition trimmings) as either dual-format or steelbook Blu-rays. Ewan Cant explained that the Blu-ray release of *The Mutilator* became his passion project – as a child, he was fascinated by the title's VIPCO sleeve. Many of the Fulci flicks that Mike was so fond of have become favourites of Arrow Video, too.

However, Ewan candidly did have this to say: "It is a struggling industry and is on the decline. [Arrow Video] have to make something the fans want to have on their shelves. Sadly, there are not too many fans like this anymore as other 'fans' think it is acceptable to download a film as a torrent off a website."

88 Films have also raided the VIPCO vaults with a number of movies receiving their UK Blu-ray debuts thanks to their efforts. Some of the lesser remembered features have been given new leases of life in Britain with *Sewage Baby* (aka *The Suckling*) (1990), *Flesh Eating Mothers* (1988), and *Zombie Flesh Eaters III* (1988) hitting the shelves in recent years.

Some of the more controversial films in the defunct VIPCO arsenal have been re-released by Shameless Screen Entertainment, a firm which employs an eye-catching yellow packaging for their DVDs and Blu-rays (no doubt Mike would have done this for VIPCO if he'd had the idea first). In 2018, Shameless unleashed high definition versions of *The Case of the Bloody Iris* (1972), *Mountain of the Cannibal God* (1978), and *Cannibal Ferox* (1981). These now join the likes of *House on the Edge of the Park* (1981), *New York Ripper* (1982), and *Cannibal Holocaust* (1980) in the Shameless catalogue.

British fans still have Salvation Films/Redemption who were once a rival, of sorts, to VIPCO. Created in 1993, around the time of the second wave of VIPCO releases, Redemption went for an audience who were interested in more than just cannibal and zombie flicks. They also sold Dario Argento and Jess Franco features – directors who were oddly lacking in the catalogue of Mike's firm (barring *Caged Women*). Former staff member, Marc Morris, said this was more than likely because Redemption went to international film markets to seek out these sorts of features, while VIPCO bought whatever was available to them in the UK. Redemption are still going strong and are always expanding and meeting the needs of their growing fanbase.

With his current firm, Nucleus Films, run with Jake West, Morris says they do not bother doing a release if they cannot give the film the best possible treatment. He says streaming rentals present nearly no money for distributors today, so the aim is to give the fans a reason to buy the actual physical copy. He admits that, even now, this is a struggle as millennials, and people who have grown up with free downloads and streaming, just assume it is a gimme that they should not have to pay. He also said that new movies which have been made in the last several years underperform; horror fans like buying retro or older content on disc.

Streaming has played a large part in keeping VIPCO wares alive, despite weakening physical DVDs power; streaming was a method of consuming film not fully realised during VIPCO's lifetime. File-sharing and primitive forms of video streaming did exist at the tail-end of the firm's history but grew significantly in the years immediately after closure.

Dozens of the features Mike had once sold in stores on VHS or DVD are now available on-demand in the home. Outlets from Amazon Prime to Shudder carry his former features, either for free, at no extra cost to the subscriber, or at a rental cost. Michael Lee, if he was still in the business of film distribution, would have found this quite the departure from the days when he would copy tapes in his office until the early hours. A VIPCO video streaming service could have been fun.

Speaking of change… The closure of VIPCO led to another business going bust: S Gold & Sons. While S Gold & Sons did distribute the films of firms outside VIPCO, including some big studios, the loss of VIPCO and the subsequent global recession caused Golds (as they were known) to suffer greatly. The challenges of being unable to compete with the internet also proved contributory. Golds entered administration in August 2008 following a period that saw business drop off greatly. Workers recall that they would often have no work to do in the factory. When Barrie himself was asked about the closure of the family-run business, he frankly said, "RBS liquidated us over £2 million, and it put 150 people out of work." Fifty-three years of S Gold & Sons' history came to an end.

As the consumption of home entertainment has changed, there has been a renewed interest in the old ways of doing things. While Blu-ray and DVD struggle in the current age, it is the older, obsolete VHS format that has seen a resurgence of sorts. The revival has led to some VIPCO tapes becoming something of collectors' items, with tatty old videos of anything from *Zombie Flesh Eaters* to *Flesh for Frankenstein* selling on eBay or similar marketplaces for extraordinary sums of money. Anything that is 'pre-cert' (pre-certification, meaning the tape was sold before the Video Recordings Act 1984 was passed, and age certificates were required by law) seems to make a VHS tape even more sought after. This money-for-old-rope fad is not limited to VIPCO, but it shows that nostalgia has been kind to the company. I myself have several pre-cert tapes in my collection.

Mike has said he thinks it is daft that some battered old videotapes with his firm's name on them should be deemed valuable and that they are being snapped up by collectors. In a recent conversation with Jason Impey, he said, "I wish I kept my tapes, I'd let you sell them all! We'd be rich!" The businessman within Mike is still alive and well!

So, would VIPCO have survived in today's commercial climate? Not a chance. "VIPCO was doomed; the business model used by Mike Lee was stuck in the eighties," explained Jay Slater. "Physical media is dying a death, [Mike] wouldn't have been able to complete." Likewise, director Jason Impey believes that the current marketplace is only kept alive by a small community of die-hard fans of horror. He feels that Mike's lack of respect for horror would have jarred with this group and led to failure.

Ewan Cant also questioned if Mike's business acumen would have been up to the strain of such a shrinking market: "He wouldn't know what to do and that probably would be because, for a long time, he didn't have to." Furthermore, "In the eighties, he just bought the films, put them on sale and waited for the money. I'm not being negative when I say this, but he was only in the business to make money." Marc Morris had similar sentiments. "Mike didn't have the knowledge or desire to learn anything outside of his comfort zone, so would have easily been defeated by new technologies like Blu-ray and streaming." The botched DVD releases were proof of this, he felt.

Whatever the criticisms of Mike – his shoddy transfers and Del Boy-like approach to the horror community being the biggest points of naysayers – it cannot be denied that VIPCO has left a positive and lasting impression on the minds of British horror fans. If the firm will only ever be remembered for one thing, it at least gave the UK *Zombie Flesh Eaters*…

…and The Nostril Picker.

20
Michael Lee – Movie Producer!

VIPCO, and Mike Lee, did more than just snap up films to be sold on video or disc. Mike also dabbled in producing movies on a couple of occasions, although the results came in for their fair share of criticism. While the heat was dying down in the UK from the Video Nasties scandal, our novice producer would go to the US to put up the cash for an over-the-top horror called *Spookies* (1986) which went so badly for him he did not try producing again until 2002, with the little-seen *The Claw* (2002). What follows is an examination of both works.

SPOOKIES (1986)

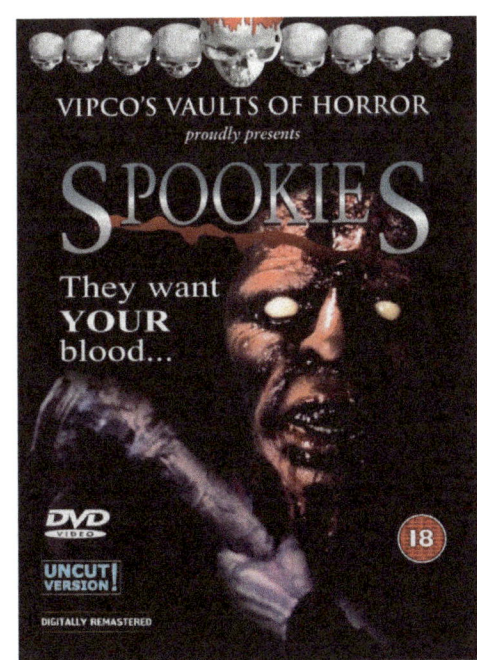

Directors: Thomas Doran (*Tortured Souls* footage), Brendan Faulkner (*Tortured Souls* footage), Genie Joseph as Eugenie Joseph

Writers: Thomas Doran, Frank M. Farel, Brendan Faulkner, Ann Burgund as Joseph Burgund

Stars: Felix Ward (Kreon), Alec Nemser (Billy), Maria Pechukas (Isabelle), Charlotte Alexandra as Charlotte Seeley (Adrienne)

VIPCO Release: 1992

Also Known As: *Tortured Souls*

VIPCO Plot Synopsis: *When young Billy's parents forgot his thirteenth birthday, he runs away from home. Soon he becomes lost in the woods, pursued by nameless things that propel him towards an old mansion, and the grisly birthday present that awaits him there. Meanwhile, a group of teenagers are driving around the woods looking for a place to party when they come across the old mansion. One by one, they too fall prey to Billy's killer, an evil sorcerer who lures his unsuspecting victims to the house with the help of his nightmarish offspring, the ones he calls the 'spookies'.*

Spookies has quite the tale behind it. Travelling to the States in the mid-eighties, Mike was on location during the making of what was originally entitled *Tortured Souls*. It was known to have had a troubled creation, and Mike is alleged to have had the title changed to *Spookies* (which, in certain parts of Britain, is slang for the supernatural) despite the protests of the crew. He also made rewrites to the script without permission, and insisted on the addition of numerous SFX sequences to grab the viewer's attention. He also, supposedly, lost his temper with the directors as they were 'wasting' his money on a film he thought to be dreadful.

Then he fired them.

It should be stated here that Mike found the whole experience to be stressful and exhausting. As a businessman investing his money, as well as travelling halfway around the world to see his project get made, it is only fair that he had an interest in the creation of his film. How he went about it, though, is another matter. Mike will not comment on it any further, other than to add that it was not a pleasant experience.

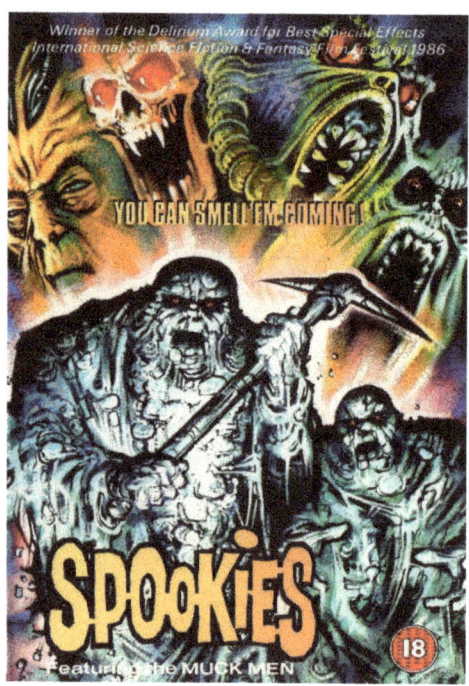

It may be Mike's hands-on approach that lent itself to the finished work's overall effect. *Spookies* is a movie that has so much going on, logical or not, that it becomes an extraordinary thing to witness. There is so much happening in such a short period of time that his demand for certain story alterations and special effects, plus the hiring of a new director (more on that later), may have had a hand in making this a super fun and over-the-top horror.

The original directors were Thomas Doran and Brendan Faulkner, and their vision was to stack the feature with monsters and ghouls galore. The two were certainly ambitious and did not let Mike's budget restrictions stop them making a visually impressive ghost-house flick.

The madness kicks off with a random guy talking to 13 year-old Billy in the woods about 'plans' – only for the random to be killed by a wolf-man, straight away. It is Billy's birthday, and he stumbles upon an old mansion with a 'party for him' after his brief encounter in the woods. Unluckily for him, he eventually ends up being buried alive. The scattershot story then cuts to a group of youths that decide to get pissed up in the same mansion and find a Ouija board; they are then attacked/chased by various monsters and ghoulies that this unleashes, including the Grim Reaper and 'the Muck Men'. Newly-shot footage is inserted next; it entertains viewers to the sight of a loony dead-man (named Kreon) trying to bring back to life his deceased wife. To top it all off, there is an outbreak of zombies! That is just half of what happens in *Spookies*.

The writing leaves a little to be desired, despite the ghost-and-monsters nature of the story; many characters feel like nothing more than walking clichés. A prime example is Duke – the ultimate braindead muscle head who spouts stereotypically stupid comments, and is annoyingly macho.

It is Kreon that is potentially the best-remembered character in the film, and he is played by Felix Ward, with something of a campy zeal, in what would turn out to be his only movie role. The late Peter Iasillo Jr gives a spirited performance as the zany Rich who is arguably the only cast member who looks like they are enjoying themselves. The rest of the cast are, like their by-the-numbers parts, bland.

Spookies is rightly remembered for its over-the-top nature, but one other memorable component also shines through. The special effects are genuinely impressive. The most infamous of all the ghouls from the movie are the Muck Men who are a group of disgusting-looking, violent ghosts that seemingly break wind non-stop. Allegedly, the addition of the farting sound effects was due to Mike's insistence, which everyone else on the production was opposed to. Graham Humphreys has said Mike told him to make sure the Muck Men were prominently featured on the VHS artwork he was commissioned to create.

As touched upon, above, the movie had been completed as *Tortured Souls* by original directors Doran and Faulkner, but after continued bad blood between them and Mike, they walked/were sacked. Lawsuits followed, and a new director was brought in: Eugenie Joseph.

Better known as Genie, she would drastically edit *Tortured Souls* (without prompting from Mike) to halve its run time. She then hired friend Bob Chappell to shoot additional scenes she had written. What Chappell would film would make up almost 50% of the finished movie and add to the mixed-up nature of proceedings. Because he could not use the original cast, he had to insert scenes and characters that did not correspond to the main plot point of the group of friends partying in an old mansion. This is what led to Billy, Kreon, and the zombie invasion.

Spookies was not originally released via VIPCO despite Mike's involvement; that honour went to Palace Premiere/Video, in 1986, with some rather nifty artwork. It is also how celebrated horror poster artist Graham Humphreys got involved with VIPCO. He was still early into his career and approached Palace with a portfolio of his work. "I was finding my way in the business of freelance design and illustration," he said of this period, "but I did *The Evil Dead* for them, and it was a massive success. Sometime later, Irving Rappaport – then working at Palace Video – called me in for a meeting with Michael Lee, based on this success." Mike had inked a deal with Palace to handle *Spookies* and thought Graham's horror work made him an ideal fit for designing the film's artwork. The only stipulation he was told to follow was that he included the farting Muck Men, and incorporate the tagline 'You can smell 'em coming!'.

"I liked Michael and was thrilled to receive the commission. Then I saw the film..." Graham would say of this venture.

Later, in the early nineties, VIPCO would reissue the title on VHS and DVD with Graham's artwork. At the turn of the new millennium, they once again reissued the movie, but minus the artwork. *Spookies* has not been released on DVD since, or even Blu-ray, which is a shame; many cult cinema fans long to see this happen.

Two reasons for the lack of a new version exist. One is Mike's declining health; the other is the lack of paperwork as to who owns the rights.

153

Ken Kelsch, one of the cinematographers for *Spookies*, experienced a true tragedy during filming when his two-week-old son died of crib death. Kelsch and his young family had been living in one of the houses on the estate where the feature was being shot.

THE CLAW (2002)

Director: Shaky Gonzalez

Writer: Shaky Gonzalez

Stars: Tolo Montana (Carlitos), Thure Lindhardt (Mike), Pat Kelman (Englishman), Zlatko Buric (Ibrahim)

VIPCO Release: 2004

Also Known As: *One Hell of a Christmas*

VIPCO Plot Synopsis: *Something discovered by an Englishman (an ancient claw) proves to have fearsome and extraordinary powers. From the sandstorms of time comes a comic strip tale of evil as never seen before.*

The story begins when Carlitos, an American criminal is released from jail. He is determined to go straight in order to reconcile with his wife and 5 year-old son. However, a friend Mikey brings to him "The Claw", & before they know it they're caught up in a mess of demons & possessed cuddly toys. Follow them from one terrifying moment to another as the forces of good and evil square off in an atmosphere of ferociously funny dread!

Standout sequences include the vengeful Zombie hooker who doles out some evil kung-fu whilst chiding Carlitos that she's got PMT, and Carlitos' ferocious battles with foot-stomping Wolfie and slick gun-fighter Cowboy Jack. The finale takes the film on a furious ride thru the horror genre, climaxing things with a truly memorable fitting end. Every horror film has a scene that scares us and everyone who's seen VIPCO films knows what we're referring to LOL!

With searing power and enduring impact "The Claw" is revolutionary cinema, paving the way for a superb edge-of-the-seat ride with its winning mix of fright and humour. Its enduring impact will entertain time and again like no other movie ever has or will. Put it on the top of your list!

Another VIPCO title with a Mike Lee 'hard sell' synopsis on the packaging, the write up here is perhaps the most hyperbolic of all. The last paragraph alone makes *The Claw* sound like a blockbuster and must-see of epic proportions. It even utilises 'LOL!', a term that was still some years away from piercing mainstream public conscious (texters and MSN users aside). Does the movie live up to the VIPCO hard sell? Of course not.

It had been almost 15 years since Mike was traumatised by producing and financing *Spookies* (1986) and, this time, he was nowhere near as hands-on. He did pay for some scenes to be reshot, and made some editing decisions, but his demands did not result in the same discord among crew as his first feature.

The production values, in general, are not overly impressive, and *The Claw* seems to have saved most of what can be assumed to be a modest budget for its special effects. There are some impressive gore effects for a few characters. These are the sole moments of interest in the feature.

Proceedings are not anything outstanding or special, and the much sought-after claw is barely seen, although the viewer is reminded, several times, that it cost '£15,000'. The movie's other title – *One Hell of a Christmas* – is perhaps more appropriate than *The Claw*; it is referenced more times.

The script is weak with many a moment of bad dialogue. Some of the actors seem to struggle with their lines, which does not help. Laughs are to be had when a character becomes possessed and starts spouting verbal abuse at the person they are harassing. "I'm gonna cut your cock off and make you suck it!" and "Suck my pussy!" are two of the gems. Readers will not be shocked to learn the character in question was created and scripted by Mike!

The star of the feature was Danish actor Tolo Montana (although he would not stay in the film industry long). Thure Lindhardt has gone on to have the most successful career out of the other cast members. Thure has been in the likes of *Angels & Demons* (2009), *Fast & Furious 6* (2013), and TV series *The Borgias* and *The Bridge*. Croatian veteran actor Zlatko Buric also appears.

The interestingly-named director Shaky Gonzalez would go onto direct/write/edit several more full-length or shorts over the next dozen years with *The Last Demon Slayer* (2011) and *Statue Collector* (2015) being part of his output.

Outside this VIPCO release, *The Claw/One Hell of a Christmas* has not been reissued on DVD/Blu-ray. It *is* available to rent on Amazon Video.

21
Deciding on Which Films to Include

When it came to which films to include in this book, I was spoilt for choice. VIPCO released *a lot* of movies from the early eighties through to the mid-noughties. I initially wanted to take a look at 20 of the biggest or best-known films it had offered, but that quickly became 30 then 45 and eventually the 'final 50'.

Admittedly, some of the features within the 50 are not some of VIPCO's most fondly-remembered releases, or even big sellers for the firm. In the eyes of the firm's owner, this would have been 'proof' the movies were terrible! The films I decided to include are here because – I hope – they are interesting, fun, obscure, or worthy in other ways.

I also have to admit that I had not seen some previously (*Rise and Fall of Idi Amin*) or I'd not watched them in many, many years (*Zombie Creeping Flesh*). For the sake of variety, and to acknowledge not everything VIPCO sold was a gem, I thought the inclusion of these films would be a sensible thing.

I believe I was right to do this as, for every classic like *Zombie Flesh Eaters* that was sold, VIPCO also sold mediocre flicks such as *King Frat*. Thankfully, taking a chance on lesser-known entries into the Cult Classics or Vaults of Horror sub-labels, I discovered and even re-discovered some diamonds in the rough. Enzo G.

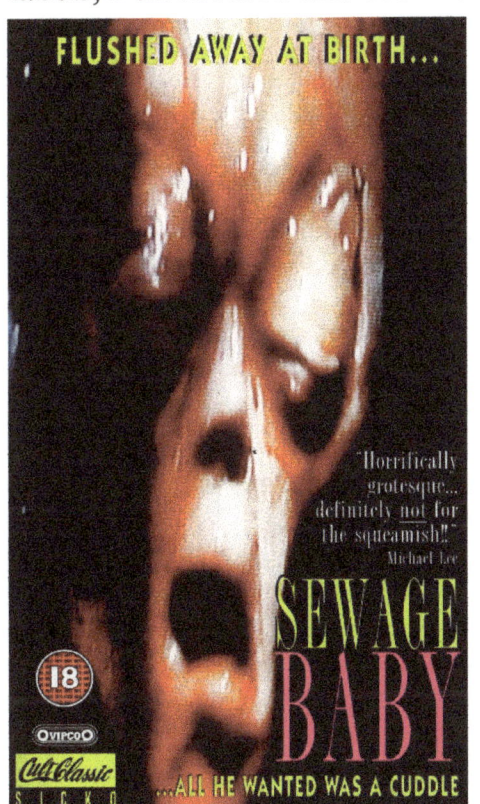

Castellari's *The Big Racket* was an absolute treat to watch and despite having seen J.S. Cardone's *The Slayer* multiple times in the past (and not been impressed by it) I fell in love with the surreal flick when re-watching it for this book.

I acknowledge there are some titles that are not featured that many may feel should have been (*Human Experiments*, *Death Trap*, and *Sewage Baby*, to name a few). This is because of time and space constraints, but it should be known I do plan to cover them, 20 other titles in total, alongside movies ranging from *Death Warmed Up* (1984) to *High Noon Part II – The Return of Will Kane* (1980), in written form one day.

When it came to VIPCO flicks that *had to be included* there was no doubt about the likes of ZFE, *Spookies*, *Driller Killer* and even *The Nostril Picker*. In research for this book these were the titles that were universally mentioned in relation to VIPCO by fans, industry insiders, and the firm's detractors.

Or did I get it wrong...?

22
Candid Thoughts on Michael Lee

Throughout the course of this book, I think it is safe to say that VIPCO founder Michael Lee is a little like Marmite. You either love him or hate him. Actually, love and hate are very strong words, and it is more accurate to say that the people who I have spoken to, or interviewed, have had divided opinions on Mike and his company. Some people are *very* pro-Mike, others not so much.

You may have already formed your own opinion about Mike; it is perhaps impossible not to have one. After all, this was the man who created VIPCO. Its journey all about his efforts and decisions. It could even be argued that VIPCO *is* Mike Lee; at times during my talks with the various names that appear within these pages, 'Mike' and 'VIPCO' were used interchangeably, yet meant the same entity.

Jay Slater, former VIPCO employee, and friend of Mike

On Mike as a person: "...a gentleman, and a lovely guy who gave the horror community *Zombie Flesh Eaters*. I miss the fella."

On an offer to work with Mike again, after leaving VIPCO: "He did ask me to come back onboard once more, to do the press and publicity for an ageing documentary for some sort of *Britain's Worst Female Drivers* video. It was – and I am being very polite due to my fondness of Mike – not his best hour. He was scraping the bottom of the barrel for fresh material. That was the last I heard from Mike."

About people, online, being negative about VIPCO and Mike: "Some forums were very anti-VIPCO to the point of me receiving a death threat for helping Mike! These forums were stalked by the same old losers and social degenerates who consider their multiple copies of *Bloody Moon* and *Zombie Lake* to be more important than life itself. Naturally, I distance myself from these socially awkward losers."

Stephen Brotherstone, co-author of the Scarred for Life books & Nasties fan

Mike and his 'political adventures': "I was gobsmacked to learn that [Mike Lee] was the original Lord Buckethead to run for MP. Now that *Gremloids* cover is starting to make sense…"

Buying VIPCO titles as a teen: "VIPCO became a seal of quality. I knew that if the VIPCO logo was on the box, I was in for a good time. VIPCO was untouchable when they got it right. They would have been the sort of video label I'd set up if I were ever in the position to do so!"

Ewan Cant, head of acquisitions for Arrow Video and VIPCO fan

Mike's approach to business: "In the eighties, he perhaps just bought the films, put them on sale, and waited for the money. I'm not being negative when I say he was only in the business to make money. If he hadn't been, the landscape of horror in the UK would have been very different."

On the changing of a movie's name to something often unrelated: "It worked. Some of these movies are better remembered by their VIPCO name in the UK, more than anywhere else, with some firms re-releasing them decades later with the VIPCO-imposed name."

Ewan on becoming a horror fan thanks to VIPCO: "VIPCO was my gateway into horror movies and the job I have today. It could be argued that it changed my life. I must have been six or seven years old and seeing them on the shelves of a Virgin Megastore. They always stood out to me from the other horror tapes. I then would buy them when I was older, usually at one tape a week."

Marc Morris, former employee of Redemption Films and co-founder of Nucleus Films

VIPCO and the continued re-release of Video Nasties: "VIPCO only survived as long as it did because it relied on the past glories of the pre-cert era, people that collected them and all the Nasties. They 'stuck around' out of loyalty and would buy the re-releases in the nineties and later on DVD. I even collected them when I thought the Video Recordings Act meant I might never see these films again!"

His thoughts when he first heard about this book: "Is VIPCO strong enough a subject to fill a book with? I'm a little shocked that people think so fondly of VIPCO."

On his only meeting with Mike, at a BBFC Christmas Party: "He didn't really stand out, he just seemed to be a typical bloke. When talking to him, I did get the impression his business style was more like that of a wheeler-dealer."

The timing of Mike entering the VHS marketplace: "I think he got lucky, especially when he talked someone into giving him the rights to *Zombie Flesh Eaters*. VIPCO should really be remembered for that. If the money hadn't been there, then he would have done something else. The market getting bigger and the growing Video Nasties scandal really helped him. He didn't like horror, but he did the rewards it brought him."

Barrie Gold, former owner of S Gold & Sons as well as a friend of Mike

Highlight of their friendship: "My memories will always be fondly of our dinners together with our wives. Good times!"

On Mike as a person: "He was very eccentric in the early days of running VIPCO!"

Graham Humphreys, movie poster artist, and former VIPCO sleeve designer

On his time with VIPCO: "Michael came across as a charming used car salesman, utterly confident in his product no matter how poor it might be. I'm happy to have enjoyed my working relationship with Michael, though, and VIPCO. It's heartening to know that there remains an interest."

Mike's car: "Although I never saw this myself, apparently he drove a Mercedes in soft metallic blue, the hubcaps missing."

'VIPCO marketing': "Michael's simple logic was to target the weekend drinking consumer. He reasoned that after several pints, groupings of inebriated young folk would order a take-away and shout, "Let's put on a VIPCO!" I had to admire his positive thinking!"

Martin Myers, friend and film distributor

If Mike was ever difficult to deal with in business: "My father never had any issues with him. He was nice and always paid on time. There were never any concerns."

On his friend's success: "He was very successful in promoting and selling his videos. Like many successful businessmen, it is about being in the right place at the right time, seeing an opportunity and going after it. That is what Mike did."

The negative opinions of Mike that some people have: "I do not have any negative thoughts of him as, to me, he will always be my friend from school. He had a successful career and then had a major setback to his life when his son died. It was terrible for him and his ex-wife Sue. I would not wish that on my worst enemy."

23
Afterword

By Jay Slater

'Can you get me *The Last Hunter*?' asked Mike Lee.

I was interviewing the VIPCO legend in a London pub, something that he was usually against, preferring to refuse publicity and lurk in the shadows as one of the UK's most prolific and infamous video distributors at the start of the video revolution. 'Sure!' was my reply without the slightest idea of where and how to find the rights for an obscure Italian action pic from the early 1980s.

And that is how my relationship with VIPCO began.

On reflection, they were fast, fun, and furious times. I had knowledge of what fans wanted to see, and Mike was a keen advocate of the horror genre and was eager to be one of the first pioneers of the digital medium. He also paid well and on time: all in all, Mike was old school and a gentleman. He is certainly missed.

Despite narrow-minded obsessiveness that hounded Mike on forums, which is sadly prevalent in horror video social circles, VIPCO never intended to short-change fans and distribute lesser quality products. Unlike today's main genre labels, which champion extras, Mike was against investing in them, preferring the film to be sold on its own merits: indeed, the DVD menu *was* an extra; however, I did convince him to invest in an audio commentary with Catriona MacColl for the digital release of *City of the Living Dead*. It worked well, all had a great time, and something clearly succeeded as the same commentary graced the recent Arrow Video releases. Sadly, VIPCO's days were numbered as horror fans, a dedicated but ageing demographic, would pay for bells and whistles releases with multiple documentaries, multiple commentaries, and pretentious pseudo-intellectual essays. But Mike soldiered on to the bitter end, and bless him for it. He was a VHS warrior dug in his Stalingrad bunker against a more sophisticated and superior enemy. His days were numbered, and he fought to the bitter end.

I recall an audio commentary for *Zombie Creeping Flesh* that did not go well with two guests spouting puerile dialogue towards the dark-skinned cast. Before I could moderate fully – and in all fairness, it was doomed by then – Mike pulled the plug and stormed off. And who could blame him? Another memory was when I received an e-mail from the director of *The Nostril Picker,* in the US, who was bemused that his film was released in the UK by VIPCO… without the rights. I can only assume that he was eventually paid? Please note that I did not acquire the feature!

I cringe at some of the new names Mike would insist his acquisitions should have. Re-titling films was something that Mike was very keen to do. They would usually happen like this:

Mike: 'So what are we going to call *Massacre in Dinosaur Valley*?'

Me: 'What about… Massacre in Dinosaur Valley?'

Mike: 'That's stupid! Who is going to buy that?'

Me: 'Cannibal Ferox 2?'

Mike (laughing): 'Brilliant!'

Please note that I fought tooth and nail to have *Burial Ground/Nights of Terror*, or whatever it is called these days, to have its original title; however, Mike decided on *The Zombie Dead*, which makes little sense as the living dead are… dead. Mike allegedly got the inspiration for this stupid and repetitive title from the equally ridiculous and stupid title of the *Doctor Who* serial, 'Mawdryn Undead', where Mawdryn simply means 'undead' in Welsh!

An issue that plagued VIPCO, from the outset of DVD, was that it had gained a notorious reputation from the horror elite for releasing a substandard product. In all fairness, *The Last Hunter* was, for its time, an impressive release as were *Bronx Warriors*, *Bronx Warriors 2* and *The New Barbarians*. VIPCO was there first as the trail-blazing behemoth it was. We did try to source *Cobra Mission* but were informed that the English language print in the vault was damaged and would cost some €50,000 to correct. I also acquired films for Mike, which were experimental and with merit, such as *Suicide*. Actually, with *Suicide*, the film bombed in the UK (as it looked like a VIPCO-packaged pic), whereas in the US it was celebrated. Go figure. He didn't enjoy that experience.

I wish Mike the very best for he was, and still is, a gentleman with so much character.

Jay Slater

London, April 2019

PS: Mike, I did forget as to how you acquired the intellectual rights for VIPCO from Ringo Starr?!

Other Books from Bennion Kearny

Write From The Start: The Beginner's Guide to Writing Professional Non-Fiction by Caroline Foster

Do you want to become a writer? Would you like to earn money from writing? Do you know where to begin?

Help is at hand with *Write From The Start* – a practical must-read resource for newcomers to the world of non-fiction writing. It is a vast genre that encompasses books, newspaper and magazine articles, press releases, business copy, the web, blogging, and much more besides.

Jam-packed with great advice, the book is aimed at novice writers, hobbyist writers, or those considering a full-time writing career, and offers a comprehensive guide to help you plan, prepare, and professionally submit your non-fiction work. It is designed to get you up-and-running fast.

One Football, No Nets by Justin Walley

In September 2017, amateur British football coach Justin Walley became the "National Team" Manager of Matabeleland, an obscure international team in western Zimbabwe.

Before him lay the seemingly impossible task of taking his group of unknown amateur footballers from an impoverished region of Africa to the "alternative world cup" – the CONIFA World Football Cup in London, the following summer. All that stood in his way was the small matter of no money, no resources, no salary, no visas, and no sponsors. There was one football, though… but no goal nets.

One Football, No Nets tells of one man's leap of faith into the unknown, swapping life with his girlfriend and a third division football team in Eastern Europe for international football management in Africa. It was to be a journey that would take Walley through the toppling of President Robert Mugabe, a collapsing financial system, and travelling to away games in rural Africa with 17 players in one pickup truck. And, oh yes, Liverpool legend Bruce Grobbelaar becomes Walley's goalkeeping coach after a meeting at an M6 motorway service station.

Tragic Magic: The Life of Traffic's Chris Wood by Dan Ropek

Traffic was the most enigmatic British band of their day. Formed in early 1967 by Chris Wood, Steve Winwood, Jim Capaldi and Dave Mason, they rejected the bright lights of London, in favor of a run-down, supposedly haunted, cottage in the country – a place to live communally and write music.

With Chris especially intent on channeling the vibes of England's landscape into their sound, days would be spent getting high, exploring, playing and working in varying proportions. Against all odds this eccentric model paid off – songs such as "Dear Mr. Fantasy" and "John Barleycorn Must Die" would lift Traffic into the upper echelons of the rock world.

Amid the clashing egos, wearing road trips, stressful break ups and a complex personal life, he vacillated precariously between bursts of exquisite creativity and torrents of self-destruction; a paradoxical dance which continued until his death in 1983. For a man who found artistic expression everything, and for whom suffering for it was an expectation, Chris would stare fully into the Medusa's face of the music industry, paying a higher price than perhaps any of his contemporaries.

Researched and written over a ten-year period, "Tragic Magic" offers the only definitive account of Traffic's story and Chris Wood's quietly extraordinary life.

Martians, Morlocks and Moon Landings: How British Science Fiction Conquered The World by Jamie Austin

Science Fiction has long been a part of popular culture. From the colour co-ordinated adventures of Captain Kirk and crew to the city chomping of Godzilla, it is very much a worldwide phenomenon.

And it all started over a century ago – in Britain.

Martians, Morlocks and Moon Landings details the influence of British Science Fiction on the world stage and is a must-read resource for anyone with an interest in the genre. Without Wells there would be no Star Wars, without Orwell there would be no Celebrity Big Brother… For good or evil, British Science Fiction has shaped our world. This book shows you how.

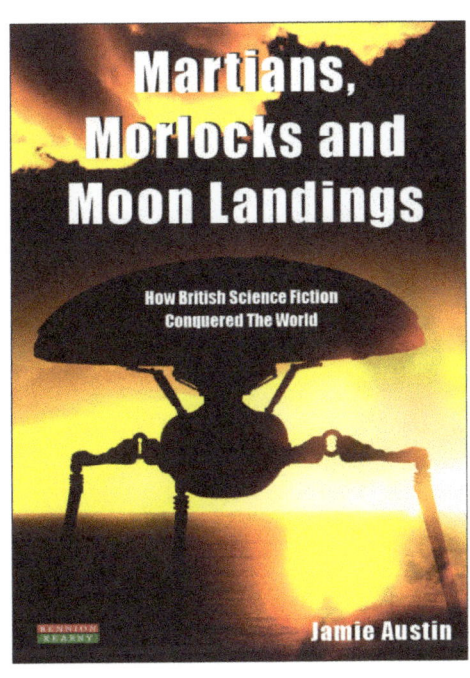